# DUMPLINGS
# ALL DAY WONG

PAGE STREET
PUBLISHING CO.

First published in 2014 by

Page Street Publishing Co.

27 Congress Street, Suite 103

Salem, MA 01970

www.pagestreetpublishing.com

Distributed by Macmillan; sales in Canada by The Canadian Manda Group; distribution in Canada by The Jaguar Book Group.

17   16   15   14      1   2   3   4   5

ISBN-13: 978-1-62414-059-4

ISBN-10: 1-62414-059-9

Library of Congress Control Number: 2013922991

Cover and book design by Page Street Publishing

Photography by Ken Goodman

Cover author image by John Mark Sorum

Printed and bound in China

Page Street is proud to be a member of 1% for the Planet. Members donate one percent of their sales to one or more of the over 1,500 environmental and sustainability charities across the globe who participate in this program.

# DUMPLINGS ALL DAY WONG

## A COOKBOOK OF ASIAN DELIGHTS FROM A TOP CHEF

### LEE ANNE WONG

CELEBRITY CHEF AND TV PERSONALITY

PAGE STREET
PUBLISHING CO.

# CONTENTS

# FOREWORD BY MARCUS SAMUELSSON

When I met Lee Anne twelve years ago, she was already an incredible badass in the kitchen. She loved flavor, had strong opinions on how and what to cook and wanted to learn, which she did fast. She came from a different mindset than a lot of chefs of that era. While they were focused on French or Italian cooking techniques, and catering to trends and audiences, Lee Anne cut right to the chase and aimed for nothing short of delicious food.

She is a bold and brave chef who continues to evolve. She really knows her Asia flavors, while at the same time, she is truly American with a mix of cultural influences evident in her incredible recipes. It's simply delicious, yummy, flavor-forward cooking.

At Aquavit, she came in as a cook, soon started writing our menu and really kicked ass. Even when we disagreed, it was a joy. She was passionate about how to cook her food and didn't back down. That energy drove her unique and special approach, and in this case, created an incredible collection of dumplings.

A lot of cooks have come and gone from my restaurants, but Lee Anne was a special chef whom I will never forget. I'm glad America gets to taste her food because I know it's going to be delicious—and unforgettable like her.

— Marcus Samuelsson

*Marcus Samuelsson is the chef and owner of Red Rooster Harlem and Ginny's Supper Club*

# INTRODUCTION

In the past 30-plus years, I have had the delight of sampling excellent versions of familiar and comforting Chinese-American classics, as well as contemporary interpretations and regionally authentic dumplings and dim sum, both in the U.S. and in Asia proper.

While I am not much of a fan of the often-bland delivery variety, it's what I knew growing up, outside of the occasional visits from my Chinese grandmother, the magical cook. Because I was raised in upstate New York suburbia, my notion of Chinese food was the local take-out place. Every now and then my parents would take me and my brother to the fancy sit-down restaurant that served the bowls of fried noodles with mustard and duck sauce on the table. These types of establishments are the most commonly recognized versions of Chinese-American cuisine, and are wildly different from the regional menus of China. But it's how I learned to love dumplings. Dumplings were as much a part of my childhood as any other snack like pizza or hot dogs. Delivery dumplings were my gateway food to every other type of dumpling out there. Xiaolongbao. Gyoza. Momos. Mandu. It was too late. I was hooked.

When I moved to New York City immediately after high school, I was enticed to stretch my culinary legs and explore neighborhoods like Flushing and Chinatown for more authentic flavors. When I turned my attention from art to cooking in my early twenties, I became obsessed with food. For a broke college student, dumplings were an economical and frequent player in my diet. Over the years and through repetition, I have honed my dumpling Jedi skills so I am no longer a slave to takeout. My friends would say I am dumpling addicted. It's the first party favor they ask for whenever I offer to cook, so needless to say being known for your dumplings is a good thing. The ability to make fresh dumplings at home will win you friends and admirers.

I personally have a solemn reverence and respect for the expert dumpling chefs I have encountered in my travels, because I am aware of the work that goes into creating that perfect bite of food. Everyone's familiar with cooking big—big roasts, big casseroles, big anything, really. We are used to making big quantities of food and then cutting it up when it is on our plates so it fits in our mouths. My admiration for dumpling and dim sum chefs stems from the dedication, repetition and intricate skill needed to make this quintessential small food in large quantities. It's why when we see a dim sum basket or plate full of perfect dumplings our eyes get wide and we start to salivate—because we have an expectation of what comes next and how that taste experience should be. Biting into a hot, fresh, juicy dumpling can be a transcendent moment, the kind that makes your eyes roll to the back of your head, and one that can be repeated (often). This dumpling euphoria is commonly achieved by dining out or ordering in, which is why making them at home for yourself is that much more special.

This book focuses on the Asian style of dumplings. The further you get into the book, the more you will begin to realize that your possibilities are truly endless. As with all styles of cooking, once you master the techniques and basic recipes, you'll have the ability to build your own dumpling arsenal.

Skilled dim sum chefs can form hundreds of different creative folds. While the idea of standing in one place all day making dumplings sounds intimidating or boring, I actually quite enjoy the repetitive motions of hand pleating dumplings. I consider it my "me time," and it gives me a chance to think about my day or what I have to do next, or how fast I am folding my dumplings (I can fold six per minute). In this book I will teach you some basic folds and cooking techniques. Where you go from there depends on how much practice you put into it. I am ever a student of the dumpling and continue to be inspired by my peers and culinary adventures.

My friend Harris, who learned the art of the dumpling from me, summed it up quite simply during a recent conversation: "You left the dumpling filling and wrappers in my fridge the last time you cooked at my place. It was awesome the day after! If I wanted a snack I could make just two dumplings. When I got hungrier, I made a dozen! That's when I realized I should keep dumpling filling in my fridge all the time, just so I can have fresh dumplings whenever I want ..." At this point Harris was wily-eyed and cackling, kinda like the Hamburglar, only he was talking about dumplings. Me: Smug grin. Take a bow. Thank you. Thank you. Yes, you have had your dumpling epiphany, my friend. It's THAT easy.

I am a huge fan of social media and how it's allowed the world to connect in an instant. Part of my passion for cooking centers around the fact that food brings people together. When it comes to dumplings, people don't just come together; they tend to swarm. I personally can drool over pictures of tasty fresh dumplings all day, so please join my dumpling community. Just add the hashtag #dumplingsalldaywong when you post pictures of your dumpling creations on Twitter, Instagram, Facebook, Vine and other social media! Be part of our dumpling family and show your dumpling love!

—Cheers, Lee Anne

# CHAPTER I

# TOOLS AND TECHNIQUES

➤ A good scout's motto is "always be prepared." The same goes for any decent cook. Like anything else in life, having the right tools and techniques available to you will make the task at hand that much easier. Below are a few highly recommended pieces of equipment you'll need to help you achieve dumpling nirvana. Most are available at houseware and cookware stores or Asian markets.

# HAND TOOLS AND SMALL WARES

**CHINESE SPIDER STRAINER:** This skimming tool is traditionally made with a long bamboo handle and a wide, shallow, wire mesh basket resembling a spidersweb, hence the name. It's great for deep-frying, as well as straining items from hot liquids.

**CHOPSTICKS:** Once you master how to hold and manipulate a set of chopsticks, these simple wooden sticks can be the perfect utensil for many applications, such as individually turning panfried dumplings, whisking and mixing ingredients and plucking perfectly fried items from hot oil. In some Asian stores you can find large chopsticks used specifically for cooking purposes.

**DEEP-FRY/CANDY THERMOMETER:** Whether you purchase a digital thermometer or a classic mercury-in-glass thermometer, I find this tool indispensable, for both candy making and especially for deep-frying. Oil temperature is key to properly frying food, letting you know when the oil is too cold (food becomes greasy and oil-laden) or too hot, which can be very dangerous in many ways. Always monitor the thermometer and adjust the heat as necessary for perfect deep-frying temperatures, which range from 325°F/162°C to 375°F/190°C.

**MANDOLINE:** This is a great tool to have for thinly slicing fruits and vegetables. I prefer the lightweight plastic Japanese models over the heavy stainless steel European versions.

**MEASURING TOOLS:** Dry measuring cups, wet measuring cups and measuring spoons are a cook's best friends. Level off the top with the straight edge of a knife for precise measurements.

**MICROPLANE:** This superfine grater is perfect for zesting, grating spices such as nutmeg and long peppercorn, and finely grating items like garlic, ginger and cheese. Look for a microplane that has a grater that resembles a wood rasp (small teeth).

**PARCHMENT PAPER:** I love parchment paper. It's a great and versatile tool for food preparation, both cold and hot applications. Available in most grocery stores, this cooking paper prevents food from sticking.

**RING CUTTERS:** You can buy them in sets of various sizes, round and square (Ateco brand is great). The cutters will help trim down fresh dough or premade wrappers to the desired size and shape.

**ROLLING PIN:** Instead of the large, two-handled rolling pin favored by bakers, shop for an Asian-style wooden dowel rolling pin. Much smaller, skinnier and more lightweight, it's perfect for rolling small delicate dumpling wrappers instead of using a cumbersome large rolling pin. The standard size Asian-style rolling pin measures 12 inches (30.5 cm) in length by ¾ inch (1.9 cm) in diameter and is usually made from a wooden dowel with a smooth, sanded surface. You can find these at restaurant and equipment supply stores, as well as gourmet cookware stores and Asian specialty markets.

# GADGETS AND STOVE-TOP GEAR

**BLENDER:** A drink blender is great tool for making smooth sauces, purees and vinaigrettes. I recommend a high-speed commercial blender like a Vitamix.

**DIGITAL KITCHEN TIMER:** If you don't already have a timer on your phone, then an inexpensive digital timer is a must in any kitchen, especially when dealing with precise (and short) cook times.

**DIGITAL SCALE:** A scale can be a handy permanent addition to your kitchen tools. Recipes can be accurately replicated through weight measurement versus volume. Try and find a digital scale that operates in grams, pounds and ounces and has at least a 5-pound weight limit.

**DIM SUM STEAMER:** This is one of the most essential tools for cooking and serving up perfectly steamed dumplings. There are two kinds available: bamboo and metal. Both function in the same way in that steam will rise from a boiling water source at the bottom of the steamer and penetrate the stacked layers, which are holding your dumplings.

➢ **BAMBOO:** A bamboo steamer is the most visually classic representation of dim sum, as the baskets are able to go from the steamer to tableside, but they require a little more love and attention to prevent them from cracking, molding and/or burning. Bamboo steamers can range from 5 inches (12.5 cm) to more than 12 inches (30.5 cm) in size, with the ability to stack multiple steamers of the same size in one tower.

➢ **METAL:** A metal dim sum steamer is handy for multiple tasks in the kitchen. Usually made from aluminum or stainless steel, the lightweight pot holds the water in the bottom and can be placed directly on the heat source. Two tightly fitted stackable trays hold your dumplings, while the pea-size holes in the tray beds lets the steam to travel upward and cook your dumplings. A domed lid lets condensation drip down the sides of the steamer rather than back onto your dumplings.

Use a small bamboo steamer at home.

**FOOD PROCESSOR:** This kitchen workhorse can be helpful when making fillings or dough for your dumplings.

**NONSTICK FRYING PAN WITH LID:** Not everyone has access to a wok, so this is my favorite piece of equipment for panfried dumplings. Make sure you have a wide-bottomed frying pan and a tight-fitting lid to capture the steaming action that will cook your dumplings. Use a 6- to 8-inch (15 to 20-cm) omelet plan if you are making dumplings just for yourself. I like to use a 10- to 12-inch (25.5 to 30.5 cm) nonstick pan for cooking larger batches of dumplings.

**ROUND STEAMING RACK:** This resembles a wire rack on which to cool baked goods, only it is round (you can still use it as a cooling rack). It is good to keep two sizes around for the recipes in this book—one that will fit the interior of a 6- to 8-quart Dutch oven or heavy-bottomed stockpot and one slightly bigger than the diameter of your pot that can sit on the top rim of the pot, creating a platform for your bamboo steamer.

**WOK:** This is one of the most widely used and versatile cooking vessels in Asian cuisine and can be used for boiling, steaming, panfrying, stir-frying, deep-frying, poaching and smoking. Traditionally made from either carbon steel or cast iron, this round-bottomed pan takes time to season and build a patina, creating a natural nonstick surface that is perfect for all types of cooking. This pan normally sits on a wok ring to stabilize the bottom over a strong gas flame, making the wok perfect for high-heat cooking. Modern versions now come preseasoned and nonstick, with flat bottoms designed to transfer the heat from an electric stove.

Panfrying in a flat-bottomed wok is one of my favorite ways to cook dumplings.

A tight-fitting lid is key to the cooking process.

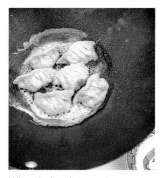

When the liquid evaporates, your dumplings should have that signature crispy/chewy texture.

# CUTTING TECHNIQUES

I'd say the most important tool in any kitchen is a sharp knife. Maintaining a sharp edge on your knives will not only help you create beautiful food but also prevent accidents and injuries, which are much more common with dull knives that can slip on food and your cutting board. Here are a few cuts employed in this book. Don't worry if your cuts aren't perfect—just remember that practice makes perfect.

**CRUSH:** Use the side of your knife and the heel of your hand to crush items like garlic or ginger to develop the juices and natural oils of the aromatic ingredient. Use a food mallet or heavy item like a small pot or pan to crush hard items such as spices and lemongrass.

**DICE:** Cut food into small cubes ranging in size from ⅛ inch (0.3 cm)(fine) to ¼ inch (0.6 cm) (small), ½ inch (1.3 cm) (medium) or ¾ inch (1.9 cm) or more (large). Cut your food item into uniform slices, then sticks of the same thickness, and then into cubes with the same diameter.

**JULIENNE:** Cut a fruit or vegetable into uniform matchsticks, usually about ⅛ inch (0.3 cm) or less in diameter, or make ribbons out of fresh herbs or leafy greens. A mandoline can be helpful in producing uniform slices before using your knife to make the thin matchsticks.

**MINCE:** Finely chop food into tiny pieces. This can be achieved with a knife, meat grinder or food processor.

# COOKING TECHNIQUES

There's more than one way to cook a dumpling. Each of these methods will produce a different texture and mouthfeel upon consumption, and to be honest, I love all four methods. Although this book has preferred methods for each recipe, the point is to cook the dumpling. If you don't feel like deep-frying, the other three methods work just as well. When you first delve into this book, make a recipe like the classic Pork and Chive Dumplings (page 37) with both premade wrappers and fresh dough, and then cook each of the dumplings by one of the four methods (premade wrapper steamed versus fresh wrapper steamed, premade wrapper panfried versus fresh wrapper panfried, and so on). This will give you a pretty immediate insight into your end results before you even get into a new recipe. It also helps you know exactly what to do when you have a craving. Sometimes I want a soft, silky, boiled dumpling; other times I am looking for that fragrant, crispy-bottomed, panfried version. The choice and the adventure are yours.

**BOILING:** The "three-boil" method was developed in China and is a good standard for cooking boiled dumplings. Bring a large pot of water to a boil (more water means the temperature won't drop as much when you put the dumplings in the water). Add your dumplings in a small batch and return the water to a boil. Add 1 cup (236 ml) of cold water to the pot and then return to a boil again. Add 1 more cup (236 ml) of cold water and after the water boils a third time, the dumplings are ready to be drained and served.

**DEEP-FRYING:** I don't care what you say, everyone loves deep-fried food, even if they won't admit it and have it once in a blue moon. The texture you are able to get with properly fried fresh and premade doughs will change the way you think about deep-frying. Deep-fried dumplings should not be ignored. Proper deep-frying is actually not all that unhealthy if done right—the oil temperature is key. When the oil is hot and ready (325°F to 375°F [162°C to 190°C]), what actually happens is the oil crisps, browns and seals the outside of whatever you are frying, creating an outer shell around the center filling, which then is essentially steamed through heat transference. Only when your oil is too cold does this outer shell not form and oil can seep into your food, making it grease-laden and heavy. You can deep-fry in a wok or heavy-bottomed Dutch oven or pot. I like to use vegetable oil because it imparts the least amount of flavor to the food, and even though peanut oil can withstand higher temperatures, I avoid using it due to peanut allergies. Use a deep-fry thermometer at all times to maintain the oil temperature. Several inches of oil is adequate for deep-frying dumplings, just make sure that the oil is well below the rim of the pot because the hot oil will bubble and expand when food is added to it. Use a Chinese spider strainer to pull your fried items out of the oil, and have a paper towel–lined surface ready to receive the hot dumplings. One of the most important things to remember when deep-frying is that oil and water do not mix. Moisture is the enemy—oil cooks at very high temperatures, while water (and most other liquids) boil and evaporate at 212°F/100°C, hence the bubbling action when you put something into hot oil. The bubbling is literally the moisture cooking out of that item in order to leave a crisp texture behind. Holes in your dumpling wrappers become dangerous when the moisture from the filling comes into contact with the hot oil. My suggestion is to pull the leaking dumpling immediately from the oil to prevent further incident. Make sure your spider strainer is always dry, too—water on the wire mesh or bamboo handle is no good. It is important to make sure your oil comes back to the desired frying temperature before adding more dumplings. Alternatively, if you happen to have a tabletop deep fryer like a FryDaddy or De'Longhi, those will work fine, too.

Always use an oil or candy thermometer to check and maintain your oil temperature.

Use a deep, heavy-bottom pot with several inches of oil for deep-frying.

Always drain anything deep-fried to a paper towel-lined surface.

**PANFRYING:** I love this method because of the dual textures it yields in the dumpling skin—crispy and chewy. Have a tight-fitting lid for the pan or wok stoveside and ready because this process happens very quickly. Add a tablespoon (15 ml) of oil to the bottom of a nonstick frying pan or wok and arrange the dumplings in the pan (you can place them spaced apart or lined up together) while heating the pan over high heat. After 1 to 2 minutes the dumplings will begin to brown on the bottoms. Add ½ cup (120 ml) of cold water to the hot pan (it will immediately steam and react with the oil in the pan, so be careful) and place the lid firmly on top of the pan to capture the steaming action. Cook the dumplings with the lid on until almost all of the water has evaporated or been absorbed by the dumplings; cooking times will vary depending on the dumpling. Remove the lid (lower the heat slightly, if necessary) and continue to cook until all of the water has evaporated from the pan and the dumpling skins begin to crisp up again. To create the lacy pancake effect on the bottom of your panfried dumplings, dissolve ½ tablespoon (4 g) of flour in the ½ cup (120 ml) of water before adding to the pan.

Line your dumplings into a lightly oiled nonstick frying pan.

When your dumplings begin to get a deep golden color on the bottom, you can add your liquid.

Carefully add the water to the pan.

A tight-fitting lid is key for steam-frying the dumplings.

When the liquid evaporates, fry your dumplings for a few seconds more until the skin crisps up.

You can add flour to your water to create a lacy pancake effect.

STEAMING: For this technique you will need a bamboo or metal dim sum steamer. Line your tray bottoms with greased parchment or blanched cabbage greens. Arrange your dumplings spaced apart in the trays, then stack your trays. If using a metal steamer, bring several inches of water to a boil in the bottom section of the pot. Fit the trays on the pot once the water is boiling and place the domed lid on top. If you are using a bamboo steamer, you have two options. I like to use a heavy-bottomed Dutch oven or stockpot with a steaming rack in conjunction with a bamboo steamer, rather than use a wok to boil the water (water can ruin the patina on a well-seasoned wok). If you are using a smaller dim sum steamer that fits the interior of the pot, then you can place a small rack inside the pot (make sure it is set above the waterline) to elevate the steaming baskets. If you are using a larger bamboo steamer (8 to 12 inches [20 to 30.5 cm]), then place a large cooling rack (it does not have to be round) on top of the rim of the pot with the boiling water. Make sure the dim sum basket is not wider than the diameter of the pot. Steaming times will vary slightly depending on how close the dim sum basket is to the steam and how vigorously the water is boiling.

# STORAGE TIPS

If you are making a large batch of dumplings for the same day it is advisable to form them within a few hours before you cook them. Moisture from the filling will soften the wrapper over the course of time, whether it is fresh or premade, which impedes the cooking process and creates problems like holes and tears in the wrapper or the wrappers sticking together. If I am having a party, I get everything ready—filling, wrappers and sauces—and either fold them right before everyone comes over or I save the labor for my friends, who usually get their hands dirty in helping fold the dumplings. Otherwise, you can form your dumplings several hours before cooking and keep them wrapped in plastic wrap in a single layer in your refrigerator. A little flour or starch dusted on the tray will help keep the dumplings from sticking later on.

Dumplings can also be made ahead of time and frozen for easy, ready-to-serve deliciousness. Clear enough space in your freezer to fit a baking tray or several large plates. Form your dumplings and then place them spaced apart in a single layer on a tray or plate. Cover with plastic wrap and place in the freezer. When the dumplings are individually frozen, you can transfer them to a zip-top freezer bag, where you can pull them one piece at a time for when you get hungry (the point is, don't freeze all the dumplings together in a pile or they will freeze into a solid mass). Dumplings will keep in an airtight bag for up to 3 months. Cook without thawing per recipe directions, but note that you will need a longer cooking time.

# CHAPTER 2

# DOUGH-HOW:
## CHOOSING THE RIGHT DUMPLING WRAPPER

➤ There's always the question of whether it is better to use fresh dumpling dough and wrappers versus the premade varieties. I believe both have their respective time and place, and I certainly do not discount the convenience of buying premade wrappers. There are dozens of varieties of premade wrappers on the market, each with a different thickness and shape; some have egg to provide a yellow hue and elasticity to the wrapper, others are made from a different combination of flours and starches to achieve a specific texture. To be honest, you can make homemade dumpling wrappers in less time than it would take to get dressed, get in your car and drive to the store. Regardless, I highly recommend experimenting with both. Here's a little Dumpling Wrapper 101 to help you on your journey to dumpling greatness.

# PREMADE DUMPLING WRAPPERS

Let's take a quick rundown of the usual players you'll find in your (Asian) grocer's freezer section and how to store and use them.

**ROUND WRAPPERS:** These are called "**dumpling** skins," "**potsticker** wrappers" and "**gyoza** skins." Every brand differs in thickness and taste once the wrapper is cooked, so you may have to shop around until you find a brand that you prefer. The average dumpling wrapper is about 3¼ to 3½ inches (8.3-8.9 cm) in diameter. With Chinese wrappers, "Shanghai style" is without egg, and the wrappers are white. "Hong Kong style" contains egg, giving the wrapper a yellow color.

**SQUARE WRAPPERS:** This shape is almost always referred to as a "**wonton** skin or wrapper." Again, thickness and consistency vary depending on the brand and whether the wrapper has egg in it. The wrappers vary in size but are usually 3¼ to 3½ inches (8.3-8.9 cm) wide. Smaller square wrappers are also available, specifically for "**shumai**," and can range from 2¾ to 3 (7-7.6 cm) inches wide.

**STORAGE:** Keep your wrappers frozen until ready to use. Give the wrappers time to properly thaw before using. I like to let them thaw for a day in the fridge first. If I need them on the same day out of the freezer, then I will leave the wrappers on my kitchen counter for a few hours. This process should not be rushed. In other words, don't put the wrappers somewhere warm, like on top of your stove. Only the top and bottom of the stack will thaw (too quickly), causing the wrappers to sweat their moisture out, leaving a mushy, gummy mess on the top and bottom while the rest are still frozen solid in the center. Do not microwave your wrappers. Do not try and peel them apart if they are still frozen. This will only lead to dumpling frustration and impede your end glory. Think ahead and know that if you are making dumplings, the first thing you need to do before you make your filling is account for your wrappers. Are they thawed and ready to go? Once you thaw your wrappers, try to use them up rather than refreezing them. Refrigerate what you are not using; in other words, if you know you are only making 12 dumplings, take out 12 thawed dumpling skins and keep the rest refrigerated versus letting the whole pack sit out.

**DUMPLING MAKING:** Let your wrappers thaw until they are pliable. Sometimes when the wrapper is too cold, the dough will tear easily. Holes in our wrappers are our enemy. Holes let out all the goodness and can make things dangerous when frying. Keep your wrappers covered; I like to use plastic wrap weighted with a damp towel. Once your dumplings are formed, keep those covered also. Dried-out dumpling skins are noticeably less tasty, especially when the dumplings are steamed or panfried.

# FRESH DOUGHS AND WRAPPERS

I cannot stress enough how easy it is to make your own dumpling wrappers from scratch. There are several advantages to homemade wrappers, especially if you have a well-stocked pantry. For one, they are more flexible and forgiving than premade wrappers—holes can be patched and wrappers can be rerolled. Consider fresh dough like dumpling Play-Doh. Second, the possibilities are endless when making fresh dough, as you can use custom combinations of flours, starches and natural color and flavor enhancers. If you have these key ingredients on hand, you can achieve dumpling wonders in the comfort of your own kitchen (see pages 22 to 31). I experimented with dozens of dough recipes. The following are the standard few that work well with almost any dumpling in this book. Note that your yield will vary depending on how thin you like to roll your dumpling wrappers. When working with fresh dough, it takes a bit of practice to master rolling them out and folding and pleating. As long as the dumpling is completely sealed, it doesn't matter what it looks like. It will still be delicious once cooked.

# BASIC DUMPLING DOUGH/ FRESH WHEAT FLOUR DOUGH

This dough is great for all types of cooking—boiling, steaming, panfrying and deep-frying—and works well with every shape in this book. The hot water or liquid provides elasticity to the dough and shape retention to the wrapper. The dough can be rolled to the desired thickness, depending on how you are using it. The amount of liquid you add will vary depending on the humidity, altitude and so on, but I like to go by feel. Although the dough can easily be made in a food processor, I prefer making it by hand, as I believe over time you can know when the dough is right simply by touch. Both ways work. All-purpose flour works best because it has a medium level of gluten, which will provide body and elasticity without being too tough or chewy.

➢ MAKES ROUGHLY 24 LARGE DUMPLINGS OR 32 MEDIUM DUMPLINGS

¾ to 1 cup (175-235 ml) water
2 cups (300g) all-purpose flour
Pinch of salt
1 tsp sesame or vegetable oil

Bring the water to a boil in a small pot over high heat. Remove from the heat and allow the water to sit for 1 minute. Place the flour and salt in a large bowl and make a well in the center. Pour ¾ cup (175 ml) of the hot water and the sesame oil into the well and stir with a wooden spoon until well incorporated with the flour. Add more water by the teaspoon as necessary to make the dough come together; there will be small lumpy pieces but the dough should not be sticky. Gently bring the warm dough together in the bowl by kneading the pieces until you get a large mass.

If using a food processor, place the flour and salt in the bowl and turn the machine on, adding the hot water and oil to the flour in a thin, steady stream until it is all incorporated. Stop the food processor immediately and check that the dough has come together and is soft and pliable. If it is too dry, add water by the teaspoonful, pulsing the food processor, until the dough comes together.

Turn the dough out onto a work surface and knead into a uniform, soft, smooth mass, about 30 seconds to a minute for machine-made dough and 2 to 3 minutes for handmade dough. The dough will be smooth and elastic and feel very dense but pliable. It should not be sticky at all and bounces back slowly when you press your finger into it, leaving a shallow impression of your finger.

Wrap the dough in plastic wrap or place in a resealable plastic bag. Allow the dough to rest for at least 15 minutes and up to 3 hours at room temperature. At this point you can make your wrappers or refrigerate your dough for up to 2 days. Before using, allow your dough to warm up to room temperature, as it will be easier to manipulate.

Mix the flour and salt.

Add the sesame oil to the boiling water.

Pour the boiling water into the flour.

Mix the flour until it begins to come together.

Gently work the flour until all of the water has been completely absorbed.

Knead the mixture until it comes together.

Turn the dough on a work surface.

Knead the dough for 2 to 3 minutes by hand.

I prefer gently folding the dough until the texture is uniform.

The dough should feel smooth and elastic but very pliable, not sticky!

Wrap the dough and let it rest before using.

# VARIATIONS

**CARROT DOUGH (ORANGE):** Substitute 100 percent carrot juice in place of the boiled water. Bring the juice to a boil and stir into the dough immediately.

Vegetable juices work well for colored doughs.

Use the same techniques as making regular fresh doughs.

Knead until color is uniform.

Continue kneading until the dough is soft and pliable.

**RED CABBAGE DOUGH (PURPLE):** Substitute the desired quantity of red cabbage juice for water: 2 tablespoons (30 ml) for a light purple color, ¼ cup (60 ml) for a deeper color. You may also use all red cabbage juice in place of water for a rich purple color. To make fresh red cabbage juice, blend 3 cups (560 g) of clean washed shredded red cabbage with ½ cup (120 ml) of water in a blender on high until well pureed. Strain through a cloth-lined or paper towel–lined fine-mesh sieve into a clean bowl. Allow the puree to hang and drip for the maximum amount of juice. Use the juice immediately. Bring the juice to a boil in place of or with the water.

**RED BELL PEPPER DOUGH (RED):** Substitute 100 percent red bell pepper juice in place of the boiled water. To make fresh red bell pepper juice, blend 1 cup (150 g) of chopped red bell pepper with ½ cup (120 ml) of water in a blender on high until well pureed. Strain through a cloth-lined or paper towel–lined fine-mesh sieve into a clean bowl. Allow the puree to hang and drip for the maximum amount of juice. Bring the juice to a boil and stir into the dough immediately.

**TOMATO DOUGH (RED):** Substitute 100 percent tomato juice in place of the boiled water. Bring the juice to a boil and stir into the dough immediately.

**TURMERIC DOUGH (GOLD):** Mix 1 teaspoon (3 g) of ground dried turmeric powder into the flour before adding the hot water.

**HONG KONG-STYLE DOUGH (WITH EGG):** Mix 2 large egg yolks with ¾ cup (175 ml) warm water (120°F/48°C) until well blended. Stir this into your dough along with the sesame or vegetable oil. Knead as usual.

**SPINACH DOUGH (SAGE GREEN TO EMERALD GREEN):** Substitute the desired quantity of spinach juice for water: 2 tablespoons (30 ml) for a light green color, ¼ cup (60 ml) for a deeper color. You may also use all spinach juice in place of water for a rich emerald color. To make fresh spinach juice, blend 3 cups (560 g) of clean washed spinach with ½ cup (120 ml) of water in a blender on high until well pureed. Strain through a cloth-lined or paper towel–lined fine-mesh sieve into a clean bowl. Allow the puree to hang and drip for the maximum amount of juice. Use the juice immediately. Bring the juice to a boil in place of or with the water. Spices may also be added in small quantities to your dough for additional flavor.

**BEET DOUGH (PINK TO DARK MAGENTA):** Substitute the desired quantity of beet juice for water: 2 tablespoons (30 ml) for a light pink color, ¼ cup (60 ml) for a deeper color. You may also use all beet juice in place of water for a dark magenta color. To make fresh beet juice, use a juice extractor with fresh raw red beets (you can also use yellow or golden beets for yellow wrappers), or blend 1 cup (135 ml) of peeled, diced raw red beets with ½ cup (120 ml) of water in a blender on high until well pureed. Strain through a cloth-lined or paper towel–lined fine-mesh sieve into a clean bowl. Allow the puree to hang and drip for the maximum amount of juice. Refrigerate the juice for up to 2 days until needed. Bring the juice to a boil in place of or with the water.

To make vegetable juice, puree your vegetables with water.

Strain the juice through a fine-mesh sieve.

Add oil to the flours.

Add hot vegetable juice to the flour.

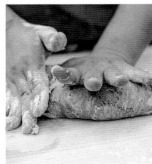

Mix as usual until the dough comes together. Knead until the dough is soft and smooth and the color is uniform.

# BASIC WHEAT STARCH DOUGH ✓

Because this dough is made with wheat starch, which is derived from wheat flour but lacking the gluten, it is inherently trickier to work with, but the end result is a delicate, translucent skin. Tapioca starch or flour helps bind the dough together and adds structure in place of the gluten. The opaque dough turns clear once fully cooked, so steaming and panfrying are the perfect cooking methods for dumplings made with this dough.

➢ MAKES ROUGHLY 30 TO 40 SMALL DUMPLINGS

1 cup (140 g) wheat starch
2 tbsp (16 g) tapioca flour or starch
1 tsp (5 ml) vegetable oil
½ cup (120 ml) plus 2 tbsp (30 ml) water

Mix the wheat starch and tapioca flour in a bowl with a whisk or fork until well combined. Make a well in the center of the flour. Bring the oil and water to a boil in a small pot and pour into the well, mixing with a spoon until the flour has absorbed all of the liquid. Cover with plastic wrap or a hot damp towel to allow the flour to soften. Turn the dough out onto a work surface or cutting board. Gently knead the dough for 1 to 2 minutes. Add more wheat starch as needed if the dough is sticky. The dough should be smooth and soft. Keep the warm dough wrapped in plastic wrap so it does not dry out.

When working with the dough, you may lightly oil your hands and work surface to prevent the dough from drying and cracking.

Color variations on this dough may be developed through the same substitutions as the Fresh Wheat Flour Dough (page 22).

# GLUTINOUS RICE FLOUR DOUGH✓

This sticky, chewy dough is great for all methods of cooking. Steaming gives the dough a translucent appearance, and deep-frying allows the dough to puff up and crisp on the outside while maintaining a chewy interior. The salt dough is great for savory dumplings (and perfect for people with wheat allergies) while the sweet dough is perfect for desserts like Sesame Jin Dui (page 209). When working with both of these doughs, feel free to use a little bit of rice flour when rolling out the dough. Remember to keep your dough covered at all stages so it does not dry out.

➢ MAKES ROUGHLY 24 TO 30 SMALL DUMPLINGS

## SALT DOUGH

1 cup (135g) glutinous rice flour
½ cup (70g) tapioca starch
½ tsp salt
¾ cup (180 ml) just-boiled water

## SWEET DOUGH

½ cup (95 g) rock sugar or demerara sugar dissolved in ¼ cup (60 ml) boiling water
1½ cups (200 g) glutinous rice flour

**SALT DOUGH:** Mix the glutinous rice flour, tapioca starch and salt in a bowl with a whisk or fork until well combined. Make a well in the center of the flour. Pour the just-boiled water into the well, mixing with a spoon until the flour has absorbed all of the liquid. Cover with plastic wrap or a hot damp towel to allow the flour to soften. Turn the dough out onto a work surface or cutting board. Gently knead the dough for 1 to 2 minutes. Add glutinous rice flour as needed if the dough is sticky. The dough should be smooth and soft. Keep the warm dough wrapped in plastic wrap so it does not dry out.

**SWEET DOUGH:** Stir the warm sugar water into the glutinous rice flour until well mixed, then turn the dough out onto a work surface or cutting board and knead until a smooth, soft dough is formed. Keep the dough covered so it does not dry out.

# SALT DOUGH ✓

Blend your glutinous rice flour, tapioca starch and salt.

Add boiling water and blend the mixture.

Knead until the dough comes together.

The dough should hold the compression when you press your finger into it.

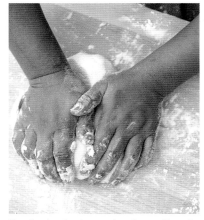

Turn the dough onto a work surface and knead until smooth.

Wrap the dough immediately to prevent from drying out.

# BAO DOUGH

It is vitally important when making the bread dough for the bao to allow the yeast and leavening agents to do their work and get a proper rise. If the dough doesn't proof properly, your bao will be tough, dense, and chewy versus the pillowy, soft texture you are looking for. Using a low-protein flour like cake flour and wheat starch allows for a super white and fluffy dough once steamed. If you don't have wheat starch available, a blend of cake flour and all-purpose flour works nicely.

➢ MAKES 32 SMALL BUNS OR 16 MEDIUM BUNS

2 cups (280 g) cake flour or Hong Kong flour

1 cup (100 g) wheat starch (or all-purpose flour)

½ cup plus 1 tbsp (90 g) confectioners' sugar

2½ tsp (9 g) baking powder

⅔ cup (160 ml) lukewarm water

2½ tsp (8 g) active dry yeast

2 tbsp (30 ml) vegetable oil

½ tsp white vinegar

In a large bowl, sift together the cake flour, wheat starch, confectioners' sugar and baking powder. Whisk the flour mixture together in the bowl after sifting. Make a well in the center of the flour.

Pour the lukewarm water over the dry yeast in a small bowl and allow the yeast to soften for 2 minutes. Whisk in the vegetable oil and vinegar. Pour the yeast and liquid into the well of the flour.

Using a wooden spoon or your fingers, slowly begin to incorporate the flour with the liquid, moving from the center toward the outer edge, gradually working in all the flour while being sure to scrape the bottom and sides of the bowl. You should have a ragged, soft dough; knead the dough several times to form a mass, and then turn the contents of the bowl out onto a work surface.

Knead the dough for 6 to 8 minutes until a smooth, soft dough forms. You shouldn't need additional flour. If the dough is still sticky after a few minutes of kneading, sprinkle a pinch of cake flour in and knead a few times until the dough is slightly tacky but no longer sticking to your fingers. The dough will feel slightly elastic and dense, and it should spring back slowly when you press your finger into it.

Transfer the dough to a lightly oiled clean bowl and cover with a large piece of plastic wrap or damp towel. Place the bowl in a warm, draft-free place to proof for 30 to 45 minutes, or until the dough doubles in size. The dough is now ready to use or you may wrap it in plastic wrap and refrigerate.

Sift flour, sugar, baking powder and starch together.

Add yeast to warm water to bloom.

Add yeast to the flour.

Bring flour together in a ball.

Knead until the dough is smooth, about 6 to 8 minutes.

Allow the dough to proof, covered, in a wam draft-free place.

# CHAPTER 3

# CLASSIC FOLDS:
## POTSTICKERS, GYOZA, MANDU AND MORE

➤ When I think of dumplings, the first image that comes to mind is that classic, plump, half-moon-shaped potsticker. There are many varieties of dumplings that use this round wrapper shape and pleating technique, names and styles varying by country and region. Having lived in New York City for the past twenty years, I've had access to the most wondrous of dumplings. There are a number of small shops in Chinatown, Koreatown and Flushing where you can actually watch a small team of cooks laboriously and meticulously hand fold Chinese-style jiaozi or Korean mandu by the hundreds, literally thousands if you were to stand there all day. At a worktable heavily dusted with flour, one cook cuts a giant ball of dough into tiny pieces and then with lightning speed rolls it into a perfectly round, thin wrapper using a small rolling pin. The cook next to the dough roller quickly stuffs, folds and seals the dumplings, arranging them compactly in neat rows on a floured tray. It's mesmerizing to watch. These particular dumpling shops usually have a line out the door, not just because you can feed a family of four for less than $20, but because everyone knows the dumplings are being made fresh that day. This chapter covers the classic cultural versions of these dumplings, as well as some new style interpretations. As soon as you get comfortable with the folding technique, you'll realize fresh dumplings are only a few minutes away from gracing your plate. Some people wish the moon was made of cheese. When there's a big half-moon hanging in the sky I like to think it's a giant potsticker.

# HOW TO FOLD

## Fold Number One

You can use fresh dough or thawed premade dumpling, mandu or gyoza wrappers, available in your grocer's freezer section. When using fresh dough, roll the dough out to the desired size and thickness specified by the recipe.

Mastering this fold takes a little bit of time and practice. The most important part is making sure you get a good seal for both safety measures so you don't lose any filling in the cooking process. Remember, especially for panfried and deep-fried dumplings, water and oil do not mix and can become dangerous when combined in a hot pan.

Hold the wrapper in the palm of your hand and lightly wet the edges of the wrapper with water using either a pastry brush or your finger. Place the desired amount of filling in the center of the wrapper, and gently fold the bottom of the wrapper toward the top half, to form a half-moon shape, then gently press the edge of the wrapper together closest to where your thumb meets your forefinger, using your thumb to seal the first ½ inch (1.3 cm) of the dumpling.

Now this is where it gets a little tricky. Using your free hand, make a small ½-inch (1.3 cm) pleat in the direction of your thumb and the sealed end with only the top wrapper, lining up the edge of the pleat with the bottom half of the wrapper, and use your thumb to press gently and seal.

Continue to gather, pleat (toward your thumb) and press the top half of the wrapper, always making sure you line the edges up with the bottom half of the wrapper, until you have made 4 or 5 pleats and the dumpling is completely sealed.

By gathering only one side of the dumpling wrapper, you will see the natural crescent shape begin to form. Place the formed dumplings on a lightly floured tray or plate. Keep a layer of plastic wrap weighted with a lightly damp towel on top of the finished dumplings so they do not dry out. Refrigerate or freeze your dumplings as needed.

## Fold Number Two

This fold is slightly easier. Hold the wrapper in the palm of your hand and lightly wet the edges of the wrapper with water using either a pastry brush or your finger. Place the desired amount of filling in the center of the wrapper, and gently fold the bottom of the wrapper toward the top half to form a half-moon shape, then gently press the edges together to seal, pressing out any air where the wrapper encases the filling.

Cut your fresh dough into portions and roll each wrapper using a rolling pin.

Fill your dumplings with the desired amount of filling.

Fold the dough in half and gently press the first corner together using your thumb and forefinger.

Make a small pleat, lining up the edges of the wrapper as you pleat and press.

Make a second pleat, lining up the edges.

Use your thumb and forefinger to seal the pleats.

Continue pleating until your have made 4 to 5 pleats and the dumpling is sealed.

When finished, the dumpling will form a natural half-moon shape.

An original plate from my great-grandfather's Chinese restaurant in New Haven.

# PORK AND CHIVE DUMPLINGS

This classic recipe is a winner every time and an MVP in my dumpling arsenal. Pork fatback plays an important role in keeping these dumplings moist and juicy. Garlic chives give the filling a robust flavor and aroma. How you cook these is up to you; they are delicious boiled, steamed, panfried and deep-fried. With this party favorite, there's no need to order Chinese takeout once you learn how easy these are to make at home.

➢ MAKES 60 DUMPLINGS
➢ Preferred Cooking Method: All methods work great!

1½ lb (680 g) ground pork

1½ cups (227 g) minced garlic or Chinese chives

¼ cup (45 g) ground fatback (if you can't find it, then make sure you are using fatty ground pork)

¼ cup (60 ml) low-sodium soy sauce

¼ cup (60 ml) Shaoxing rice wine

2 tbsp (30 g) finely grated or minced ginger

2 tsp (8 g) sugar

1 tsp (4 g) salt

½ tsp ground white pepper

60 round dumpling wrappers or 2x recipe Fresh Wheat Flour Dough (page 22)

Oil if frying (optional)

Chopped scallion for garnish

Soy Ginger Dipping Sauce (page 219)

In a large mixing bowl, combine the pork, garlic or chives, fatback, soy sauce, wine, ginger, sugar, salt and white pepper. Mix the ingredients until the filling is well combined and homogenous.

Fill each dumpling with 1 tablespoon (12 g) of filling. Lightly wet the edges of the wrapper and form the dumpling using the classic pleat technique. Keep the dumplings covered on a lightly floured tray or plate.

## CHOOSE YOUR COOKING METHOD:

**BOILED:** Bring a large pot of salted water to a boil over high heat. Add half the dumplings to the pot. When the water boils again, add ½ cup (120 ml) of cold water. When the water boils again, add another ½ cup (120 ml) of cold water. When the water boils again (the dumplings should be floating), strain out the dumplings and repeat with the remaining dumplings. Garnish with the chopped scallion and serve hot with the dipping sauce.

**STEAMED:** Arrange the dumplings 1 inch (2.5 cm) apart in a dim sum basket lined with greased parchment paper. Place the covered dim sum steamer over a boiling water bath until the filling and dumpling skins are cooked through, about 6 minutes. Repeat with the remaining dumplings. Garnish with the chopped scallion and serve hot with the dipping sauce.

**PANFRIED:** In a liquid measuring cup, mix 2 cups (475 ml) of water and 2 tablespoons (12 g) of flour well until the flour has dissolved into the water and the mixture is cloudy. Heat a small nonstick pan over medium-high heat. Add 1 tablespoon (15 ml) of vegetable oil to the pan and place the dumplings in the pan, lined up next to each other, and cook until the bottoms of the dumplings turn golden brown, about 1 to 2 minutes. Add ½ cup (120 ml) of the flour and water mixture to the pan; it will react with the hot pan and steam and splatter a bit; be ready with a lid to fit the pan. As soon as you add the flour and water mixture, cover the pan with a tight-fitting lid. Cook the dumplings, covered, until almost all of the water has evaporated and a thin golden crust begins to form in the bottom of the pan, about 4 to 5 minutes. Remove the lid and cook until all the water has evaporated. Carefully remove the dumplings from the pan and repeat with the remaining dumplings. Garnish with the chopped scallion and serve hot with the dipping sauce.

**DEEP-FRIED:** Preheat a large pot of oil to 350°F/176°C. Carefully drop the dumplings one by one into the hot oil, frying in small batches and being sure not to overcrowd the oil. Cook the dumplings for 2 minutes, until the filling is cooked and the exterior is golden brown. Drain on paper towels. Repeat with the remaining dumplings until all are cooked, making sure the oil temperature returns to 350°F/176°C before frying the next batch. Garnish with the chopped scallion and serve hot with the dipping sauce.

# FIVE-SPICE PORK BELLY DUMPLING WRAPS

The difficulty with this recipe is in not eating all of the filling first. The recipe for the pork belly is a staple of mine, and you can make a master batch of belly and keep it in your freezer for uses such as dumplings, ramen, buns and hundreds of other snack-tastic applications. I love eating these dumplings in a lettuce leaf; the crunchy freshness and the addition of a dipping sauce or dressing cuts through the richness of the pork belly.

➤ MAKES 60 DUMPLINGS
➤ Preferred Cooking Method: Deep-fried

## PORK BELLY FILLING

2 tbsp (30 g) five-spice powder

½ tsp crushed red pepper flakes

1 tsp (5 g) salt

1 tsp (5 g) cracked black pepper

¼ cup (60 g) brown sugar

6 cloves garlic, sliced

2 lb (910 g) pork belly, slab or thick slices, skin removed

1 cup (150 g) sliced yellow onion or chopped scallion greens

2" (5 cm) piece ginger, thinly sliced

2 tbsp (30 ml) rice or apple cider vinegar

2 tbsp (30 ml) sesame oil

¼ cup (60 ml) soy sauce

½ cup (120 ml) sake, Shaoxing wine or dry sherry

2 cups (475 ml) water

½ cup (25 g) minced scallion

2 to 3 tbsp (30 to 45 ml) pork belly braising liquid

60 round dumpling wrappers

Oil for deep-frying

60 small Bibb lettuce leaves

Cilantro for garnish

Hoisin sauce, Sweet Chili Sauce (page 223), or Black Vinegar Dipping Sauce (page 219)

To make the pork belly filling, combine the five-spice powder, red pepper flakes, salt, black pepper, sugar and garlic slices in a bowl. Stir well to combine, and then rub all sides of the pork belly in the spice mixture, reserving any extra rub that falls off.

Place the onion and ginger in the bottom of a 2- to 3-inch (5- to 7.5-cm)-deep ovenproof baking dish and nestle the spice rubbed pork belly on top. Mix the remaining spice rub, vinegar, sesame oil, soy sauce, sake and water together and pour over the pork belly and onions, tossing gently to coat. Allow the pork to marinate, covered, overnight in the refrigerator if time allows.

Preheat the oven to 450°F/232°C. Cover the baking dish tightly with aluminum foil. Place the pork belly in the oven on the middle rack and bake for 30 minutes before turning the heat down to 300°F/148°C. Bake the belly for 2 to 2 ½ hours, until fork-tender, checking the pork halfway through (add more water to the braising liquid if it is evaporating too quickly).

Carefully remove the pork and onions from the braising liquid, reserve the liquid, drain on paper towels and then transfer to a cutting board. Chop the pork and onions into small pieces until the pork begins to naturally shred and fall apart. Transfer the chopped mixture to a mixing bowl. Add the minced scallion and braising liquid to taste. Cover and refrigerate the pork filling until it is cold.

You may use fresh dough, but I like the delicate feel of Hong Kong–style dumpling wrappers (the yellow ones with egg yolk). Place a heaping teaspoon (4 g) of filling in the wrapper and form the dumpling with a classic potsticker pleat. Because the filling is already cooked you only need to worry about making sure the wrapper is thoroughly cooked.

Preheat the deep-frying oil to 350°F/176°C. Carefully fry the dumplings in small batches until the skin is golden brown and the dumplings are floating in the oil, about 2 to 3 minutes, gently tossing the dumplings in the oil so all sides cook evenly. Drain on paper towels. Allow the oil to come back to 350°F/176° before frying the next batch.

Serve the crispy dumplings with fresh lettuce leaves, cilantro and the dipping sauce of your choice.

# XO PORK POTSTICKERS

XO sauce is one of my favorite Chinese condiments, a spicy sauce made from dried seafood, Chinese ham and sausage, and chiles. Take all that flavor and put it in a dumpling and you can't go wrong!

▷ MAKES 60 DUMPLINGS
▷ Preferred Cooking Method: Panfried

1 oz (30 g) dried scallop

1 oz (30 g) dried tiny shrimp

1 tbsp (15 ml) sesame oil

3 tbsp (45 g) minced shallot

1 tbsp (15 g) minced garlic

1 tbsp (15 g) minced ginger

1 tbsp (15 g) brown sugar

4 oz (115 g) Chinese bacon or ham, cut into ¼" (0.6 cm) dice

2 links Chinese lap cheong sausage, cut into ¼" (0.6 cm) dice

2 tbsp (21 g) seeded and minced fresh red chile, or 1 tsp (3 g) crushed red pepper flakes

½ cup (120 ml) Shaoxing rice wine or dry sherry

8 oz (226 g) ground pork

4 oz (120 g) raw shrimp, peeled and finely chopped

2 tbsp (30 ml) dark soy sauce

1 tbsp (10 g) cornstarch

½ cup (25 g) minced scallion

½ tsp ground white pepper

2 recipes Fresh Wheat Flour Dough (page 22)

Oil for panfrying

Black Vinegar Dipping Sauce (page 219)

Bring 2 cups (475 ml) of water to a boil and pour over the dried scallop and shrimp. Allow the dried seafood to rehydrate for an hour, then drain and pat dry. Mince the scallop and shrimp and set aside.

Heat a large sauté pan over medium-high heat. Add the sesame oil and the shallot and stir-fry for 30 seconds, then add the garlic and ginger and stir-fry for another 30 seconds. Add the dried seafood, brown sugar and Chinese ham and sausage and cook for 2 minutes. Add the minced chile, and deglaze the pan with the wine. Cook until all of the liquid has evaporated, stirring often, about 3 minutes. Transfer the contents of the pan to a sheet tray or dish to cool.

Once the mixture has cooled to room temperature (or preferably chilled in the fridge), combine in a bowl with the ground pork, chopped shrimp, dark soy sauce, cornstarch, scallion and white pepper. Mix well. Refrigerate until needed.

Divide your dough into 4 pieces. Roll each piece into a 1-inch (2.5-cm)-thick rope and cut into ½-inch (1.3 cm) pieces. Keep the dough covered with a damp towel.

Roll each dough ball into a 3-inch (7.5-cm) round wrapper using a rolling pin. Fill each dumpling with 1 tablespoon (12 g) of filling. Lightly wet the edges of the wrapper and form the dumpling using the classic pleat technique. Keep the dumplings covered on a lightly floured tray or plate.

Heat a wok or large nonstick frying pan over high heat. Add ½ tablespoon (7.5 ml) of oil to the hot pan, tilting the pan to coat the bottom. Place the dumplings in a single layer in the hot pan and cook until the bottoms are golden brown, 1 to 2 minutes. Add ½ cup (125 ml) of water and immediately cover the pan with a tight-fitting lid. Cook until all of the water has been absorbed and the dumpling skins have cooked through, about 4 to 5 minutes. Repeat with the remaining dumplings. Serve with the dipping sauce.

# GARLIC PORK AND KALE DUMPLINGS

Kale is all the rage now, so there's no reason why you can't have this super green in your dumplings. I like to marinate the kale briefly before mixing it in the filling. This gives it time to tenderize before going into the quick-cooking filling. I love these dumplings simply steamed; they are juicy and flavorful on their own but certainly pair well with any number of dipping sauces, including red vinegar dipping sauce or soy ginger dipping sauce.

➢ MAKES 60 DUMPLINGS
➢ Preferred Cooking Method: Steamed

½ lb (230 g) green kale, stems removed, finely shredded into small pieces

1 tsp (5 g) salt

2 tbsp (30 g) sugar

2 tbsp (30 ml) rice vinegar or apple cider vinegar

1 tbsp (15 ml) sambal chile paste

2 tbsp (30 ml) oyster sauce

3 tbsp (30 g) minced garlic

3 tbsp (45 ml) sesame oil

Zest of 1 lemon

1 lb (450 g) ground pork

½ cup (90 g) finely grated Parmesan cheese

Pinch of salt and white pepper

2 recipes Fresh Wheat Flour Dough (page 22) or Basic Wheat Starch Dough (page 27)

Red Vinegar Dipping Sauce (page 219) or Soy Ginger Dipping Sauce (page 219)

Place the kale in a large bowl. In a small bowl, combine the salt, sugar, vinegar, sambal, oyster sauce, garlic, sesame oil and lemon zest. Mix well and then combine with the shredded kale. Toss to coat and allow the kale to marinate, covered, at room temperature for 1 hour to soften.

Add the ground pork and Parmesan cheese. Mix the filling well. Season to taste with salt and pepper. Refrigerate until needed.

Divide your dough into 4 pieces. Roll each piece into a 1-inch (2.5-cm)-thick rope and cut into ½-inch (1.3-cm) pieces. Keep dough covered with a damp towel.

Roll each dough ball into a 3-inch (7.5-cm) round wrapper using a rolling pin. Fill each dumpling with 1 tablespoon (12 g) of filling. Lightly wet the edges of the wrapper and form the dumpling using the classic pleat technique. Keep the dumplings covered on a lightly floured tray or plate.

Place the dumplings in a steamer basket lined with punched parchment or wax paper, or blanched cabbage leaves. Cover and steam for 8 minutes. Serve with the dipping sauce of your choice.

# BRUSSELS SPROUTS AND BACON DUMPLINGS

This dumpling pays homage to the fried brussels sprouts and pork craze. Forget the soggy, overcooked brussels sprouts that make you wrinkle your nose in disdain. The deep-fried brussels sprout leaves develop a caramelized nutty flavor that pairs beautifully with the salty, smoky bacon. This tasty filling is great any way you decide to cook your dumplings.

➤ MAKES 60 DUMPLINGS
➤ Preferred Cooking Method: Panfried

1 lb (450 g) bacon, diced into ¼" (0.6 cm) pieces
Oil for deep-frying
2 pints (1½ lb) fresh brussels sprouts
Salt and black pepper
3 tbsp (30 g) minced garlic
3 tbsp (40 g) brown sugar
2 tbsp (20 g) cornstarch
2 tbsp (30 ml) fish sauce
2 tbsp (30 ml) black vinegar or balsamic vinegar
2 tbsp (30 ml) reserved bacon fat
60 round dumpling wrappers
Fish Sauce Caramel (page 226)

In a large sauté pan, render the bacon over medium-high heat until it is completely cooked and crispy. Strain and cool the cooked bacon on a paper towel–lined plate. Reserve the bacon fat.

Preheat a small pot of oil to 375°F/190°C. Trim the bottom ends and old leaves from the brussels sprouts. Reserve any fresh leaves that may have fallen. Quarter the brussels sprouts, leaving the root ends intact.

Divide the trimmed brussels sprouts in half. Deep-fry half of the brussels sprouts in small batches, cooking each batch for 2 to 3 minutes until the leaves are caramelized and brown. Drain on paper towels and season lightly with salt. Once cool, chop the fried brussels sprouts into small pieces or pulse in a food processor.

Bring a pot of salted water to a boil. Blanch the remaining brussels sprouts until tender, about 3 minutes. Refresh in ice water to stop the cooking and then drain on paper towels. Dry the blanched brussels sprouts well with paper towels and then chop finely (or pulse in the food processor).

Combine the cooked bacon, fried chopped brussels sprouts, blanched chopped brussels sprouts and minced garlic in a large bowl. In a small bowl, sift together the brown sugar and cornstarch until it is well mixed. Sprinkle this mixture evenly over the filling, add the fish sauce, vinegar and bacon fat and mix until well combined. Season with salt and pepper to taste. Refrigerate the filling for at least an hour.

Fill and form the dumplings in the classic pleat style. I prefer using premade wrappers for this dumpling. Heat a wok or large nonstick frying pan over high heat. Add ½ tablespoon (7.5 ml) of oil to the hot pan, tilting the pan to coat the bottom. Place the dumplings in a single layer in the hot pan and cook until the bottoms are golden brown, 1 to 2 minutes. Add ½ cup (125 ml) of water and immediately cover the pan with a tight-fitting lid. Cook until all of the water has been absorbed and the dumpling skins have cooked through, about 4 to 5 minutes. Repeat with the remaining dumplings. Serve with the Fish Sauce Caramel.

# SZECHUAN EGGPLANT AND PORK DUMPLINGS

I love the earthy flavor and silky texture of cooked eggplant and savory pork. The heat from the chiles and tingle from the Szechuan peppercorns are addictive. These dumplings are great when you use the Wheat Starch Dough and panfry them. However you decide to cook them, the classic XO Sauce and Red Vinegar Dipping Sauce are perfect accompaniments.

➤ MAKES 30 DUMPLINGS
➤ Preferred Cooking Method: Panfried

1 lb (450 g) eggplant, peeled and cut into ¼" (0.6 cm) dice

1 tbsp (15 g) salt

3 tbsp (45 ml) sesame oil

2 tbsp (20 g) minced garlic

2 tbsp (20 g) minced ginger

1 tbsp (10 g) minced red chile pepper or sambal chile paste

1 tsp (3 g) ground Szechuan peppercorns

2 tbsp (30 ml) red vinegar

2 tbsp (30 ml) dark soy sauce

1 tbsp (15 ml) lite soy sauce

2 tbsp (30 g) sugar

1 tbsp (15 ml) hot bean paste or miso

½ lb (225 g) ground pork

½ cup (75 g) minced garlic chives

2 tbsp (20 g) cornstarch

1 recipe Basic Wheat Starch Dough (page 27)

Oil for panfrying

Red Vinegar Dipping Sauce (page 220)

In a large bowl, sprinkle the diced eggplant with the salt and toss to coat. Allow the eggplant to sit for at least an hour; you will see beads of moisture on the eggplant. Rinse the eggplant under cold water and dry thoroughly, pressing the eggplant between clean dry towels or paper towels to remove all excess moisture.

In a large wok or sauté pan, heat the sesame oil over high heat. Add the garlic, ginger and chile pepper; it should sizzle immediately. Cook for 30 seconds, or until fragrant. Add the eggplant and Szechuan pepper to the pan and stir-fry to coat. Reduce the heat to medium-high and continue to stir-fry the eggplant until it is soft and tender, about 5 minutes. Remove the eggplant from the pan, transfer to a bowl and allow to cool in the refrigerator.

In a separate mixing bowl, combine the vinegar, dark and lite soy sauces, sugar and bean paste, whisking thoroughly until smooth. Add the ground pork, garlic chives, cornstarch and chilled cooked eggplant to the bowl. Mix thoroughly but gently, so as not to crush the eggplant. Refrigerate the filling until needed.

Roll the dough into a 1-inch (2.5-cm)-thick rope and cut into 3 pieces. Cover the dough pieces with plastic wrap and a hot, damp towel.

Lightly spray a small piece of plastic wrap or two small sheets of parchment paper with cooking spray. Place the dough piece on the greased plastic wrap and fold the plastic wrap in half over the dough ball, or place between the two pieces of parchment paper.

Using a rolling pin or a meat cleaver, flatten or roll each piece into a 3- to 4-inch (7.5- to 10-cm) round. The dough should be fairly thin (about 1/16 inch). Gently unpeel the wrapper from the plastic wrap or parchment and fill the wrapper immediately with 1 tablespoon (12 g) of filling. Lightly wet the edges of the wrapper and form the dumpling using the classic pleat technique. Keep the dumplings covered on a lightly floured tray or plate.

Heat a wok or large nonstick frying pan over high heat. Add ½ tablespoon (7.5 ml) of oil to the hot pan, tilting the pan to coat the bottom. Place the dumplings in a single layer in the hot pan, making sure they are not crowded in the pan and do not touch each other. Cook until the bottoms are golden brown, about 2 minutes. Add ½ cup (125 ml) of water and immediately cover the pan with a tight-fitting lid. Cook until all of the water has been absorbed and the dumpling skins have cooked through, about 4 to 5 minutes. Repeat with the remaining dumplings. Serve with the dipping sauce.

# MISO SHORT RIB DUMPLINGS

These decadent dumplings take a few steps and several days to make, but this is the one that will win you friends and admirers for sure, especially the beef lovers. These dumplings are best with wheat flour dough, and I love the panfrying method that keeps the skin slightly crispy and chewy. The light heat from the wasabi and horseradish makes this French-Asian mash-up complete.

≫ MAKES 60 DUMPLINGS
≫ Preferred Cooking Method: Panfried

## DUMPLINGS

2 lb (900 g) boneless short ribs
Kosher salt and black pepper
Vegetable oil for panfrying
6 cloves garlic, sliced
2 tbsp (30 g) minced ginger
2 cups (300 g) sliced yellow onion
¼ cup (60 ml) red miso
3 tbsp (45 g) brown sugar
½ cup (120 ml) red wine
½ cup (120 ml) dry sake
½ cup (120 ml) mirin
3 cups (700 ml) beef stock or chicken stock, store-bought or homemade (page 217 or 215)
1 sprig thyme
1 cup (50 g) minced scallion, white and green parts
1 tbsp (15 g) butter
2 recipes Fresh Wheat Flour Dough (page 22)

## HORSERADISH CREAM

2 cups (240 g) sour cream
¼ cup (30 g) prepared horseradish
2 tbsp (30 ml) prepared wasabi paste
2 tbsp (30 ml) lemon juice
½ tsp freshly cracked black pepper
½ tsp salt

To make the dumplings, preheat the oven to 325°F/162°C. Heat a large ovenproof pot (like a Dutch oven) over high heat. Season the short ribs generously with salt and pepper. Add a few tablespoons of oil to the hot pot to coat the bottom and sear the short ribs on all sides, about 3 to 4 minutes per side, until you have developed nice caramelization on the short ribs. Remove from the pot and set aside. Pour off the excess fat from the pot and discard.

Return the pot to the heat, turned down to medium, and add 1 tablespoon (15 ml) of oil. Sweat the garlic and ginger, stirring, until fragrant, 2 minutes. Add the onion and continue to sweat until softened, about 5 minutes. Stir in the miso and brown sugar until everything is well coated and then add the red wine, sake, mirin, stock and thyme, stirring well.

Place the short ribs back into the pot and return the heat to high until the liquid begins to boil. Place a tight-fitting lid on the pot and place the pot in the oven on the middle rack. Braise the short ribs until fork-tender, about 3½ hours. When the ribs are fully cooked, remove them from the braising liquid and transfer to a cutting board. Roughly chop the short ribs into small pieces and place in a large bowl. Add the minced scallion to the bowl.

Strain the braising liquid, reserving the solids; discard the thyme sprig. Skim any excess fat off the top of the braising liquid; set aside. Bring the remaining braising liquid to boil in a small pot and reduce until there is only ½ cup (120 ml) of liquid remaining. Whisk in the butter and then pour into a blender with the strained solids from the braise. Start the blender on low speed (make sure the cover is on tightly) and then increase to high until you have a loose puree. Add the puree to the short ribs and mix well. Refrigerate the mixture overnight.

Meanwhile, make the horseradish cream. Mix all the ingredients in a bowl until well combined. Refrigerate in an airtight container until needed.

Divide your dough into 4 pieces. Roll each piece into a 1-inch (2.5-cm)-thick rope and cut into ½-inch (1.3 cm) pieces. Keep the dough covered with a damp towel.

Roll each dough ball into a 3-inch (7.5-cm) round wrapper using a rolling pin. Fill each dumpling with 1 tablespoon (12 g) of filling. Lightly wet the edges of the wrapper and form the dumpling using the classic pleat technique. Keep the dumplings covered on a lightly floured tray or plate.

Heat a wok or large nonstick frying pan over high heat. Add ½ tablespoon (7.5 ml) of oil to the hot pan, tilting the pan to coat the bottom. Place the dumplings in a single layer in the hot pan and cook until the bottoms are golden brown, 1 to 2 minutes. Add ½ cup (125 ml) of water and immediately cover the pan with a tight-fitting lid. Cook until all of the water has been absorbed and the dumpling skins have cooked through, about 4 to 5 minutes. Repeat with the remaining dumplings. Serve with the horseradish cream on the side.

# BEEF AND BLACK PEPPER DUMPLINGS

People ask me all the time what my favorite spice is, and black pepper happens to be at the top of my list. Freshly toasted and cracked or ground, pepper has a natural aroma and heat that can enhance virtually any food. One of my favorite dishes at any Chinese restaurant is beef short ribs in black pepper sauce. Lightly sweet and salty, the pungent black pepper creates the pleasant burn that keeps me coming back for more. You can eat these dumplings alone; I like them sautéed in black pepper sauce.

➤ MAKES 30 DUMPLINGS
➤ Preferred Cooking Method: Panfried

## DUMPLINGS

¾ lb (340 g) ground beef, 80% to 85% lean

½ cup (100 g) grated yellow onion

½ cup (75 g) diced water chestnuts

2 tsp (6 g) minced garlic

1 tsp (5 g) freshly cracked black pepper

1 tbsp (15 ml) Shaoxing rice wine

2 tbsp (30 ml) soy sauce

1 tbsp (15 g) sugar

½ tsp salt

1 tbsp (10 g) cornstarch

1 recipe Fresh Wheat Flour Dough (page 22)

Sesame oil for panfrying

## SAUCE

1 cup (50 g) 2"- (5 cm)-long scallion, green and white parts

1 red or green chile, thinly sliced

1 tbsp (15 g) sugar

1 tbsp (10 g) cornstarch

1 tbsp (15 ml) Shaoxing rice wine

3 tbsp (45 ml) lite soy sauce

¼ cup (60 ml) low-sodium chicken or beef broth

1 tsp (5 g) freshly cracked black pepper

To make the dumplings, in a large bowl combine the ground beef, grated onion, water chestnuts, garlic, black pepper, wine, soy sauce, sugar, salt and cornstarch. Mix until well combined.

Divide your dough into 4 pieces. Roll each piece into a 1-inch (2.5-cm)-thick rope and cut into ½-inch (1.3-cm) pieces. Keep the dough covered with a damp towel.

Roll each dough ball into a 3-inch (7.5-cm) round wrapper using a rolling pin. Fill each dumpling with 1 tablespoon (12 g) of filling. Lightly wet the edges of the wrapper and form the dumpling using the classic pleat technique. Keep the dumplings covered on a lightly floured tray or plate.

Heat a wok or large nonstick frying pan over high heat. Add ½ tablespoon (7.5 ml) of oil to the hot pan, tilting the pan to coat the bottom. Place half of the dumplings in a single layer in the hot pan and cook until the bottoms are golden brown. Add ½ cup (125 ml) of water and immediately cover the pan with a tight-fitting lid. Cook until all of the water has been absorbed and the dumpling skins have cooked through, about 4 to 5 minutes. Repeat with the remaining dumplings. Set the dumplings aside on a plate.

To make the sauce, add a few more tablespoons of sesame oil to the hot pan. Add the scallion batons and sliced chile and sauté for 1 minute. Mix the sugar and cornstarch together, sprinkle over the sautéed vegetables, then add the wine, soy sauce, chicken broth and black pepper. Stir well and bring to a boil until the sauce thickens. Add the dumplings back to the pan and stir well to coat. Serve immediately.

# VIETNAMESE BEEF POTSTICKER SALAD

I love how aromatic these dumplings are. Served with a little nuoc cham dipping sauce, these dumplings satisfy my Asian food craving on so many different levels. The dumplings are great on their own, but I like pairing them with a bitter green and some nuoc cham to make it a potsticker salad.

➢ MAKES 30 DUMPLINGS
➢ Preferred Cooking Method: Deep-fried

---

¾ lb (340 g) ground beef, 80% to 85% lean

2 tbsp (6 g) finely minced fresh lemongrass

1 tbsp (10 g) minced garlic

¼ cup (50 g) minced shallot

2 tbsp (30 g) brown sugar

2 tbsp (30 ml) soy sauce

3 tbsp (45 ml) fish sauce

3 tbsp (5 g) finely minced mint

¼ tsp salt

½ tsp ground white pepper

1 tsp (5 g) crushed red pepper flakes

30 round dumpling wrappers

Oil for panfrying

6 cups (1,080 g) watercress or baby arugula or salad greens, cleaned and trimmed

⅓ cup (65 g) Pickled Red Onions (page 230)

Fried Shallots (page 231) for garnish

½ cup (120 ml) Nuoc Cham (page 227)

In a large bowl, combine the ground beef, lemongrass, garlic, shallot, brown sugar, soy sauce, fish sauce, mint, salt, white pepper and red pepper. Mix well and refrigerate until needed.

Fill each wrapper with 1 tablespoon (12 g) of filling. Lightly wet the edges of the wrapper and form the dumpling using the classic pleat technique. Keep the dumplings covered on a lightly floured tray or plate.

Heat a wok or large nonstick frying pan over high heat. Add 1 tablespoon (15 ml) of oil to the hot pan, tilting the pan to coat the bottom. Place the dumplings in a single layer in the hot pan and cook until the bottoms are golden brown, 1 to 2 minutes. Add ⅓ cup (80 ml) of water and immediately cover the pan with a tight-fitting lid. Cook until all of the water has been absorbed and the dumpling skins have cooked through, about 5 to 6 minutes. Carefully remove from the pan. Repeat with the remaining dumplings.

To serve, divide the greens and dumplings among 5 or 6 plates. Top with the pickled onions and fried shallots. Drizzle with the nuoc cham or serve the sauce on the side.

# BEEF AND RADISH MANDU WITH KIMCHI VINAIGRETTE

Every culture has a name for their dumplings. In Korea, dumplings are called "mandu." They range from bite-size to giant pillows that take three or four bites to consume. I've only been to Korea once, for nine hours on a long layover. I took the bus into downtown Seoul, the Insa-dong neighborhood, and met a friend from New York who happened to be living there. As we wandered around looking for our first place to lunch we happened upon this busy shop, Koong, which had a large picture of Korean mandu and a lovely Korean grandmother on the door. As we sat down to eat the waiter tried to explain that there was no menu that day, only set dishes. We couldn't understand what was happening when food began hitting the table (we hadn't even ordered) until another diner next to us, a Korean lady who happened to speak English, explained that the matriarch and resident chef of the house had just passed away. That day, everyone was invited in and fed free of charge by the family who continues to run the restaurant, to honor this woman's lifetime in food and her part in the community. We were so blown away and humbled that we got to experience this heartfelt act of sharing, me as a complete stranger to the country, beyond the fact that the food was incredible. Grandmother's signature recipe was her Gae-song-style beef mandu, which we consumed in a hot steaming bowl of broth with garlic chives and cabbage. These mandu were literally perfect: hot, tender, filling and comforting, just the way Grandma would have made them. Far and away one of my most memorable dumpling moments, this recipe pays homage to that family, and every grandmother's spirit of feeding the soul.

➢ MAKES 30 DUMPLINGS
➢ Preferred Cooking Method: Boiled

6 oz (170 g) Chinese radish, grated (large holes)

½ tbsp salt

½ lb (225 g) ground beef, 80% lean

4 oz (110 g) firm tofu, crumbled

¼ cup (50 g) finely minced yellow onion

¼ tsp black pepper

1 tsp (5 g) sugar

1 tbsp (15 ml) dark soy sauce

1 recipe Fresh Wheat Flour Dough (page 22)

Sliced scallions for garnish

Minced kimchi for garnish

Kimchi Vinaigrette (page 227)

In a small bowl, toss the grated radish with the salt. Allow the radish to sit for 30 minutes. Rinse the radish briefly under cold water and then squeeze completely dry using a clean towel.

Combine the radish with the ground beef, crumbled tofu, minced onion, black pepper, sugar and dark soy sauce. Mix well, and refrigerate as needed.

Divide your dough into 4 pieces. Roll each piece into a 1-inch (2.5-cm)-thick rope and cut into ½-inch (1.3-cm) pieces. Keep the dough covered with a damp towel.

Roll each dough ball into a 3-inch (7.5-cm) round wrapper using a rolling pin. Fill each dumpling with 1 tablespoon (12 g) of filling. Lightly wet the edges of the wrapper and form the mandu using the classic pleat technique. Keep the dumplings covered on a lightly floured tray or plate.

Bring a large pot of water to a boil. Add half the dumplings to the pot. When the water boils again add ½ cup (120 ml) of cold water. When the water boils again add another ½ cup (120 ml) of cold water. When the water boils again (the dumplings should be floating), strain out the dumplings. Repeat with the remaining dumplings. Serve hot on a plate garnished with scallions, sliced kimchi and kimchi vinaigrette.

# LEMONGRASS CHICKEN DUMPLING SOUP

Coconut milk adds a rich taste to the fragrant filling and pairs perfectly with the peppers and turmeric. It's important that you crush the lemongrass with the heavy end of your knife or a rolling pin to release the aromatic juices before you mince the firm stalk. I love these dumplings with Peanut Sesame Sauce (page 223) or Nuoc Cham (page 227). You can always substitute boxed chicken stock if you don't have time to make your own.

➢ MAKES 30 DUMPLINGS
➢ Preferred Cooking Method: Boiled

## DUMPLINGS

¾ lb (340 g) ground white meat chicken

2 tbsp (6 g) finely minced lemongrass

2 tbsp (25 g) finely minced shallot

2 tbsp (20 g) finely minced garlic

1 tbsp (10 g) seeded and minced jalapeño pepper

1 tsp (5 g) ground turmeric

1 tbsp (15 g) brown sugar

1 tbsp (10 g) cornstarch

1 tbsp (15 ml) fish sauce

¼ cup (60 ml) full-fat coconut milk

Zest of ½ lime

1 tbsp (15 ml) lime juice

½ tsp salt

30 round dumpling wrappers

## LEMONGRASS BROTH

8 cups (1,900 ml) chicken stock, store-bought or homemade (page 215)

½ cup (65 g) sliced yellow onion

1 stalk lemongrass, crushed and chopped

3 cloves garlic, crushed

2" (5-cm) piece ginger, sliced

1 piece lime zest ½" x 2" (1.3 x 5 cm)

1 tbsp (15 ml) lime juice

Salt and sugar to taste

1 cup (50 g) thinly sliced scallion greens, soaked in ice water

1 cup (26 g) cilantro leaves and stems

Fried Shallots (page 231) for garnish

To make the dumplings, in a large bowl combine the ground chicken, lemongrass, shallot, garlic and jalapeño pepper. In a small bowl, mix together the turmeric, sugar and cornstarch, then sprinkle evenly over the filling. Add the fish sauce, coconut milk, lime zest, lime juice and salt to the bowl and mix the filling well. Refrigerate until needed.

Fill each wrapper with 1 tablespoon (12 g) of filling. Lightly wet the edges of the wrapper and form the dumpling using the classic pleat technique. Keep the dumplings covered on a lightly floured tray or plate.

To make the broth, in a pot, bring the chicken stock, sliced onion, lemongrass, garlic, ginger and lime zest to a boil over high heat. Reduce the heat to a rolling simmer and cook for 30 minutes. Strain the broth through a fine-mesh sieve and season to taste with the lime juice and salt and sugar. Keep warm.

Bring a large pot of water to a boil over high heat. Add half the dumplings to the pot. When the water boils again, add ½ cup (120 ml) of cold water. When the water boils again, add another ½ cup (120 ml) of cold water. When the water boils again (the dumplings should be floating), drain the dumplings and add to the chicken broth. Cook the remaining dumplings and add to the broth. Add the scallion and cilantro and serve the soup hot, garnished with the fried shallots.

# SPICY CHICKEN YUZU GYOZA

*I love these delicate but spicy little flavor bombs, perfect served simply with Kewpie mayonnaise or Ponzu Dipping Sauce.*

➢ MAKES 30 GYOZA
➢ Preferred Cooking Method: Panfried

¾ lb (340 g) ground dark meat chicken

½ tsp togarashi pepper blend

½ tsp salt

1 tsp (5 g) sugar

1 tbsp (10 g) cornstarch

2 tbsp (20 g) seeded and finely minced jalapeño pepper

1 tbsp (15 g) finely grated ginger

2 tbsp (30 ml) soy sauce

2 tbsp (30 ml) yuzu juice (see page 235)

3 tbsp (10 g) minced scallion whites

3 tbsp (5 g) minced cilantro

1 large egg white, lightly beaten until foamy

30 gyoza wrappers

1½ cup (355 ml) water

1½ tbsp (9 g) flour

Oil for panfrying

Kewpie mayonnaise or Ponzu Dipping Sauce (page 221) for serving

Place the ground chicken in a mixing bowl. In a small bowl whisk together the togarashi, salt, sugar and cornstarch. Sprinkle evenly over the ground chicken. Add the jalapeño, ginger, soy sauce, yuzu, scallion, cilantro and beaten egg white. Mix until well combined. Refrigerate as needed.

Fill each wrapper with 1 tablespoon (12 g) of filling. Lightly wet the edges of the wrapper and form the dumpling using the classic pleat technique. Keep the dumplings covered on a lightly floured tray or plate.

In a liquid measuring cup, mix the water and flour until the flour has dissolved into the water and the mixture is cloudy. Heat a large wok or nonstick pan over medium-high heat. Add 1 tablespoon (15 ml) of oil to the pan and place 10 of the dumplings in the pan, lined up next to each other, and cook until the bottoms of the dumplings turn golden brown, about 1 to 2 minutes. Add ½ cup (125 ml) of the flour and water mixture to the pan; it will react with the hot pan and steam and splatter a bit; be ready with a lid to fit the pan. As soon as you add the flour and water mixture, cover the pan with a tight-fitting lid.

Cook the dumplings, covered, until almost all of the water has evaporated and a thin golden crust begins to form in the bottom of the pan, about 5 to 6 minutes. Remove the lid and cook until all the water has evaporated. Carefully remove the dumplings from the pan and repeat with the remaining dumplings. Serve immediately with Japanese mayonnaise or ponzu sauce.

# KOREAN FRIED CHICKEN DUMPLINGS √

Sometimes people ask me what my favorite foods are and what I can eat a lot of. Okay, dumplings would be first. And Korean fried chicken is a close second.

➢ MAKES 30 DUMPLINGS
➢ Preferred Cooking Method: Deep-fried

## GOCHUJANG SAUCE

2 tbsp (30 g) butter

2 tbsp (30 ml) sesame oil

1 tsp (4 g) minced garlic

1 tsp (5 g) finely grated ginger

1 tbsp (15 ml) rice vinegar

1 tbsp (15 ml) honey

2 tbsp (30 ml) gochujang red pepper paste

2 tbsp (30 ml) soy sauce

## DUMPLINGS

1 tbsp (10 g) finely minced garlic

1 tbsp (15 g) finely minced ginger

1 tbsp (15 ml) soy sauce

1 tbsp (15 ml) gochujang red pepper paste

2 tbsp (30 ml) sesame oil

¼ cup (12 g) minced scallion whites

1 tbsp (10 g) toasted black sesame seeds

1 tbsp (10 g) cornstarch

1 egg white, beaten

¾ lb (340 g) ground dark meat chicken

30 gyoza wrappers

Oil for deep-frying

Sliced scallions for garnish

Pickled Daikon Radish (page 231) for garnish

To make the sauce, in a small sauté pan, melt the butter and sesame oil together over medium heat. Add the garlic and ginger and simmer until fragrant, about 2 minutes. Whisk in the vinegar, honey, red pepper paste and soy sauce until smooth and emulsified. Keep warm until needed. If the sauce separates, add 1 tablespoon (15 ml) of cold water and whisk until it comes together again.

To make the dumplings, in a large bowl whisk together the garlic, ginger, soy sauce, gochujang paste, sesame oil, minced scallion, sesame seeds, cornstarch and beaten egg white. Whisk vigorously until well blended. Add the ground chicken to the bowl and mix until well combined. Refrigerate as needed.

Fill each wrapper with 1 tablespoon (12 g) of filling. Lightly wet the edges of the wrapper and form the dumpling using the classic pleat technique. Keep the dumplings covered on a lightly floured tray or plate.

Preheat the deep-frying oil to 350°F/176°C. Add the dumplings to the oil and deep-fry in small batches until golden and crispy, about 3 minutes. Drain the dumplings into a large mixing bowl. Add a few tablespoons of the warm gochujang sauce to the bowl and toss until well coated. Garnish with sliced scallions and serve with pickled radish.

# CHICKEN CAESAR DUMPLING SALAD

Here's a fun new take on a classic favorite. These dumplings are terrific panfried, but I love the crunch of the deep-fried version.

➤ MAKES 30 DUMPLINGS
➤ Preferred Cooking Method: Deep-fried

## DUMPLINGS

¾ lb (340 g) ground white meat chicken

1 large egg white, lightly beaten until foamy

1 tsp (3 g) lemon zest

1 tbsp (10 g) finely minced garlic

1 tbsp (10 g) finely minced anchovies

1 tbsp (15 ml) soy sauce

1 tbsp (15 ml) lemon juice

2 tbsp (30 ml) sesame oil

½ tsp salt

1 tsp (5 g) sugar

1 tsp (5 g) freshly cracked black pepper

1 tbsp (10 g) cornstarch

½ cup (90 g) finely grated Parmesan cheese

30 dumpling wrappers

Oil for deep-frying

## LEMON CAESAR DRESSING

1 egg yolk

1 clove garlic

3 tbsp (45 ml) lemon juice

1 tsp (5 ml) soy sauce

½ tsp sugar

¼ cup (60 ml) sesame oil

¾ cup (175 ml) canola oil

Salt and pepper

## SALAD

6 cups (1,080 g) hearts of romaine, cut into 1" (2.5 cm) pieces

1 cup (180 g) Parmesan cheese shavings

Salt and black pepper

Toasted black sesame seeds for garnish

To make the dumplings, in a large bowl combine the ground chicken, beaten egg white, lemon zest, garlic, anchovies, soy sauce, lemon juice and sesame oil. In a separate small bowl whisk together the salt, sugar, black pepper, cornstarch and grated Parmesan cheese. Add this to the chicken filling and mix until well combined.

Fill each wrapper with 1 tablespoon (12 g) of filling. Lightly wet the edges of the wrapper and form the dumpling using the classic pleat technique. Keep the dumplings covered on a lightly floured tray or plate.

Preheat the deep-frying oil to 350°F/176°C. Carefully fry the dumplings in small batches until the skin is golden brown and the dumplings are floating in the oil, about 2 to 3 minutes, gently tossing the dumplings in the oil so all sides cook evenly. Drain on paper towels. Allow the oil to come back to 350°F/176°C before frying the next batch.

To make the dressing, combine the egg yolk, garlic, lemon juice, soy sauce and sugar in a food processor or blender. Blend until smooth, then begin to add the sesame oil in a thin stream, forming an emulsion. Follow with the canola oil until all of the oil has been added. The vinaigrette should be very thick. Season with salt and pepper to taste. Refrigerate until serving time.

To make the salad, toss the romaine hearts and Parmesan cheese shavings with one-third of the lemon Caesar dressing. Season with salt and pepper, sprinkle with black sesame seeds, and toss to coat. Top with the fried chicken dumplings and serve with the remaining dressing on the side as a dipping sauce.

# KARAAGE FRIED DUMPLINGS WITH CARROT GINGER SALAD

Karaage, Japanese marinated fried chicken, is one of my favorite snacks. Dark meat chicken is seasoned with soy sauce, sake and mirin to give it a rich aromatic flavor and juicy texture. The same ingredients are used here to give that classic flavor. The deep-fried dumpling skin provides the crunchy texture.

➤ MAKES 32 DUMPLINGS
➤ Preferred Cooking Method: Deep-fried

## DUMPLINGS

8 oz (225 g) boneless, skinless chicken thighs, diced into 1" (2.5 cm) pieces

1 tbsp (15 g) finely grated ginger

1 tsp (5 g) minced garlic

1 tbsp (15 ml) sake

1 tbsp (15 ml) mirin

1 tbsp (15 ml) soy sauce (preferably usukuchi)

1 large egg white

2 tbsp (20 g) cornstarch

32 round dumpling wrappers

## CARROT GINGER SALAD

4 oz (115 g) carrots, peeled and chopped into small pieces

2 tbsp (30 g) minced ginger

3 tbsp (45 ml) rice vinegar

1 tbsp (15 ml) soy sauce

1 tbsp (15 ml) honey

1 tbsp (15 ml) sesame oil

½ cup (120 ml) vegetable oil

Salt and pepper to taste

¼ cup (30 g) thinly sliced sweet onion, rinsed under cold water

Fresh salad greens

Oil for deep-frying

To make the dumplings, place the chicken in a food processor and pulse until the meat is in small pieces. Add the ginger, garlic, sake, mirin, soy sauce, egg white and cornstarch. Pulse again until the ingredients are well incorporated. Refrigerate the filling for at least an hour.

Form your dumplings, using 1 tablespoon (12 g) of filling and keeping them covered on a lightly floured tray as you make them (see page 34).

To make the salad, place the carrots, ginger, rice vinegar, soy sauce and honey in a blender. Start the blender on low speed and eventually increase to high speed until a smooth puree begins to form. Slowly drizzle in the sesame oil and vegetable oil. Season with salt and pepper to taste. Toss the onion with the salad greens and set aside.

Preheat the deep-frying oil to 350°F/176°C. Carefully fry the dumplings in small batches until the skin is golden brown and the dumplings are floating in the oil, about 3 to 4 minutes, gently tossing the dumplings in the oil so all sides cook evenly. Drain on paper towels. Allow the oil to come back to 350°F/176°C before frying the next batch.

To serve, place the dumplings on a bed of the lettuce tossed with onion and drizzle with the carrot dressing. Serve immediately.

# MISO DUCK AND RICOTTA DUMPLINGS WITH STONE FRUIT SALAD

I love the richness of duck meat paired with creamy ricotta. Marinated fruit and peppery arugula pair nicely with these panfried beauties. You can substitute shredded cooked duck confit for the duck breast for a slightly different take.

➤ MAKES 30 DUMPLINGS
➤ Preferred Cooking Method: Panfried

## DUMPLINGS

8 oz (225 g) ground duck breast

4 oz (115 ml) full-fat ricotta cheese, drained

2 tbsp (25 g) minced shallot

1 tbsp (15 g) finely grated ginger

1 tbsp (10 g) finely minced dried apricot

1 tbsp (15 ml) dry sake

2 tbsp (30 ml) shiro white miso

1 tbsp (15 g) finely minced tarragon

2 tbsp (12 g) all-purpose flour

1 tsp (5 g) sugar

½ tsp salt

¼ tsp ground white pepper

30 round dumpling wrappers

Oil for panfrying

## SALAD

1 tbsp (15 ml) honey

2 tbsp (30 g) sugar

¼ cup (60 ml) rice vinegar

1 tbsp (15 ml) ginger juice

1 tbsp (15 ml) mirin

1 tbsp (15 ml) extra virgin olive oil

¼ tsp salt

2 cups (400 g) thinly sliced stone fruit, such as plums, nectarines or peaches

3 tbsp (5 g) tarragon leaves

3 cups (540 g) baby arugula

Salt and black pepper

Sweet soy sauce for drizzling

To make the dumplings, in a mixing bowl, combine the ground duck, ricotta cheese, shallot, ginger, apricot, sake, miso, tarragon, flour, sugar, salt and pepper. Mix well. Refrigerate until needed.

Fill each wrapper with 1 tablespoon (12 g) of filling. Lightly wet the edges of the wrapper and form the dumpling using the classic pleat technique. Keep the dumplings covered on a lightly floured tray or plate.

To make the salad, in a separate small bowl whisk together the honey, sugar, rice vinegar, ginger juice, mirin, olive oil and salt until well blended. Pour the vinaigrette over the sliced stone fruit, add the tarragon leaves, toss to coat and allow the fruit to sit at room temperature for 20 to 30 minutes.

Heat a wok or large nonstick frying pan over high heat. Add 1 tablespoon (15 ml) of oil to the hot pan, tilting the pan to coat the bottom. Place the dumplings in a single layer in the hot pan and cook until the bottoms are golden brown, 1 to 2 minutes. Add ½ cup (125 ml) of water and immediately cover the pan with a tight-fitting lid. Cook until all of the water has been absorbed and the dumpling skins have cooked through, about 4 to 5 minutes. Repeat with the remaining dumplings.

To serve, place the dumplings on a bed of baby arugula. Dress with the marinated fruit, season with salt and pepper and drizzle with the sweet soy sauce.

# THANKSGIVING DUMPLINGS

This recipe is inspired by decades of the day-after-Thanksgiving-everything burrito. I usually try to find five different ways every year to deal with leftover Thanksgiving goodies. You can easily take a little bit of everything and mix it in a bowl and voilà: instant dumpling filling. If you happen to want that holiday flavor and don't happen to have a turkey carcass lying around, here's a recipe that will deliver that comforting taste, with the stuffing and mashed potato all inside. Mmmm, fried turkey bites and craaaaanberry sauce!

➢ MAKES 60 DUMPLINGS
➢ Preferred Cooking Method: Deep-fried

## CRANBERRY SOY DIPPING SAUCE

½ cup (50 g) minced dried cranberries

1 tbsp (12 g) minced shallot

1 tsp (5 g) finely grated ginger

1 small fresh chile, split

1 tbsp (15 ml) sesame oil

2 tbsp (30 g) brown sugar

¼ cup (60 ml) mirin

¼ cup (60 ml) rice vinegar

¼ cup (60 ml) soy sauce

1½ cups (350 ml) water

Pinch of salt

## DUMPLINGS

1 large russet potato (about 8 oz/225 g), skin on

Oil for deep-frying

1½ tsp (8 g) salt, plus extra for sprinkling on potato

¼ cup (60 ml) sour cream

¼ cup (60 g) butter

1 cup (200 g) minced yellow onion

½ cup (100 g) minced celery

3 cloves garlic, minced

2 cups (120 g) dry ¼" (0.6 cm) bread cubes

¼ cup (60 ml) Madeira, dry sherry or white wine

¾ cup (180 ml) rich chicken broth

1 tsp (5 g) poultry seasoning

1 tsp (5 ml) Worcestershire sauce

½ tsp ground black pepper

2 tsp (2 g) minced thyme leaves

2 tsp (2 g) minced sage leaf

1 large egg, beaten

1 lb (450 g) ground turkey

60 round dumpling wrappers

To make the dipping sauce, combine all the ingredients in a small pot. Bring to a boil over high heat, and then lower to a simmer and cook until the liquid has reduced by half. Blend the ingredients in a blender until smooth.

To make the dumplings, preheat the oven to 400°F/204°C. Scrub the potato under cold water. Pat dry and pierce the potato with a fork or small sharp knife in 4 or 5 places, at least 1 inch (2.5 cm) apart. Rub a little bit of oil all over the surface of the skin, then season the entire potato with salt and place on a tray on the middle rack in the oven. Bake for 50 to 60 minutes, until the skin is crisp and the interior is light and flaky.

Transfer the potato to a cutting board and split the potato in half. Scoop the cooked flesh from the skins and pass the cooked potato through a ricer or fine-mesh sieve using a spatula. Fold in the sour cream until well incorporated, being careful not to overwork the potatoes. You can snack on the skins or make potato skins. Cover the mashed potatoes with a damp paper towel and set aside to cool.

Heat a large sauté pan over medium-high heat, and add the butter once the pan is hot. Once the butter melts, add the onion and celery and cook for 5 minutes, stirring often. Stir in the garlic and cook for another minute. Add the diced bread and cook for another minute, stirring so the bread begins to absorb moisture. Deglaze the pan with the Madeira, allowing the alcohol to cook off and reduce, for 1 minute. Add the chicken stock and cook until most of the liquid has evaporated except for 2 to 3 tablespoons (30-45 ml) when you tilt the pan. Transfer the mixture to a bowl and cool in the refrigerator.

Once the mixture has cooled, add the riced potato, poultry seasoning, salt, Worcestershire sauce, pepper, thyme, sage, beaten egg and ground turkey to the bowl. Mix well to combine. Refrigerate if needed.

Fill each wrapper with 1 tablespoon (12 g) of filling. Lightly wet the edges of the wrapper and form the dumpling using the classic pleat technique. Keep the dumplings covered on a lightly floured tray or plate.

Preheat the deep-frying oil to 350°F/176°C. Carefully fry the dumplings in small batches until the skin is golden brown and the dumplings are floating in the oil, about 2 to 3 minutes, gently tossing the dumplings in the oil so all sides cook evenly. Drain on paper towels. Allow the oil to come back to 350°F/176°C before frying the next batch. Serve with the Cranberry Soy Dipping Sauce.

# TERIYAKI SALMON GYOZA

This simple seafood dumpling is one of my favorites. You can substitute other seafood, such as tuna, shrimp or minced scallop. The gyoza can be sautéed in a little bit more teriyaki or served with ponzu sauce on the side.

➤ MAKES 30 GYOZA
➤ Preferred Cooking Method: Panfried

12 oz (340 g) salmon fillet, skinned and boned
½ cup (25 g) minced scallion whites
1 tbsp (10 g) cornstarch
1 tbsp (10 g) toasted black sesame seeds
1 tbsp (15 ml) honey
1 tbsp (15 g) brown sugar
1 tbsp (15 ml) dry sake
2 tbsp (30 ml) mirin
¼ cup (60 ml) soy sauce
30 round gyoza wrappers
1½ cup (355 ml) water
1½ tbsp (9 g) flour
Oil for panfrying
Ponzu Dipping Sauce (page 221)
Salmon Roe for garnish (optional)

Mince the salmon fillet by hand or cut it into small chunks and pulse it into a paste in a food processor. Add the minced scallion whites to the salmon. Mix the cornstarch and sesame seeds in a separate bowl and then sprinkle evenly over the salmon. In another small bowl, whisk together the honey, sugar, sake, mirin and soy sauce until well combined. Pour over the salmon and mix until the filling is well combined. Refrigerate until needed.

Fill each wrapper with 1 tablespoon (12 g) of filling. Lightly wet the edges of the wrapper and form the dumpling using the classic pleat technique. Keep the dumplings covered on a lightly floured tray or plate.

In a liquid measuring cup, mix the water and flour until the flour has dissolved into the water and the mixture is cloudy. Heat a large wok or nonstick skillet over medium-high heat. Add 1 tablespoon (15 ml) of vegetable oil to the pan and place 10 dumplings in the pan, lined up next to each other, and cook until the bottoms of the dumplings turn golden brown, about 1 to 2 minutes. Add ½ cup (125 ml) of the flour and water mixture to the pan. It will react with the hot pan and steam and splatter a bit; be ready with a lid to fit the pan. As soon as you add the flour and water mixture, cover the pan with a tight-fitting lid.

Cook the dumplings, covered, until almost all of the water has evaporated and a thin golden crust begins to form in the bottom of the pan, about 5 to 6 minutes. Remove the lid and cook until all the water has evaporated. Carefully remove the dumplings from the pan and repeat with the remaining dumplings. Serve immediately with the ponzu sauce.

# MIXED SEAFOOD DUMPLINGS

This filling has a classic Chinese flavor that reminds me of Sunday mornings at dim sum. You can alter the ratios of seafood, depending on what you like. I love the texture of shrimp and scallop for this filling, which is great for any type of wrapper you choose. The slick texture when these are boiled lends itself to a juicy filling.

➢ MAKES 40 DUMPLINGS
➢ Preferred Cooking Method: Boiled

8 oz (225 g) sea scallops, sliced into ¼" (0.6 cm) dice

8 oz (225 g) raw shrimp, peeled and deveined, sliced into ¼" (0.6 cm) dice

½ cup (25 g) finely sliced garlic chives

4 large dried shiitake mushrooms, rehydrated (see page 239), stems removed, and finely diced

1 tbsp (15 ml) Shaoxing rice wine

1 tbsp (15 ml) oyster sauce

1 tbsp (15 ml) soy sauce

1 tbsp (10 g) cornstarch

¼ tsp ground white pepper

½ tsp sugar

40 round dumpling wrappers

Soy Ginger Dipping Sauce or Chinese mustard (page 219 or 226)

Combine the scallops, shrimp, garlic chives and shiitake mushrooms in a mixing bowl. In a separate bowl, whisk the wine, oyster sauce, soy sauce, cornstarch, white pepper and sugar until well combined. Add to the seafood mix and stir well. Refrigerate for at least 30 minutes.

Fill each wrapper with 1 tablespoon (12 g) of filling. Lightly wet the edges of the wrapper and form the dumpling using the classic pleat technique. Keep the dumplings covered on a lightly floured tray or plate.

Bring a large pot of water to a boil. Add half the dumplings to the pot. When the water boils again, add ½ cup (120 ml) of cold water. When the water boils again, add another ½ cup (120 ml) of cold water. When the water boils again (the dumplings should be floating), drain the dumplings and serve hot with the dipping sauce.

# CALIFORNIA ROLL GYOZA

In Japan, the universal name for dumplings is "gyoza." This sushi-inspired dumpling gets the flavorful addition of toasted nori layered in the wrapper. Peekytoe crab is my crabmeat of choice, for its natural sweetness. Backfin and claw meat are also fine for this tasty dumpling, as well as the kani crab stick used in sushi.

➢ MAKES 32 GYOZA
➢ Preferred Cooking Method: Panfried

8 oz (225 g) crabmeat, cleaned and picked through, excess liquid gently squeezed out

4 oz (110 g) ripe avocado, diced into ¼" (0.6 cm) pieces

4 oz (120 g) English cucumber, peeled and diced into ⅛" (0.3 cm) pieces

3 tbsp (45 ml) Kewpie mayonnaise

1 tbsp (15 ml) finely minced pickled ginger

2 sheets nori seaweed

32 gyoza wrappers

1½ cup (355 ml) water

1½ tbsp (9 g) flour

Oil for panfrying

Soy sauce

Freshly grated or prepared wasabi

Combine the crabmeat, diced avocado, diced cucumber, mayonnaise and minced pickled ginger in a bowl, stirring gently to combine. Refrigerate until needed.

Place a nonstick pan over high heat. When the pan is hot, place 1 sheet of nori into the dry pan. Toast the seaweed for 10 seconds and then turn it over to the other side, toasting for another 5 seconds. Set aside to cool and repeat with the remaining sheet of nori. When the nori has cooled, cut each sheet into 16 squares with a knife or pair of scissors.

Place a wrapper in one hand and lightly brush the entire surface of the wrapper with water using a pastry brush or your finger. Place a square of nori in the center of the wrapper. Fill each wrapper with 1 tablespoon (12 g) of filling. Form the dumpling using the classic pleat technique. Keep the dumplings covered on a lightly floured tray or plate.

In a liquid measuring cup, mix the water with the flour well until the flour has dissolved into the water and the mixture is cloudy. Heat a large wok or nonstick pan over medium-high heat. Add 1 tablespoon (15 ml) of oil to the pan and place 10 to 12 dumplings in the pan, lined up next to each other, and cook until the bottoms of the dumplings turn golden brown, about 1 to 2 minutes. Add ½ cup (125 ml) of the flour and water mixture to the pan; it will react with the hot pan and steam and splatter a bit; be ready with a lid to fit the pan. As soon as you add the flour and water mixture, cover the pan with a tight-fitting lid.

Cook the dumplings, covered, until almost all of the water has evaporated and a thin golden crust begins to form in the bottom of the pan. Remove the lid and cook until all the water has evaporated. Carefully remove the dumplings from the pan and repeat with the remaining dumplings. Serve immediately with soy sauce and wasabi.

# CALIFORNIA ROLL GYOZA (CONTINUED)

Lightly brush your wrapper with water.

Place a small square of nori seaweed on the wrapper.

Fold and pleat your dumpling as usual.

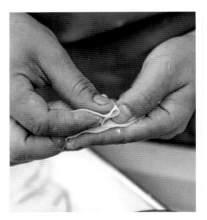

Line up your dumpling edges.

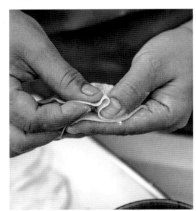

Pleat and press.

Pleat and press.

Make 4 to 5 tight pleats.

Press the pleats tightly to seal.

The pleating action will make the dumplings form its natural half-moon shape.

# CRISPY BBQ EEL GYOZA

Unagi, a popular fish prized for its fatty rich flavor and texture, is the perfect filling for this sushi-inspired dumpling. I don't recommend trying to butcher a live eel at home. Instead, you can find it in your Asian grocer's freezer section, labeled "unagi kabayaki," the traditional Japanese preparation of broiled eel dipped in a sweet shoyu marinade.

➣ MAKES 36 DUMPLINGS
➣ Preferred Cooking Method: Deep-Fried

½ cup (65 g) grated (large holes) seedless cucumber

1 tsp (5 g) salt

1 (14-oz [400 g]) package unagi kabayaki

4 oz (110 g) ripe avocado, diced into ¼" (0.6 cm) pieces

3 tbsp (45 ml) cream cheese, softened to room temperature

1 tbsp (15 ml) Kewpie mayonnaise

1 tbsp (15 ml) soy sauce

½ tbsp (6 g) granulated sugar

2 tbsp (25 g) minced red onion

2 tbsp (4 g) minced cilantro

36 gyoza wrappers

Oil for deep-frying

Ponzu Dipping Sauce (page 221)

In a small bowl, combine the grated cucumber and salt. Stir well and allow the cucumber to sweat for 15 to 20 minutes. Rinse the cucumber briefly under cold water and then gently press dry between clean paper towels.

Remove the skin from the cooked eel fillet. Mince the eel into small pieces using a large knife. Place the eel in a mixing bowl and combine with the grated cucumber and diced avocado.

In a separate bowl, combine the softened cream cheese, mayonnaise, soy sauce, sugar, red onion and cilantro. Mix well and then combine with the eel, avocado and cucumber. Using a rubber spatula, gently fold the ingredients together. Refrigerate for at least 30 minutes before forming dumplings.

Fill each wrapper with 1 tablespoon (12 g) of filling and form the dumpling with a classic potsticker pleat. Because the filling is already cooked you only need to worry about making sure you get a good seal and thoroughly cooking the wrapper.

Preheat the deep-frying oil to 350°F/176°C. Carefully fry the dumplings in small batches until the skin is golden brown and the dumplings are floating in the oil, about 2 to 3 minutes, gently tossing the dumplings in the oil so all sides cook evenly. Drain on paper towels. Allow the oil to come back to 350°F/176°C before frying the next batch. Serve warm with the dipping sauce.

# SCALLOP NORI DUMPLINGS

The addition of nori seaweed to the wheat starch dough brings flavor and a really cool texture to the translucent dough when it cooks. The delicate sweetness of the scallops is simply accented by the light scent of ginger and a few other aromatic ingredients. I love this dumpling served with ponzu sauce or Chinese mustard.

➤ MAKES 32 DUMPLINGS
➤ Preferred Cooking Method: Steamed

## FILLING

½ lb (226 g) fresh dry sea scallops

1 tsp (4 g) cornstarch

1 tbsp (15 ml) sake

1 tbsp (15 ml) soy sauce

½ tsp salt

Pinch of ground white pepper

1 tsp (5 g) finely grated ginger

2 tbsp (6 g) finely minced scallion, white parts only

## NORI WHEAT STARCH DOUGH

½ sheet nori seaweed

¾ cup (75 g) wheat starch flour

2 tbsp (15 g) tapioca flour or starch

1 tsp (5 ml) lard or vegetable oil

½ cup (120 ml) plus 1 tsp (5 ml) water, boiling

To make the filling, remove the small muscle from the side of the scallops and discard. Rinse the scallops under cold water and pat dry. Place the scallops and remaining filling ingredients in a food processor. Pulse until the scallops are finely chopped and the paste is well blended, being sure to scrape down the sides of the bowl with a spatula in between pulsing. Refrigerate the mixture for at least an hour.

To make the dough, heat a dry sauté pan over high heat. When the pan is hot, using a pair of tongs or chopsticks, briefly toast the nori sheet for about 5 seconds on each side. Remove from the pan and allow to cool slightly. Crumble the nori slightly and place in a spice or coffee grinder, blender or food processor. Pulse until the nori is finely ground.

Place the ground nori, wheat starch flour, tapioca flour and lard in a bowl and mix well. Pour the boiling water over the mix and stir until well combined. Cover with plastic wrap or a hot, damp towel to allow the flour to soften. Turn the dough out onto a work surface or cutting board. Gently knead the dough for 1 to 2 minutes. Add wheat starch as needed if the dough is sticky. The dough should be smooth and soft. Keep the dough wrapped in plastic wrap so it does not dry out.

To form your wrappers, roll your dough into a 1-inch (2.5-cm)-thick rope and cut into 32 pieces. Cover the dough pieces with plastic wrap and a hot, damp towel.

Form your dumplings, using a heaping teaspoon (4 g) of filling, making them one at a time as you roll out each wrapper. Because the dough is delicate I usually just fold the dough in half to make half-moons rather than pleated dumplings.

Place the formed dumplings into a steamer lined with lightly greased parchment or waxed paper punched with holes, ensuring the dumplings are not touching each other in the steamer basket. Keep a layer of plastic wrap weighted with a lightly damp towel on top of the finished dumplings so they do not dry out. Remove the plastic wrap and towel before cooking. Cover and steam the dumplings for 6 to 8 minutes, until they are fully cooked and the wrappers are translucent. Serve with the dipping sauce of your choice.

# EDAMAME AND SWEET PEA GYOZA WITH WASABI CREAM

These dumplings will satisfy both vegetarians and meat eaters alike. I like using edamame and extra-firm tofu to give the filling a creamy nuttiness, while dried seaweed, most commonly found in miso soup, adds salinity and the fresh green peas add a delicate sweetness and pop to the overall taste experience. You can buy shelled edamame and even the green peas in your grocer's freezer section. I happen to love frozen vegetables, not only for their convenience, but also for the fact that most are harvested and frozen at their peak of perfection. These are great both panfried and deep-fried, and perfect with pea shoots for an extra "salad-y" crunch.

➢ MAKES 50 DUMPLINGS
➢ Preferred Cooking Method: Panfried

## DUMPLINGS

¼ cup (85 g) dried wakame seaweed

7 oz (200 g) superfirm tofu (half block)

2 cups (300 g) shelled cooked edamame (cooled)

1 clove garlic, minced

2 tbsp (30 ml) pickled ginger

3 tbsp (45 ml) soy sauce

1 tbsp (15 g) sugar

½ tbsp salt

2 tbsp (3 g) mint or cilantro leaves (optional)

2 cups (300 g) shelled petite green peas, fresh or frozen

50 round gyoza wrappers

2 cups (475 ml) water

2 tbsp (12 g) all-purpose flour

Vegetable oil for frying

## WASABI CREAM

1 cup (235 ml) sour cream

3 tbsp (45 ml) milk

1 tbsp (15 ml) lemon juice

1 tbsp (15 ml) prepared wasabi paste

¼ tsp salt

Pinch of sugar

To make the dumplings, add the dried seaweed to the bowl of a food processor. Pulse until the seaweed has broken up into small pieces. Add the tofu, edamame, garlic, pickled ginger, soy sauce, sugar, salt and fresh herbs to the food processor bowl. Pulse the mixture until it is chunky but well mixed (it should have the texture of a thick tapenade). Transfer the filling to a large mixing bowl. Refrigerate for 10 minutes to allow the seaweed to rehydrate.

While the filling is chilling, bring a medium pot of salted water to a boil. Blanch the peas for 1 minute, then drain and chill in an ice bath to stop the cooking (stir for 15 to 20 seconds). Remove the peas from the ice bath as soon as they are cold and drain well. Add the cooked peas to the filling, stirring well until combined.

Using water to seal the gyoza, add ½ tablespoon (6 g) of filling to each wrapper and form the gyoza using single side pleats (page 70). Place the formed gyoza on a lightly floured baking pan lined with parchment paper. Cover and refrigerate until ready to cook.

To make the wasabi cream, combine all the ingredients in a bowl and whisk until the mixture is smooth. Refrigerate until needed.

In a small container, mix the water and flour well until the flour has dissolved into the water and the mixture is cloudy. Heat a small nonstick pan over medium-high heat. Add 1 tablespoon (15 ml) of vegetable oil to the pan and place the gyoza in the pan, lined up next to each other, and cook until the bottoms of the gyoza turn golden brown, about 1 to 2 minutes. Add ½ cup (125 ml) of the flour and water mixture to the pan; it will react with the hot pan and steam and splatter a bit, so be ready with a lid to fit the pan. As soon as you add the flour and water mixture, cover the pan with a tight-fitting lid. Cook the gyoza, covered, until almost all of the water has evaporated and a thin golden crust begins to form in the bottom of the pan. Remove the lid and cook until all the water has evaporated. Carefully remove the gyoza from the pan and repeat with the remaining gyoza. Serve immediately with the wasabi cream.

# SWEET CORN TAMALE DUMPLINGS

I spent my twenties traveling annually to Mexico to explore and learn all about Mexican cuisine. One of my favorite places to visit is Oaxaca, where I guest chef regularly at a lovely hotel and restaurant, Casa Oaxaca. The chef, Alejandro Ruiz, first took me to a small café in the Reforma neighborhood, La Teca, where I was introduced to the owner's famous Tamale de Elote (corn tamale). It has become one of my must-haves every time I visit Oaxaca and serves as my inspiration for this fun and tasty Mexico-meets-Asia mash-up.

> MAKES 60 DUMPLINGS
> Preferred Cooking Method: Panfried

## SESAME-AVOCADO SAUCE

2 ripe avocados, flesh removed from skin, pits reserved

½ cup (13 g) cilantro leaves

Juice of 1 lime

2 tbsp (18 g) chopped onion

2 tbsp (30 ml) water

1 tbsp (10 g) seeded and diced jalapeño pepper

1 tbsp (15 ml) sesame oil

½ tsp salt

1 tsp (5 g) sugar

## DUMPLINGS

2 cups (200 g) maseca corn flour

1½ cups (355 ml) chicken broth or vegetable broth

1 cup (230 g) butter or lard, at room temperature

1 cup (150 g) sweet corn kernels (canned or frozen and thawed is fine)

¼ cup (40 g) diced onion, sautéed

1 tbsp (10 g) minced garlic

1 tbsp (15 g) sugar

1 tbsp (12 g) baking powder

1 tsp (5 g) salt

½ tsp white pepper

60 round dumpling wrappers

Oil for panfrying

Kecap manis (Indonesian sweet soy sauce) for garnish

Mexican crema for garnish

Queso fresco cheese for garnish

Cilantro leaves for garnish

To make the sauce, combine all the ingredients in a food processor and blend until smooth. Transfer to a small container or piping bag and add the whole pit back into the puree (it will prevent the avocado from oxidizing and turning brown). Refrigerate until needed.

To make the dumplings, combine the maseca, chicken broth, butter, corn kernels, sautéed onion, garlic, sugar, baking powder, salt and white pepper in a stand mixer (you may also mix by hand). Using the paddle attachment, mix the ingredients until they are well combined and the dough is fluffy.

Using water to seal the dumplings, add 1 tablespoon (12 g) of filling to each wrapper and form the dumplings using single side pleats (see page 70). Place the formed dumplings on a lightly floured baking pan lined with parchment paper. Cover and refrigerate until ready to cook.

Heat a small nonstick pan over medium-high heat. Add 1 tablespoon (15 ml) of vegetable oil to the pan and place the dumplings in the pan, lined up next to each other, and cook until the bottoms of the dumplings turn golden brown, about 1 to 2 minutes. Add ½ cup (125 ml) of water and immediately cover the pan with a tight-fitting lid. Cook until all of the water has been absorbed and the dumpling skins have cooked through, about 4 to 5 minutes. Remove the lid and cook until all the water has evaporated. Carefully remove the dumplings from the pan. Repeat with the remaining dumplings.

Garnish the dumplings by drizzling the sesame-avocado sauce on top, followed by the kecap manis, Mexican crema, a few tablespoons of queso fresco and cilantro leaves. Serve immediately.

# MUSHROOM AND TRUFFLE DUMPLINGS

This recipe is adapted from one of my good friends, Chef Marja Samsom, otherwise known as "The Dumpling Diva". Mushrooms are one of my favorite ingredients for their natural earthiness. The addition of rehydrated dried mushrooms gives the filling an extra richness. Truffles are also part of the fungus family and are prized for their aroma and flavor. If you happen to have a fresh truffle lying around, then make it rain all over your dumplings. Truffle paste or oil, however, is perfectly fine to use for this recipe to achieve that rich truffle bouquet.

> MAKES 36 DUMPLINGS
> Preferred Cooking Method: Boiled

## FILLING

2 tbsp (30 ml) sesame oil

½ lb (225 g) fresh mushrooms, trimmed and cleaned, cut into ¼" (0.6 cm) pieces

4 dried shiitake mushrooms, rehydrated (see page 239), minced, soaking liquid reserved

1 tbsp (10 g) minced garlic

1 tbsp (15 g) minced ginger

2 cups (680 g) finely shredded and chopped napa cabbage

2 tbsp (30 ml) Shaoxing rice wine

1 tbsp (15 ml) mushroom soy sauce or dark soy sauce

1 tbsp (15 ml) truffle puree, truffle oil or minced preserved truffles

1 tbsp (12 g) cornstarch

1 tsp (5 g) salt

½ tsp sugar

½ tsp ground white pepper

¼ cup (12 g) minced scallion, white and green parts

½ cup (30 g) crumbled firm tofu

## CREAM SAUCE

¼ cup (60 ml) shiitake soaking liquid

2 tbsp (30 ml) mushroom-cabbage liquid

1 cup (235 ml) heavy cream

¼ cup (45 g) finely grated Parmesan cheese

½ tsp truffle oil or truffle paste

Salt and pepper

1 recipe Fresh Wheat Flour Dough (page 22)

To make the filling, heat a large sauté pan over medium-high heat. Add the sesame oil to the hot pan and then the fresh mushrooms. Stir-fry for 5 minutes, until they begin to soften and shrink in size. Add the rehydrated shiitakes, garlic and ginger to the pan and stir-fry for another minute. Add the cabbage to the pan and cook until the cabbage wilts, about 4 minutes. Transfer the mixture to a fine-mesh sieve positioned over a bowl to allow the cooking liquid to drain from the cooked cabbage and mushrooms while it cools. Reserve the cooking liquid.

Once the mixture has cooled, transfer it to a clean bowl and mix in the wine, soy sauce, truffle puree, cornstarch, salt, sugar, pepper, scallion and tofu until well combined. Refrigerate the filling until needed.

To make the sauce, in a small pot, combine the shiitake-soaking liquid, mushroom-cabbage liquid and heavy cream. Bring to a simmer and reduce the liquid by half. Stir in the Parmesan cheese and truffle oil and blend briefly with an immersion blender. Season with salt and pepper to taste. Keep warm until needed.

Divide your dough into 4 pieces. Roll each piece into a 1-inch (2.5-cm)-thick rope and cut into ½-inch (1.3-cm) pieces. Keep the dough covered with a damp towel.

Roll each dough ball into a 3-inch (7.5-cm) round wrapper using a rolling pin. Fill each dumpling with 1 tablespoon (12 g) of filling. Lightly wet the edges of the wrapper and form the dumpling using the classic pleat technique. Keep the dumplings covered on a lightly floured tray or plate.

Bring a large pot of water to a boil. Add half the dumplings to the pot. When the water boils again, add ½ cup (120 ml) of cold water. When the water boils again, add another ½ cup (120 ml) of cold water. When the water boils again (the dumplings should be floating), strain out the dumplings and repeat with the remaining dumplings. Serve hot in the cream sauce.

# KIMCHI MANDU

There's a little shop on 32nd Street in Koreatown in New York City that makes fresh, plump mandu (the Korean word for "dumpling") right in the front window. Pork and kimchi is one of their top-selling varieties, beloved for its spicy sour flavor. I love kimchi for its health properties, and yes, it's just plain delicious, although riding home on the subway with a quart of it in your handbag tends to get you dirty looks and a five-foot circle of space. Be aware that the best kimchi is usually the stinkiest, so make sure it's kept in an airtight container with a tight-fitting lid (preferably screw cap) wrapped in an airtight plastic zip bag. This will help prevent odor transfer in your fridge and avoid any exploding containers of kimchi, as the fermentation is still live and active. This recipe uses tofu, but you can substitute pork, beef, chicken, or even fish for a meatier texture. I like adding Korean red pepper flakes and carrot juice to the dough for extra spice and a little color.

➤ MAKES 32 DUMPLINGS
➤ Preferred Cooking Method: Panfried

1 cup (340 g) finely chopped cabbage kimchi

7 oz (200 g) firm tofu, excess moisture pressed out and crumbled

4 oz (115 g) cooked cellophane noodles, chopped into ½" (1.3 cm) pieces

¼ cup (85 g) finely shredded carrot

½ cup (40 g) finely chopped fresh shiitake mushrooms, stems removed

½ cup (25 g) chopped garlic chives or scallion greens

1 tbsp (10 g) cornstarch

1 tbsp (15 ml) soy sauce

1 tbsp (15 ml) sesame oil

1 large egg, beaten

1 recipe Basic Wheat Starch Dough (page 27) colored with carrot juice (see page 25) and mixed with 2 tsp (10 g) Korean red pepper flakes

Oil for panfrying

Soy Ginger Dipping Sauce (page 219)

Squeeze the excess liquid from the kimchi and reserve for future use, such as Kimchi Vinaigrette (page 227). In a mixing bowl, combine the kimchi, tofu, cooked cellophane noodles, carrot, shiitake mushrooms, garlic chives, cornstarch, soy sauce, sesame oil and egg. Mix the filling well and then refrigerate until needed.

Divide your dough into 4 pieces. Roll each piece into a 1-inch (2.5-cm)-thick rope and cut into ¼-inch (0.6 cm) pieces. Keep the dough covered with a damp towel.

Roll each dough ball into a 3-inch (7.5-cm) round wrapper using a rolling pin. Fill each dumpling with 1 tablespoon (12 g) of filling. Lightly wet the edges of the wrapper and form the dumpling using the classic pleat technique. Keep the dumplings covered on a lightly floured tray or plate.

Heat a wok or large nonstick frying pan over high heat. Add ½ tablespoon (7.5 ml) of oil to the hot pan, tilting the pan to coat the bottom. Place the dumplings in a single layer in the hot pan and cook until the bottoms are golden brown, 1 to 2 minutes. Add ½ cup (125 ml) of water and immediately cover the pan with a tight-fitting lid. Cook until all of the water has been absorbed and the dumpling skins have cooked through, about 4 to 5 minutes. Repeat with the remaining dumplings. Serve with the dipping sauce.

# WHITE CHOCOLATE WASABI PRETZEL DUMPLINGS

The flavors of white chocolate and wasabi are surprisingly well matched. The crunchy, yeasty pretzels make this salty-sweet dumpling familiar and fun, like biting into a candy store confection.

➢ MAKES 32 DUMPLINGS
➢ Preferred Cooking Method: Deep-fried

8 oz (225 g) high-quality white chocolate

¾ cup (175 ml) heavy cream

1 tsp (5 ml) prepared wasabi paste

6 tbsp (40 g) all-purpose flour

6 oz (170 g) salted thin pretzels, chopped into small bits

32 round dumpling wrappers

Oil for deep-frying

¼ cup (50 g) turbinado sugar

1 tsp (5 g) pretzel salt or kosher salt

Chop the white chocolate into very small pieces and place in a bowl. Heat the cream to boiling and then pour over the white chocolate. Stir until the chocolate melts completely, then whisk in the wasabi paste and flour until smooth; the chocolate will seize up a bit. Refrigerate the mixture until it is pliable and cool but not completely set.

Fold in the chopped pretzels. Refrigerate the filling until completely set, about 30 minutes more.

Fill each wrapper with 1 tablespoon (12 g) of filling. Lightly wet the edges of the wrapper and form the dumpling using the classic pleat technique. It is important that you get a good seal. Keep the dumplings covered on a lightly floured tray or plate.

Preheat the deep-frying oil to 340°F/171°C. Mix the turbinado sugar and pretzel salt in a small dish. Set aside. Carefully fry the dumplings in small batches until the skin is golden brown and the dumplings are floating in the oil, about 2 to 3 minutes, gently tossing the dumplings in the oil so all sides cook evenly. Drain on paper towels and then immediately roll the cooked dumplings in the sugar-salt mix. Allow the oil to come back to 340°F/171°C before frying the next batch. Allow the dumplings to cool slightly before serving.

# BANANA CARAMEL DUMPLINGS ✓

I love fried bananas, a favorite childhood snack growing up. My mother made banana lumpia/spring rolls for us when we were young, a treat she had known in the Philippines. The addition of smoked almonds gives these dumplings a salty crunchy note. Finish with some whipped cream for absolute decadence.

➤ MAKES 32 DUMPLINGS
➤ Preferred Cooking Method: Deep-fried

## DUMPLINGS

2 cups (360 g) ripe bananas, diced ¼" (0.6 cm) thick

1 tbsp (15 ml) fresh lemon juice

2 tbsp (30 g) turbinado sugar

1 tbsp (15 ml) rum

¼ tsp vanilla bean paste or extract

¼ cup (40 g) hickory-smoked almonds, chopped into small pieces

32 dumpling wrappers

## CARAMEL SAUCE

1 cup (190 g) granulated sugar

¼ cup (60 ml) water

½ cup (115 g) butter

½ cup (120 ml) heavy cream

¼ tsp salt

Oil for deep-frying

Whipped cream for garnish

To make the dumplings, toss the diced bananas with the lemon juice. Take ½ cup (90 g) of the diced bananas and mash with a fork in a separate bowl with the sugar, rum and vanilla paste. Fold the mashed banana back into the diced bananas and stir in the chopped almonds.

Fill each wrapper with 1 tablespoon (12 g) of filling. Lightly wet the edges of the wrapper and form the dumpling using the classic pleat technique. Keep the dumplings covered on a lightly floured tray or plate.

For the caramel sauce, have everything ready to go by the side of the stove. In a small, heavy-bottomed pot, melt the sugar and water over medium-high heat, stirring occasionally. Once the sugar comes to a boil, stop stirring. The sugar crystals will eventually melt and the sugar will turn a dark amber color.

As soon as the color is dark amber, about 5 to 7 minutes, carefully whisk in the butter and remove the pan from the heat. Add the heavy cream while whisking (the caramel will foam up), and then season with the salt. Allow the caramel to cool down to a warm temperature before serving.

Preheat the deep-frying oil to 350°F/176°C. Carefully fry the dumplings in small batches until the skin is golden brown and the dumplings are floating in the oil, about 2 to 3 minutes, gently tossing the dumplings in the oil so all sides cook evenly. Drain on paper towels. Allow the oil to come back to 350°F/176°C before frying the next batch. Keep the dumplings warm until serving time. Serve with the caramel sauce and whipped cream.

# YUZU BLINTZ DUMPLINGS

I'm a sucker for cheese desserts, so these creamy, blintz-inspired dumplings hit the spot when I want a quick, tasty sweet snack. Frozen fruit is perfect for making instant sauce.

➢ MAKES 40 DUMPLINGS
➢ Preferred Cooking Method: Panfried

## MIXED BERRY SAUCE

1 (8-oz [225 g]) bag frozen mixed berries, thawed

1 tsp (5 ml) yuzu juice (see page 235)

1 tbsp (15 ml) honey

1 tsp (5 g) sugar

Pinch of salt

1 tbsp (15 g) butter

## DUMPLINGS

1½ cups (354 ml) full-fat ricotta cheese, drained

½ cup (120 ml) cream cheese, softened

¼ cup (30 g) confectioners' sugar

5 vanilla wafer cookies, pulsed to a fine crumb in a food processor

1 large egg, beaten

1 tsp (5 ml) yuzu juice (see page 235)

1 tbsp (10 g) minced candied yuzu or lemon zest (optional)

¼ vanilla bean, seeds scraped from the pod, or ¼ tsp vanilla extract

40 round dumpling wrappers

1½ cup (355 ml) water

1½ tbsp (23 g) granulated sugar

1½ tbsp (9 g) flour

Butter for panfrying

To make the sauce, place the thawed berries and their juice in a nonreactive pan. Stir in the yuzu juice, honey, sugar and salt. Reduce over medium heat until the berries have a saucelike consistency. Whisk in the butter. Keep the sauce warm until needed.

To make the dumplings, in a bowl, combine the ricotta cheese, cream cheese, confectioners' sugar, vanilla wafer crumbs, beaten egg, yuzu juice and zest, and vanilla bean seeds. Refrigerate the filling until it firms up, about an hour.

Fill each wrapper with 1 tablespoon (12 g) of filling. Lightly wet the edges of the wrapper and form the dumpling using the classic pleat technique. Keep the dumplings covered on a lightly floured tray or plate.

In a liquid measuring cup, mix the water with granulated sugar and flour until the sugar and flour have dissolved into the water and the mixture is cloudy. Heat a large wok or nonstick pan over medium-high heat. Add 1 tablespoon (15 g) of butter to the pan and place a third of the dumplings in the pan, lined up next to each other, and cook until the bottoms of the dumplings turn golden brown, about 1 to 2 minutes. Add ½ cup (125 ml) of the sugar-flour-water mixture to the pan. It will react with the hot pan and steam and splatter a bit; be ready with a lid to fit the pan. As soon as you add the liquid, cover the pan with a tight-fitting lid.

Cook the dumplings, covered, until almost all of the water has evaporated and a thin golden crust begins to form in the bottom of the pan, 5 to 6 minutes. Remove the lid and cook until all the water has evaporated. Carefully remove the dumplings from the pan. Repeat with the remaining dumplings. Serve with the warm mixed berry sauce.

# CHAPTER 4

# CUP-SHAPED FOLD: SHUMAI

➤ One of my favorite dining experiences is going out for dim sum with my family and friends. These traditional Cantonese restaurants are known for their dizzying and bountiful style of service, as rolling carts stacked with bamboo steamer baskets and small plates of baked and fried treats breeze by you while you eagerly try to smell and see what you want to order for your table (and the tea hasn't even been poured yet!).

A popular favorite, and one of the most well-known types of dim sum, is shumai. This open-faced-style dumpling is traditionally made with pork and/or seafood in a thin wonton skin shaped like a cup. It is often topped with some sort of fish roe or vegetable decoration. I am a huge fan of shumai because you can make them small enough to be a single bite of heaven, and their flowerlike shape allows them to stand on their own, with the exposed filling just begging for a creative decoration or sauce.

Countries including Japan, Thailand and Mongolia all have their own variations of shumai, differing by ingredients, cooking methods and serving styles. If you happen to like the ease of forming these tasty gems, then your culinary possibilities are endless.

# HOW TO FOLD

Trim your wonton wrappers to 3-inch (7.5-cm) rounds or squares. Gently cup one of your hands and place the wrapper in that hand. Place a spoonful of filling in the center of the wrapper and then gently gather the sides of the wrapper up and around the filling, forming the sides of the shumai by circling your forefinger and thumb together. Using a small knife or spatula, smooth down the top of the filling (it should come to the edges of the wrapper, and will be exposed) while continuing to gently squeeze and form the sides and bottom of the cup-shaped dumpling. Gently tap the finished shumai on the work surface to flatten the bottom so it stands up and the shumai resembles a short cylinder. At this point you may decorate the exposed filling before it cooks, or you have the option to top the shumai after they are done cooking. Lightly grease or spray a parchment-lined tray or platter with cooking oil. Place the formed shumai on the greased parchment and cover with plastic wrap. Refrigerate or freeze until needed.

Cup one of your hands.

Press the wrapper into your hand.

Use a small spatula to fill the wrapper.

Use the spatula to compress and pack the filling into the wrapper.

Smooth out the top while using your hand to form the barrel or cup-shaped dumpling.

The finished dumpling should look like a tulip or cup shape with a flat bottom.

# PORK AND SHRIMP SHUMAI

This is the most classic style of shumai, a dim sum superstar. My earliest memories of shumai are when I was a child, haplessly stabbing at them with my chopsticks until I just picked one up with my hands and crammed it into my mouth. I'm a little more coordinated these days and can eat them twice as fast. Use your imagination to garnish these juicy dumplings. Chinese mustard and a little sambal are my weapons of choice to clear the sinuses and accentuate the combination of pork and shrimp.

➤ MAKES 40 DUMPLINGS
➤ Preferred Cooking Method: Steamed

## FILLING

½ lb (225 g) shrimp, peeled, deveined, and cut into ¼" (0.6 cm) dice

¼ lb (115 g) ground pork

¼ cup (40 g) diced water chestnuts

½ cup (25 g) minced scallion, white and green parts

1 tbsp (15 g) finely grated ginger

1 tbsp (10 g) minced garlic

1 tbsp (15 g) sugar

1 tbsp (10 g) cornstarch

2 tbsp (30 ml) Shaoxing rice wine

3 tbsp (45 ml) soy sauce

1 tsp (5 ml) sesame oil

40 shumai wrappers

Garnish options: baby shrimp, fish roe, green peas, diced carrot or diced red bell pepper

Chinese mustard (page 226) and sambal for serving

To make the filling, in a mixing bowl combine all of the ingredients and stir until well incorporated. Refrigerate until needed.

Place 1 tablespoon (12 g) of filling in the center of the wrapper and then gently gather the sides of the wrapper up and around the filling, forming the sides of the shumai by circling your forefinger and thumb together.

Using a small knife or spatula, smooth down the top of the filling (it should come to the edges of the wrapper, and will be exposed) while continuing to gently squeeze and form the sides and bottom of the cup-shaped dumpling. Gently tap the finished shumai on the work surface to flatten the bottom so it stands up and the shumai resembles a short cylinder.

Finish the shumai by pressing the garnish of your choice gently into the top of the filling. Refrigerate the shumai for at least an hour before cooking.

Prepare a steamer basket lined with blanched cabbage leaves or lightly greased parchment paper. Place the shumai in the steamer basket, being careful to space them apart so they are not touching. Cover with a lid and steam the shumai for 6 to 8 minutes, until they are cooked through. Serve with Chinese mustard and sambal.

# CHICKEN AND MUSHROOM SHUMAI

Chinese mushrooms have such great texture and the dried varieties are bursting with flavor. It's always best to give your dried mushrooms a quick rinse and then a long soak overnight; this allows the mushrooms to fully rehydrate. If for some reason you are short on time, bring water to a boil, pour over the mushrooms and soak for an hour. Panfrying shumai is fantastic—I love the chewy-crispy bottom!

➢ MAKES 40 DUMPLINGS
➢ Preferred Cooking Method: Panfried

## FILLING

¾ lb (340 g) ground chicken meat

4 dried shiitake mushrooms or wood fungi, rehydrated (see page 239) and minced (½ cup [40 g])

¼ cup (50 g) finely minced yellow onion

¼ cup (65 g) finely minced fresh bamboo shoots

¼ cup (85 g) finely minced green cabbage

3 tbsp (30 g) finely minced carrot

1 large egg white, lightly beaten

2 tbsp (30 ml) oyster sauce

1 tbsp (15 ml) soy sauce

1 tbsp (10 g) cornstarch

1 tsp (5 ml) Shaoxing rice wine

½ tsp white pepper

40 shumai wrappers

Decoratively cut carrots for garnish

Oil for panfrying

Black Vinegar Dipping Sauce (page 219) and Chile Oil (page 225) for serving

To make the filling, in a mixing bowl combine all of the ingredients. Refrigerate if needed.

Place 1 tablespoon (12 g) of filling in the center of the wrapper and then gently gather the sides of the wrapper up and around the filling, forming the sides of the shumai by circling your forefinger and thumb together.

Using a small knife or spatula, smooth down the top of the filling (it should come to the edges of the wrapper, and will be exposed) while continuing to gently squeeze and form the sides and bottom of the cup-shaped dumpling. Gently tap the finished shumai on the work surface to flatten the bottom so it stands up and the shumai resembles a short cylinder.

Finish the shumai by pressing the carrot garnish gently into the top of the filling. Refrigerate the shumai for at least an hour before cooking.

Heat a wok or large nonstick frying pan over high heat. Add ½ tablespoon (7.5 ml) of oil to the hot pan, tilting the pan to coat the bottom. Place the shumai in a single layer in the hot pan and cook until the bottoms are golden brown. Add ½ cup (125 ml) of water and immediately cover the pan with a tight-fitting lid. Cook until all of the water has been absorbed and the dumpling skins have cooked through, about 4 to 5 minutes. Repeat with the remaining shumai. Serve with the dipping sauce and chile oil.

# CHICKEN PARM SHUMAI

This Italian-Asian mash-up comes from the culinary team at the Hurricane Club: chefs Craig Koketsu and Lawrence Knapp. I featured this dumpling on my one-hour special *Food Crawl*, dedicated to my dumpling and noodle obsession. There's a great blend of flavors and the surprise addition of mozzarella cheese. A gingery tomato chutney acts as the perfect condiment for this reinvented comfort food.

➤ MAKES 30 SHUMAI
➤ Preferred Cooking Method: Steamed

## SHUMAI

2 tbsp (30 ml) extra virgin olive oil

½ cup (75 g) finely diced celery

2 tbsp (20 g) minced garlic

½ tsp crushed red pepper flakes

1 tsp (2 g) minced thyme leaves

12 oz (340 g) ground chicken breast

¼ cup (45 g) grated Parmesan cheese

¼ cup (45 g) shredded mozzarella cheese

½ tsp salt

¼ tsp ground black pepper

30 shumai wrappers or 1 recipe Basic Wheat Starch Dough (page 27) colored with spinach juice (page 25)

## TOMATO GINGER CHUTNEY

1 tbsp (15 ml) extra virgin olive oil

¼ cup (60 g) minced shallot

2 tsp (5 g) minced garlic

2 cups (475 ml) canned diced tomatoes in juice

1 cup (240 ml) tomato puree

1 tbsp (15 g) brown sugar

3 tbsp (45 g) minced pickled ginger

1 tbsp (15 ml) pickled ginger juice (from the jar of pickled ginger)

Salt

To make the shumai, in a small sauté pan heat the olive oil over medium heat. Sweat the celery until translucent, about 3 minutes, then stir in the garlic, red pepper flakes and thyme. Cook for another 3 minutes, then transfer the mixture to a plate to cool down in the refrigerator.

Once the celery has cooled, add it to the ground chicken, Parmesan cheese, mozzarella, salt and black pepper, mixing until well incorporated.

Place 1 tablespoon (12 g) of filling in the center of a wrapper and then gently gather the sides of the wrapper up and around the filling, forming the sides of the shumai by circling your forefinger and thumb together.

Using a small knife or spatula, smooth down the top of the filling (it should come to the edges of the wrapper, and will be exposed) while continuing to gently squeeze and form the sides and bottom of the cup-shaped dumpling. Gently tap the finished shumai on the work surface to flatten the bottom so it stands up and the shumai resembles a short cylinder. Refrigerate the shumai on a lightly floured tray wrapped in plastic wrap until needed.

To make the tomato chutney, combine the olive oil, shallot, garlic, diced tomatoes with liquid, tomato puree and brown sugar in a small pot. Simmer over medium heat, stirring occasionally, until the liquid has reduced and the sauce is thick and rich. Stir in the pickled ginger and pickled ginger juice. Season to taste with salt. The chutney may be served warm or cold with the shumai.

Prepare a steamer basket lined with blanched cabbage leaves or lightly greased parchment paper. Place the shumai in the steamer basket, being careful to space them apart so they are not touching. Cover with a lid and steam the shumai for 6 to 8 minutes, until they are cooked through. Serve with a dollop of the chutney on top.

# LAMB SATAY SHUMAI

I'm a huge fan of lamb for its rich, meaty flavor and versatility. I recently visited Kuala Lumpur, Malaysia, where street food is a way of life. Shumai on a stick was one of my favorite snacks during my three weeks there. This recipe combines the best of both worlds and is fantastic served with peanut sauce and pickled cucumbers. Hey, most people love meat on a stick. Think about how your friends are going to react when you put shumai on a stick. You'll need 12 wooden skewers for this recipe.

➢ MAKES 12 SKEWERS
➢ Preferred Cooking Method: Steamed and grilled

1 lb (450 g) ground lamb shoulder
¼ cup (60 g) minced shallot
1 tbsp (10 g) minced garlic
1 tsp (5 g) ground coriander
1 tsp (5 g) ground turmeric
½ tsp ground ginger
1 tbsp (5 g) brown sugar
3 tbsp (45 g) tamarind concentrate
3 tbsp (45 ml) kecap manis (sweet soy sauce)
36 shumai wrappers
Oil for grilling
Quick Pickled Cucumbers (page 230)
Peanut Sesame Sauce (page 223)
Cilantro leaves for garnish

Combine the ground lamb, shallot, garlic, coriander, turmeric, ginger, brown sugar, tamarind and kecap manis in a bowl. Mix thoroughly.

Place 1 tablespoon (12 g) of filling in the center of the wrapper and then gently gather the sides of the wrapper up and around the filling, forming the sides of the shumai by circling your forefinger and thumb together.

Using a small knife or spatula, smooth down the top of the filling (it should come to the edges of the wrapper and will be exposed) while continuing to gently squeeze and form the sides and bottom of the cup-shaped dumpling. Gently tap the finished shumai on the work surface to flatten the bottom so it stands up and the shumai resembles a short cylinder. Thread 3 shumai onto each skewer. Refrigerate on a lightly floured tray wrapped in plastic wrap for at least an hour.

Prepare a steamer basket lined with blanched cabbage leaves or lightly greased parchment paper. Place the shumai skewers in the steamer basket, being careful to space them apart so they are not touching. Cover with a lid and steam the shumai for 4 minutes, until the wrappers are cooked. Transfer the skewers to a sheet tray and refrigerate until cold. *If the skewers are not able to fit inside the steamer, steam the shumai first, chill them, then thread 3 per skewer afterward.

Heat a grill* or grill pan over medium-high heat until very hot. Brush the grill grates well with oil. Brush the tops and bottoms of the shumai lightly with oil. Grill the shumai bottoms until the grill marks are distinct. Be careful not to move the shumai while they are cooking, as the wrappers will tear. As the grill marks begin to caramelize and the wrapper begins to crisp slightly, turn it over and grill the open-faced meat side. Grill for another 3 to 4 minutes, until the top has caramelized. Serve the shumai skewers with pickled cucumbers, peanut sauce and fresh cilantro leaves.

* Most backyard grills tend to have very large grates, and food will sometimes fall through the grates, forever lost to the hot coals below. One of my favorite tricks is to put a metal cooling rack (used for cooling cakes and cookies) on the grill. Make sure the cooling rack is not coated in plastic or another material that will melt on the grill. Aluminum or stainless steel works best and I like to use racks with a crosshatch grate rather than parallel wires. The rack will heat and discolor over time, but keep it clean and it will forever be your barbecue friend, perfect for grilling vegetables, delicate items like seafood and small items like dumplings and shumai!

# THAI SHRIMP SHUMAI

These little gems are great any which way you decide to cook them. Kaffir lime leaves are a secret weapon for a burst of lime freshness, and coconut milk gives a buttery taste to the filling. You can use homemade dough colored with a vegetable juice for an extra special look and taste. Any number of dipping sauces work with these.

➤ MAKES 40 SHUMAI
➤ Preferred Cooking Method: Steamed

---

¾ lb (340 g) raw shrimp, peeled and deveined

1 large egg white

1 tbsp (10 g) potato starch

1 tbsp (15 ml) Thai fish sauce

2 tbsp (30 ml) coconut milk

½ tsp salt

½ tsp sugar

¼ tsp ground white pepper

¼ cup (65 g) minced bamboo shoots

¼ cup (15 g) minced scallion, white parts only

1 tsp (3 g) minced garlic

1 tsp (2 g) minced kaffir lime leaves

40 shumai wrappers or 1 recipe Basic Wheat Starch Dough (page 27) colored with carrot juice (page 25)

Small Thai basil leaves for garnish

Place ¼ pound (115 g) of the shrimp in a food processor with the egg white, potato starch, fish sauce, coconut milk, salt, sugar and white pepper. Pulse until a paste forms.

Dice the remaining ½ pound (225 g) shrimp into tiny pieces and combine with the shrimp paste in a mixing bowl along with the bamboo shoots, scallion, garlic and kaffir lime leaf.

Place 1 tablespoon (12 g) of filling in the center of the wrapper and then gently gather the sides of the wrapper up and around the filling, forming the sides of the shumai by circling your forefinger and thumb together.

Using a small knife or spatula, smooth down the top of the filling (it should come to the edges of the wrapper and will be exposed) while continuing to gently squeeze and form the sides and bottom of the cup-shaped dumpling. Gently tap the finished shumai on the work surface to flatten the bottom so it stands up and the shumai resembles a short cylinder. Refrigerate the shumai for at least an hour before cooking.

Prepare a steamer basket lined with blanched cabbage leaves or lightly greased parchment paper. Place the shumai in the steamer basket, being careful to space them apart so they are not touching. Cover with a lid and steam the shumai for 7 to 8 minutes, until they are cooked through. Garnish with fresh Thai basil leaves and a dipping sauce of your choice.

# SCALLOP AND WATER CHESTNUT SHUMAI

This is one of my favorite fillings. The natural sweetness of the scallops pairs so well with the garlicky chives and crunchy water chestnuts. If you don't want to use pork fat for the mousse, feel free to substitute unsalted butter. These are perfect with black or red vinegar dipping sauce.

▷ MAKES 40 SHUMAI
▷ Preferred Cooking Method: Steamed

¾ lb (340 g) dry sea scallops

¼ lb (115 g) pork fat or unsalted butter, softened

1 tsp (5 ml) sesame oil

1 tbsp (15 ml) Shaoxing rice wine

1 tbsp (15 ml) soy sauce

½ tsp salt

1 tsp (5 g) sugar

¼ tsp white pepper

½ cup (75 g) water chestnuts, cut into ¼" (0.6 cm) dice

½ cup (25 g) chopped garlic chives

40 shumai wrappers

Garnish options: baby shrimp, fish roe, green peas, diced carrot or diced red bell pepper

Watercress leaves for garnish

Black or Red Vinegar Dipping Sauce (page 219 or 220)

Pat the scallops dry between clean towels or paper towels.

Combine ½ pound (225 g) of the scallops and the pork fat in a food processor and pulse briefly. Add the sesame oil, wine, soy sauce, salt, sugar and white pepper. Pulse the scallops until a smooth mousse is formed, being careful not the let the food processor run for a long time (the heat of the friction will warm the mousse).

Dice the remaining ¼ pound (115 g) scallops into ¼-inch (0.6-cm) dice. Add the water chestnuts, garlic chives and scallop mousse to the diced scallops and mix well. Chill the filling for at least 30 minutes.

Place 1 tablespoon (12 g) of filling in the center of the wrapper and then gently gather the sides of the wrapper up and around the filling, forming the sides of the shumai by circling your forefinger and thumb together.

Using a small knife or spatula, smooth down the top of the filling (it should come to the edges of the wrapper, and will be exposed) while continuing to gently squeeze and form the sides and bottom of the cup-shaped dumpling. Gently tap the finished shumai on the work surface to flatten the bottom so it stands up and the shumai resembles a short cylinder.

Finish the shumai by pressing the garnish of your choice gently into the top of the filling. Refrigerate the shumai for at least an hour before cooking.

Prepare a steamer basket lined with blanched cabbage leaves or lightly greased parchment paper. Place the shumai in the steamer basket, being careful to space them apart so they are not touching. Cover with a lid and steam the shumai for 5 to 6 minutes, until they are cooked through. Garnish with the watercress leaves. Serve with the dipping sauce of your choice.

# PAELLA SHUMAI

Saffron is one of the oldest, most versatile and valued spices on the market, the rehydrated threads giving a beautiful golden yellow color to its multiple uses. For thousands of years, saffron has been prized for its homeopathic benefits, and it was used as a natural vegetable dye, cosmetic and textile, as well as for religious purposes. Of course, it can also be found in cuisines all over the world. One of my favorite places to find saffron is in a giant pan of paella, a traditional rice dish from Spain and the inspiration for this recipe.

➤ MAKES 40 SHUMAI
➤ Preferred Cooking Method: Steamed

1 tbsp (15 ml) olive oil

½ cup (45 g) dried Spanish chorizo, cut into ⅛" (0.3 cm) dice

¼ cup (50 g) Yukon gold potato, cut into ⅛" (0.3 cm) dice

¼ cup (15 g) fennel bulb, cut into ⅛" (0.3 cm) dice

¼ cup (60 g) minced shallot

1 tbsp (10 g) minced garlic

½ tsp saffron threads

¼ cup (60 ml) dry white wine

¼ cup (60 ml) heavy cream

¾ lb (340 g) raw shrimp, peeled and deveined

1 large egg white

1 tbsp (10 g) cornstarch

1 tsp (5 ml) lime juice

1 tsp (5 g) salt

½ tsp sugar

¼ tsp ground white pepper

¼ tsp crushed red pepper flakes

1 tbsp (2 g) minced cilantro

1 tbsp (2 g) minced parsley

40 shumai wrappers or 1 recipe Basic Wheat Starch Dough (page 27) colored with spinach or red bell pepper juice (page 25)

40 baby shrimp

40 green peas

Yuzu Aioli (page 228)

Crispy Rice (page 229) for garnish

Heat a large sauté pan over medium-high heat. When the pan is hot, add the olive oil, chorizo and potato. Sauté the mixture for 3 minutes, then add the fennel and cook, stirring occasionally, for another 3 minutes. Add the shallot and garlic and cook for another 2 minutes.

While you are cooking the vegetables, soak the saffron threads in the white wine. Add the white wine and saffron to the pan after the shallot and garlic. Allow the liquid to reduce until it has almost evaporated completely. Add the heavy cream to the pan and reduce again until the cream is coating the vegetables and has thickened and reduced by half. When you tilt the pan there should only be 1 or 2 tablespoons (15 or 30 ml) of liquid in the pan. Transfer the mixture to a bowl and then refrigerate to cool.

In a food processor, pulse ¼ pound (115 g) of the peeled shrimp with the egg white, cornstarch, lime juice, salt, sugar and white pepper. Pulse until well blended and fairly smooth, being careful not to let the food processor run for more than 5 seconds at a time. Transfer the mixture to a mixing bowl.

Chop the remaining ½ pound (225 g) of shrimp into tiny pieces. Fold the shrimp mousse together with the chorizo mixture until they are well combined, then fold in the chopped shrimp, red pepper flakes and minced cilantro and parsley.

Place 1 tablespoon (12 g) of filling in the center of the wrapper and then gently gather the sides of the wrapper up and around the filling, forming the sides of the shumai by circling your forefinger and thumb together.

Using a small knife or spatula, smooth down the top of the filling (it should come to the edges of the wrapper and will be exposed) while continuing to gently squeeze and form the sides and bottom of the cup-shaped dumpling. Gently tap the finished shumai on the work surface to flatten the bottom so it stands up and the shumai resembles a short cylinder.

Finish the shumai by pressing a baby shrimp gently but firmly into the top of the filling and then the green pea into the center of each shrimp. Refrigerate the shumai for at least an hour before cooking.

Prepare a steamer basket lined with blanched cabbage leaves or lightly greased parchment paper. Place the shumai in the steamer basket, being careful to space them apart so they are not touching. Cover with a lid and steam the shumai for 5 to 6 minutes, until they are cooked through. Serve with the yuzu aioli and crispy rice.

# LOBSTER CORN SHUMAI

The taste of lobster and summer rolls rolled up in a dumpling. You can use frozen raw lobster meat if you can't get fresh. Garnish with a little soy ginger and yuzu aioli: it's New England meets Asia!

➢ MAKES 40 SHUMAI
➢ Preferred Cooking Method: Panfried

1 tbsp (15 g) salted butter
¼ cup (40 g) diced celery
¼ cup (50 g) minced shallot
1 clove garlic, minced
½ cup (75 g) corn kernels
¾ lb (340 g) lobster meat
¼ lb (115 g) unsalted butter, softened
1 large egg white
1 tbsp (10 g) cornstarch
1 tbsp (15 ml) dry sake
1 tbsp (15 ml) dashi stock (page 218)
½ tsp salt
½ tsp sugar
¼ tsp ground white pepper
1 tsp (5 ml) lemon juice
1 tbsp (2 g) minced dill
1 tbsp (2 g) minced chives
40 shumai wrappers
Oil for panfrying
Soy Ginger Dipping Sauce (page 219)
Yuzu Aioli (page 228) for garnish
Dill fronds for garnish

In a small sauté pan, heat the salted butter and sweat the celery and shallot over medium heat until translucent, about 4 minutes. Add the garlic, cook for 2 minutes more, then add the corn kernels and cook for another 3 minutes. Transfer the mixture to a bowl to cool. Refrigerate until needed.

Combine ½ pound (225 g) of the lobster meat with the softened unsalted butter in a food processor. Pulse until well blended and fairly smooth, being careful not to let the food processor run for more than 5 seconds at a time. Add the egg white, cornstarch, sake, dashi stock, salt, sugar, white pepper and lemon juice. Pulse until well blended.

Mince the remaining ¼ pound (115 g) lobster meat and fold into the lobster mousse along with the corn mixture and the minced dill and chives.

Place 1 tablespoon (12 g) of filling in the center of the wrapper and then gently gather the sides of the wrapper up and around the filling, forming the sides of the shumai by circling your forefinger and thumb together.

Using a small knife or spatula, smooth down the top of the filling (it should come to the edges of the wrapper and will be exposed) while continuing to gently squeeze and form the sides and bottom of the cup-shaped dumpling. Gently tap the finished shumai on the work surface to flatten the bottom so it stands up and the shumai resembles a short cylinder.

Heat a wok or large nonstick frying pan over high heat. Add ½ tablespoon (7.5 ml) of oil to the hot pan, tilting the pan to coat the bottom. Place the shumai in a single layer in the hot pan and cook until the bottoms are golden brown, 1 to 2 minutes. Add ½ cup (125 ml) of water and immediately cover the pan with a tight-fitting lid. Cook until all of the water has been absorbed and the dumpling skins have cooked through, about 4 to 5 minutes. Repeat with the remaining shumai. Garnish with a drizzle of dipping sauce, a small dollop of aioli and a dill frond.

# CHAPTER 5

# MULTI-PLEAT FOLD: HAR GOW

⇾ One of most widely recognized types of dim sum is Cantonese har gow. Otherwise known as "crystal shrimp" dumplings, these eye-appealing bites are known for their delicate translucent skin, fine multitude of pleats and perfectly cooked shrimp filling. Originating in the Guangzhou province, this specialty is said to have been created by a masterful chef at a teahouse for the Empress Dowager Cixi toward the end of the Qing dynasty.

The beauty is in the wheat starch dough. The dough is tricky to handle and it will take a bit of practice to master the folding technique. But once the opaque dough is steamed, it turns translucent, like a frosted window, allowing you a glimpse of what's inside. The recipes that follow have some fun with that dough, adding vegetable juice for color and ingredients such as seaweed and green tea for texture and flavor. If you are able to master this particular dumpling, it will be your showstopper every single time.

# HOW TO FOLD

It takes quite a bit of practice to form har gow's signature multi-pleat bonnet shape. It is similar to the potsticker fold, but the dough itself is more delicate and must be freshly rolled while still warm and the har gow formed immediately. The warm dough is more pliable and easier to handle.

To form your wrappers, roll your single batch of dough into a 1-inch (2.5-cm)-thick rope and cut into 32 pieces. Cover the dough pieces with plastic wrap and a hot, damp towel.

Lightly oil your work surface and your rolling pin, or use two small sheets of parchment paper. Place a dough ball on the greased surface or between the two pieces of parchment paper.

Using a lightly oiled rolling pin or lightly oiled meat cleaver, flatten each piece into a 3- to 4-inch (7.5-to 10-cm) round shape. The dough should be fairly thin (about $1/16$ inch [0.2 cm]). The thinner you roll the dough, the more translucent the wrapper will be when it steams. Gently unpeel the wrapper from the parchment. It is best to fill the wrapper immediately to form the dumpling, but you can make all of the wrappers first and then fill them afterward, as long as you keep the wrappers covered in a layer of plastic wrap weighted with a hot, damp towel to prevent them from drying out.

Rub a little vegetable oil into your hands. Using a similar technique as with the potsticker fold, hold the wrapper in the palm of your hand. Place the desired amount of filling (usually a heaping teaspoon [4 g]) in the center of the wrapper and gently fold the bottom of the wrapper toward the top half, to form a half-moon shape. Gently press the edges of the wrapper together closest to where your thumb meets your forefinger, using your thumb to seal the first ½ inch (1.3 cm) of the dumpling.

Using your free thumb and forefinger, make a series of small ¼-inch (0.6 cm) pleats in the direction of your thumb with only the top wrapper, lining up the edge of the pleat with the bottom half of the wrapper and using your thumb on your opposite hand (the one holding the dumpling) to press gently and seal.

Continue to gather, pleat (toward your thumb), and press the top half of the wrapper, always making sure you line up the edges with the bottom half of the wrapper, until you have made seven to ten pleats and the dumpling is completely sealed.

By gathering only one side of the dumpling wrapper, you will see the natural bonnet shape begin to form. Place the formed dumplings into a steamer lined with lightly greased parchment or waxed paper punched with holes, ensuring the dumplings are not touching each other in the steamer basket. Keep a layer of plastic wrap weighted with a lightly damp towel on top of the finished dumplings so they do not dry out. Cover and steam the har gow per the recipe directions.

Roll your dough using a lighly oiled surface or between two pieces of parchment paper.

The dough should be 1/16 inch thick.

Use a ring cutter and gently peel away the parchment.

Fill the dough with a small amount of filling.

Begin to form tiny pleats.

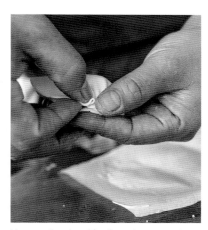

Use your thumb and forefinger to press and seal the dough.

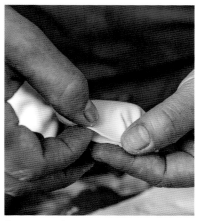

Line up your edges.

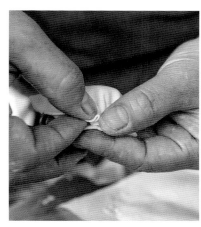

Great har gow have 7 to 10 pleats.

Press and pinch the finished dumpling to seal.

# CRYSTAL SHRIMP HAR GOW

This is one of the most classic dim sum dumplings and always a regular on my table. The translucent white skin surrounds plump and firm steamed shrimp cut with fragrant bamboo shoots. The best dim sum chefs can use as many as fifteen pleats to form this popular delicacy. Obviously, this particular fold takes some time to master, so a potsticker pleat is fine, too. With plenty of practice (and many har gow later), you will become familiar with how to handle the dough, at which point you can really get creative with dumpling shapes and ideas.

➤ MAKES 32 DUMPLINGS
➤ Preferred Cooking Method: Steamed

## FILLING

½ lb (225 g) raw shrimp, peeled, deveined, and finely minced

1 tbsp (15 g) finely minced pork fatback

1 tbsp (3 g) minced scallion, white parts only

2 tbsp (35 g) minced bamboo shoots

2 tsp (10 ml) soy sauce

1 tbsp (15 ml) Shaoxing rice wine

1½ tsp (5 g) cornstarch

1 tsp (5 ml) sesame oil

½ tsp sugar

½ tsp salt

1 large egg white

Pinch of ground white pepper

1 recipe Basic Wheat Starch Dough (page 27)

To make the filling, combine all of the ingredients in a bowl and mix until well blended. Refrigerate for at least an hour.

To form your wrappers, roll your dough into a 1-inch (2.5-cm)-thick rope and cut into 32 pieces. Cover the dough pieces with plastic wrap and a hot, damp towel. Form your har gow, using a heaping teaspoon (4 g) of filling, making them one at a time as you roll out each wrapper (see page 100).

Place the formed dumplings into a steamer lined with lightly greased parchment or waxed paper punched with holes, ensuring the dumplings are not touching each other in the steamer basket. Keep a layer of plastic wrap weighted with a lightly damp towel on top of the finished dumplings so they do not dry out. Remove the plastic wrap and towel before cooking. Cover and steam the har gow for 6 to 8 minutes, until they are fully cooked and the wrappers are translucent. Serve with the dipping sauce of your choice.

# LOBSTER AND KAFFIR LIME HAR GOW

Kaffir lime can be commonly found in Southeast Asian cuisine. While the juice of the kaffir lime is very tart, it's really the leaves and zest that contain the powerful natural oils and provide the distinctive taste and fragrance. You can usually find the leaves and fruit in Asian and specialty grocery stores. I always have a small bag of kaffir lime leaves in my freezer, as a little goes a long way.

➢ MAKES 32 DUMPLINGS
➢ Preferred Cooking Method: Steamed

## FILLING

½ lb (225 g) raw lobster meat

2 kaffir lime leaves, fresh or frozen, finely minced

¼ cup (15 g) minced scallion, white parts only

1 large egg white, lightly beaten

1 tsp (3 g) cornstarch

1 tsp (5 ml) soy sauce

1 tsp (5 ml) fish sauce

½ tsp salt

½ tsp sugar

¼ tsp white pepper

1 recipe Basic Wheat Starch Dough (page 27) colored with ½ cup (120 ml) carrot juice (page 25)

Nuoc Cham or Sweet Chili Sauce (page 227 or 223)

To make the filling, combine all of the ingredients in the food processor. Pulse until well blended and fairly smooth. Refrigerate for at least an hour.

To form your wrappers, roll your dough into a 1-inch (2.3-cm)-thick rope and cut into 32 pieces. Cover the dough pieces with plastic wrap and a hot, damp towel. Form your har gow, using a heaping teaspoon (4 g) of filling, making them one at a time as you roll out each wrapper (see page 100).

Place the formed dumplings into a steamer lined with lightly greased parchment or waxed paper punched with holes, ensuring the dumplings are not touching each other in the steamer basket. Keep a layer of plastic wrap weighted with a lightly damp towel on top of the finished dumplings so they do not dry out. Remove the plastic wrap and towel before cooking. Cover and steam the har gow for 5 to 6 minutes, until they are fully cooked and the wrappers are translucent. Serve with the dipping sauce of your choice.

# BEET AND TOFU HAR GOW

The addition of beet juice to the dough creates a beautiful pink color for these vegetarian delights. Dried wakame seaweed and pickled ginger add a briny, pungent scent to the dumplings. Panfrying adds a really nice crispiness to the translucent skin. These dumplings are beautiful with a little bit of sea salt and sesame oil for dipping but also pair well with Soy Ginger Dipping Sauce.

➢ MAKES 40 DUMPLINGS
➢ Preferred Cooking Method: Panfried

## FILLING

6 oz (170 g) red beet, peeled and trimmed

2 tbsp (10 g) chopped dried wakame seaweed

6 oz (170 g) extrafirm tofu

1 tbsp (10 g) minced pickled ginger

2 tbsp (5 g) minced scallion, white parts only

1 tbsp (15 ml) mirin

2 tsp (10 ml) soy sauce

2 tbsp (20 g) cornstarch

½ tsp salt

¼ tsp togarashi pepper

1 recipe Basic Wheat Starch Dough (page 27) colored with 2 tbsp (30 ml) beet juice (page 25)

Oil for panfrying
Sesame oil and sea salt

To make the filling, slice the beet into ⅛-inch (0.3 cm)-thick slices. Add 1 inch (2.5 cm) of water to the bottom of a large pot and bring the water to a boil over high heat. Place the sliced beets in a steamer basket, then the basket in the pot, lower the heat to medium, and cover. Cook the beets for 5 minutes, until tender. Transfer the beets to a cutting board and allow them to cool. Mince the beets into ⅛-inch (0.3 cm) dice.

Add the dried wakame to a food processor and pulse into small pieces slightly smaller than a grain of rice. Gently press the tofu dry with a paper towel. Add the tofu to the food processor along with the remaining ingredients for the filling. Pulse until well incorporated. Transfer to a bowl and fold in the minced beets. Cover and refrigerate for at least an hour to allow the filling to firm up and the seaweed to hydrate.

To form your wrappers, roll your single batch of dough into a 1-inch (2.5-cm) thick rope and cut into 32 pieces. Cover the dough pieces with plastic wrap and a hot, damp towel. Form your har gow, using a heaping teaspoon (4 g) of filling, making them one at a time as you roll out each wrapper (see page 100).

Heat a wok or large nonstick frying pan over high heat. Add ½ tablespoon (7.5 ml) of oil to the hot pan, tilting the pan to coat the bottom. Place the dumplings in a single layer in the hot pan, making sure they are not touching, and cook until the bottoms are golden brown, about 1 minute. Add ½ cup (125 ml) of water and immediately cover the pan with a tight-fitting lid. Cook until all of the water has been absorbed and the dumpling skins have cooked through, about 5 to 6 minutes. Repeat with the remaining dumplings. Serve with sesame oil and sea salt.

# GREEN TEA AND RED BEAN HAR GOW

This dessert dumpling is very much like green tea mochi, and you can substitute Basic Glutinous Rice Flour Dough (page 28) for the wheat starch dough if you want. Sweetened red bean paste is sold in cans at Asian and specialty grocery stores if you don't have time to make your own. Because you are using a wheat starch dough, these are best served warm, freshly steamed.

➢ MAKES 32 DUMPLINGS
➢ Preferred Cooking Method: Steamed

## FILLING
¾ cup (150 g) dried red adzuki beans
½ cup (95 g) sugar
3 tbsp (45 ml) vegetable oil

## GREEN TEA WHEAT STARCH DOUGH
¾ cup (75 g) wheat starch flour
2 tbsp (15 g) tapioca flour or starch
2 tbsp (15 g) matcha green tea powder
1 tsp (5 ml) vegetable oil
½ cup (120 ml) plus 1 tbsp (15 ml) water

To make the filling, sort through the dried adzuki beans to remove any stones or broken beans. Rinse the beans in cold water and then soak them in a bowl overnight, with water covering the beans by 2 inches (5 cm).

The next day, drain the beans and rinse again in cold water. Transfer them to a heavy-bottomed saucepan. Cover the beans with water and bring to a boil over high heat. Reduce the heat to a simmer and cook the beans until they are soft, 1½ to 2 hours, adding more water if needed. The beans are done when they can be easily smashed between your thumb and forefinger. Drain the beans, reserving the cooking liquid.

Add the cooked beans, sugar and 1 tablespoon (15 ml) of the cooking liquid to a food processor. Pulse until you have a chunky paste.

Heat a small sauté pan over medium-low heat and add the vegetable oil to the pan. Add the bean paste to the pan and cook for 4 to 5 minutes, mashing and stir-frying the beans with a wooden spoon, until they begin to dry out a little. Transfer the bean paste to a flat surface and spread it out to cool, covering with a piece of plastic wrap. Wrap the bean paste tightly in plastic wrap and refrigerate until needed.

To make the dough, mix the wheat starch, tapioca flour and matcha powder in a bowl with a whisk or fork until well combined. Make a well in the center of the flour. Bring the oil and water to a boil and pour into the well, mixing with a spoon until the flour has absorbed all of the liquid. Cover with plastic wrap or a hot damp towel to allow the flour to soften. Turn the dough out onto a work surface or cutting board. Gently knead the dough for 1 to 2 minutes. Add wheat starch as needed if the dough is sticky. The dough should be smooth and soft. Keep the warm dough wrapped in plastic wrap so it does not dry out.

To form your wrappers, roll your dough into a 1-inch (2.5-cm)-thick rope and cut into 32 pieces. Cover the dough pieces with plastic wrap and a hot, damp towel.

Form your har gow, using a heaping teaspoon (4 g) of filling, making them one at a time as you roll out each wrapper (see page 110).

Place the formed dumplings into a steamer lined with lightly greased parchment or waxed paper punched with holes, ensuring the dumplings are not touching each other in the steamer basket. Keep a layer of plastic wrap weighted with a lightly damp towel on top of the finished dumplings so they do not dry out. Remove the plastic wrap and towel before cooking. Cover and steam the har gow for 5 to 6 minutes, until they are fully cooked and the wrappers are translucent. Serve warm.

# GREEN TEA AND RED BEAN HAR GOW (CONTINUED)

Roll your dough between two sheets of parchment. Use a ring cutter to cut a round shape.

Place the red bean filling in the center and fold the dough in half.

Begin making small pleats.

Continue pleating, 7 to 10 pleats until the dumpling is formed.

# TEA-SMOKED CHICKEN HAR GOW

You can use any type of black tea, such as jasmine or oolong, to smoke your chicken. For an even smokier flavor, you can grind up a little bit of Lapsang Souchong, a smoky Chinese tea, and add ½ teaspoon to the filling. I like using dark meat chicken for the filling, as it stays tender and moist when cooked twice.

➤ MAKES 32 DUMPLINGS
➤ Preferred Cooking Method: Steamed

1 tsp (5 g) Szechuan peppercorns

¼ cup (60 ml) loose-leaf black tea, such as jasmine or oolong

¼ cup (50 g) uncooked rice, such as jasmine

2 tbsp (30 g) brown sugar

½ lb (225 g) ground dark meat chicken

1 tbsp (15 ml) sesame oil

1 tsp (5 g) minced ginger

2 tbsp (30 ml) Shaoxing rice wine

1 tbsp (15 ml) dark soy sauce

1 large egg white, beaten

2 tbsp (20 g) cornstarch

1 tsp (5 g) salt

½ tsp granulated sugar

4 dried shiitake mushrooms, rehydrated* and minced

¼ cup (15 g) minced garlic chives

1 recipe Basic Wheat Starch Dough (page 27)

Chinese mustard (page 226) and sambal for serving

Toast the Szechuan peppercorns in a dry sauté pan over medium heat for 5 minutes, gently shaking the pan frequently, until fragrant. Coarsely grind the peppercorns in a spice grinder or with a mortar and pestle. Set aside and wipe out the sauté pan with a paper towel.

Prepare a large heavy-bottomed pot (a pasta pot with an insert works well for this), dim sum steamer or wok by placing a double layer of heavy-duty aluminum foil inside to fit the bottom. Mix the tea, rice and brown sugar together and place in the bottom of the pot in the center of the foil.

Mix the ground chicken with the sesame oil, ginger, wine, soy sauce and ground peppercorns. Place the ground chicken on a small plate that fits the interior of the steamer or pasta insert, gently spreading the chicken evenly on the plate. If you are using a pasta pot, place the plate in the bottom of the insert. If you don't have a pot with a pasta or steamer insert or a dim sum steamer, place a large tall ring mold or cookie cutter in the bottom of the pot with the smoking mixture.

Place the plate of chicken on the ring mold, or place the insert in the pot. Cover the pot with a tight-fitting lid. Cook over high heat for 8 to 10 minutes, smoking the chicken until it takes on a golden brown color and has a smoky aroma. Transfer the chicken and the cooking liquid to a bowl. Crumble the cooked chicken with a spoon or fork. Allow the chicken to cool slightly.

Add the beaten egg white, cornstarch, salt, granulated sugar, minced shiitakes and garlic chives to the chicken meat. Mix well and refrigerate the filling for an hour.

To form your wrappers, roll your dough into a 1-inch (2.5-cm)-thick rope and cut into 32 pieces. Cover the dough pieces with plastic wrap and a hot, damp towel. Form your har gow, using a heaping teaspoon (4 g) of filling, making them one at a time as you roll out each wrapper (see page 100).

Place the formed har gow into a steamer lined with lightly greased parchment or waxed paper punched with holes, ensuring the dumplings are not touching each other in the steamer basket. Keep a layer of plastic wrap weighted with a lightly damp towel on top of the finished dumplings so they do not dry out. Remove the plastic wrap and towel before cooking. Cover and steam the har gow for 6 to 8 minutes, until they are fully cooked and the wrappers are translucent. Serve with the Chinese mustard and sambal.

* To rehydrate dried shiitake mushrooms, rinse the dried mushrooms briefly under cold water. Place in a bowl or sealable container. Pour enough cold water over the mushrooms to cover them by at least 1 inch (2.5 cm). Place a folded paper towel over the mushrooms and water and press down until the paper towel saturates and keeps the dried mushrooms submerged. Allow the mushrooms to rehydrate overnight. Drain and remove the stems before using. Reserve the mushroom liquid for future use. If you are in a hurry, bring a small pot of water to a boil and pour over the dried mushrooms. Submerge the mushrooms with a paper towel and allow to soak for at least an hour.

# CHAPTER 6

# ROUND FOLD/ PUCK-SHAPED FOLD

➤ I love this style of dumpling because it's a two or three biter. The most recognized version of this fold comes in the form of a dim sum favorite known as gau choi gao. The wrapper is made from Basic Wheat Starch Dough (page 27) or Basic Glutinous Rice Flour Dough (page 28), although you can substitute frozen wrappers, too. The dumpling is then formed in the shape of a mini puck, the skin surrounding the traditional filling of minced shrimp and garlic chives. It is usually steamed or boiled, then optionally panfried or deep-fried. The shape of the dumpling gives maximum surface area for getting the outer skin crispy, which is one of my favorite dumplings mottos—"Crispy on the outside, juicy on the inside."

# HOW TO FOLD

If using Basic Wheat Starch Dough or Basic Glutinous Rice Flour Dough, the procedure is the same as for har gow (page 100).

To form your wrappers, roll your dough into a 1-inch (2.5-cm)-thick rope and cut into 32 pieces. Cover the dough pieces with plastic wrap and a hot, damp towel.

Place a piece of dough between two sheets of parchment paper or plastic wrap. Using a rolling pin or a meat cleaver, flatten or roll each piece into a 4- to 5-inch (10- to 12.5-cm) round shape. Use a little wheat starch if the dough is sticky. The dough should be fairly thin (about 1⁄16 inch [0.2 cm]). Gently unpeel the wrapper from the plastic wrap or parchment and fill the wrapper immediately to form the dumpling.

Hold the wrapper in the palm of one hand and place 1 to 2 teaspoons (4 to 8 g) of filling in the center of the wrapper. Dampen the edges of the wrapper with some water using your finger or a pastry brush. Fold one edge of the wrapper toward the center of the filling and hold in place with your thumb.   Continue to bring the edges of the dumpling toward the center in small increments, overlapping and gently pressing the seal until a pleated puck-shaped dumpling has formed. Pinch the center where the edges come together to complete the seal.

Place the filling in the center and fold the edges in toward the center.

Bring all of the edges to the center until they meet.

Gently pinch and seal the center of the dumpling.

# CRISPY SHRIMP AND CHIVE DUMPLINGS

This is ultimately one of my favorite dumplings. My friend Shannon and I judge how good a dim sum restaurant is by the quality of this traditional panfried wonder. I love the heft of this dumpling with the round fold, usually a two to three biter. It's all about the crispy wheat starch wrapper encasing the garlicky chives and shrimp. You can use either bamboo shoots or water chestnuts, which I prefer for their crunchy texture.

➤ MAKES 24 DUMPLINGS
➤ Preferred Cooking Method: Panfried

## FILLING

1 tbsp (15 ml) vegetable oil

3 cups (150 g) garlic chives, cut into 2" (5 cm) pieces

4 oz (115 g) raw shrimp, peeled, deveined, and minced

¼ cup (70 g) minced water chestnuts or bamboo shoots

2 tbsp (30 ml) Shaoxing rice wine

2 tbsp (30 ml) sesame oil

1 tbsp (15 ml) oyster sauce

1 tbsp (15 ml) soy sauce

1 tsp (5 g) sugar

½ tsp salt

½ tsp ground white pepper

2 tbsp (20 g) cornstarch

1 recipe Basic Wheat Starch Salt Dough (page 27) or Glutinous Rice Flour Salt Dough (page 28)

Vegetable oil for panfrying

To make the filling, heat the vegetable oil in a sauté pan or wok over high heat. Add the cut garlic chives and stir-fry for 1 minute, until the chives wilt slightly. Transfer to a plate or sheet tray to cool.

Once the chives are cool, stir in the remaining ingredients for the filling until well mixed. Refrigerate the filling for at least an hour.

To form your wrappers, roll your dough into a 1-inch (2.5-cm) thick rope and cut into 24 pieces. Cover the dough pieces with plastic wrap and a hot, damp towel.

Form your dumplings, using a heaping teaspoon (4 g) of filling, making them one at a time as you roll out each wrapper (see page 114).

Place the formed dumplings into a steamer lined with lightly greased parchment or waxed paper punched with holes, ensuring the dumplings are not touching each other in the steamer basket. Keep a layer of plastic wrap weighted with a lightly damp towel on top of the finished dumplings so they do not dry out. Remove the plastic wrap and towel before cooking.

To panfry, heat a wok or large sauté pan over medium-high heat. Add a few tablespoons of oil to coat the bottom of the pan. Line the dumplings in the hot pan, ensuring that they are not touching each other. Fry the dumplings until they begin to brown on the bottom, about 1 to 2 minutes. Add ½ cup (125 ml) of water and immediately cover the pan with a tight-fitting lid. Cook until all of the water has been absorbed and the dumpling skins have cooked through, about 4 to 5 minutes. When the water has evaporated let the bottoms crisp up again then flip the dumplings to brown on the opposite side, another 1 to 2 minutes. Drain on paper towels and serve hot with the dipping sauce of your choice.

# AHI DUMPLINGS WITH AVOCADO

This dumpling showcases fresh ahi tuna, accented with simple garnishes. You can deep-fry or panfry these for the crispy texture that will complement the chunky avocado. Smooth miso sauce is a great option as a dipping sauce. I like using the premade wrappers for this dumpling; the thin skins lend themselves to quick cooking time.

➤ MAKES 32 DUMPLINGS
➤ Preferred Cooking Method: Panfried

## FILLING
¾ lb (340 g) fresh ahi tuna, cut into ¼" (0.6 cm) dice
2 tbsp (30 g) minced shallot
1 tbsp (3 g) minced chives
1 tsp (5 ml) sesame oil
1 tsp (5 ml) chile oil (page 225)
1 tbsp (15 ml) soy sauce

32 round dumpling wrappers

## AVOCADO MIXTURE
1½ cups (270 g) diced avocado
1 tsp (5 ml) yuzu or lime juice
½ tsp salt
¼ tsp sugar
¼ tsp ground black pepper

Oil for panfrying
Miso Mustard Sauce, optional (page 220)

To make the filling, combine all the ingredients in a mixing bowl. Stir until well combined. Refrigerate for at least an hour.

Form your dumplings, using a heaping teaspoon (4 g) of filling (page 114). Keep the dumplings covered on a lightly floured tray or plate.

To make the avocado mixture, in a separate bowl, combine the avocado, yuzu juice, salt, sugar and pepper. Lightly mash with a fork until well mixed; the avocado should still be slightly chunky. Keep refrigerated and covered until needed.

Heat a wok or large nonstick frying pan over high heat. Add ½ tablespoon (7.5 ml) of oil to the hot pan, tilting the pan to coat the bottom. Place the dumplings in a single layer in the hot pan and cook until the bottoms are golden brown, about 1 to 2 minutes. Add ⅓ cup (80 ml) of water and immediately cover the pan with a tight-fitting lid. Cook until all of the water has been absorbed and the dumpling skins have cooked through, about 5 to 6 minutes. Repeat with the remaining dumplings.

To serve, top each dumpling with ½ teaspoon of avocado mixture and serve with sauce.

# TEMPURA WHITEFISH AND ASPARAGUS DUMPLINGS WITH PONZU DIPPING SAUCE

The combination of whitefish mousse and diced asparagus makes a fresh and light filling, very much like traditional Japanese fish cake, kamaboko. Quickly blanch these beauties before you dunk them in tempura batter for a crispy and airy exterior. This recipe is really all about taking two favorite things and marrying the techniques for an unusually delicious result.

> MAKES 32 DUMPLINGS
> Preferred Cooking Method: Boiled, then deep-fried

## DUMPLINGS

12 oz (340 g) whitefish fillets, skinned

1 large egg white

1 tbsp (15 ml) dashi stock (page 218)

2 tbsp (30 ml) mirin

1 tbsp (10 g) cornstarch

½ tsp salt

2 or 3 pencil asparagus spears, fibrous stems removed, sliced into 1/16" (0.2 cm) rounds (½ cup [80 g])

32 round gyoza wrappers

## TEMPURA BATTER

½ cup (50 g) all-purpose flour

½ cup (50 g) rice flour

½ tsp baking powder

1 tsp (4 g) cornstarch

1½ cups (355 ml) cold club soda

Oil for deep-frying

Flour for dusting

Ponzu Dipping Sauce (page 221)

To make the dumplings, dice the fish fillet into small pieces and place in a food processor with the egg white, dashi, mirin, cornstarch and salt. Pulse until a homogenous paste is formed. Transfer to a bowl and mix in the diced asparagus. Cover and refrigerate the fish paste for at least an hour.

Fill each wrapper with 1 heaping teaspoon (4 g) of filling. Lightly wet the edges of the wrapper and form the dumpling (see page 114). Keep the dumplings covered on a lightly floured tray or plate.

Bring a pot of water to a boil. Working in small batches, carefully add the fish dumplings to the pot. Once the water comes to a boil again, strain out the dumplings and allow them to cool on a baking sheet or tray, making sure they are not touching each other. Repeat with the remaining dumplings, bringing the water to a boil again before adding each batch.

To make the tempura batter, whisk the flours, baking powder and cornstarch together in a bowl. Add the cold club soda, stirring gently to combine; the batter should be slightly lumpy. Allow the batter to rest for 5 minutes, and then give it one more stir. Keep the batter cold by placing it over an ice bath.

Preheat a small pot or wok with several inches of oil to 375°F/190°C for deep-frying.

Dredge the cooled dumplings in a little bit of flour, shaking off extra flour. Using chopsticks or a fork, dip the dumplings one at a time into the tempura batter, making sure the batter adheres to all sides of the dumpling and allowing the excess to drip off over the bowl for a few seconds before carefully adding the dumpling to the hot oil. Fry the dumplings a few pieces at a time, turning in the oil often, until the dumplings float and the exterior is lightly golden and crispy, about 2 minutes. Drain on paper towels. Repeat with the remaining dumplings, ensuring the oil temperature returns to 375°F/190°C. Serve the dumplings hot with the dipping sauce.

# BROCCOLI AND BLACK BEAN DUMPLINGS

The first thing I ever learned to cook for myself was broccoli, which I now deem "my gateway food." I love the fresh green flavor of the broccoli combined with the saltiness of Chinese dried black beans and creamy tofu.

➤ MAKES 32 DUMPLINGS
➤ Preferred Cooking Method: Pan-fried

## FILLING

2 tbsp (30 ml) peanut oil

¼ cup (15 g) minced scallion, white and green parts

1 tbsp (10 g) minced garlic

2 tbsp (30 g) minced ginger

3 tbsp (40 g) chopped dried fermented black beans

¼ cup (60 ml) sake

¼ cup (60 ml) vegetable stock or dashi stock (page 218)

2 tbsp (30 g) unsalted butter

4 oz (115 g) firm tofu, crumbled

8 oz (225 g) broccoli florets, pulsed to small pieces in a food processor

1 tbsp (15 g) brown sugar

2 tsp (10 g) cornstarch

1 recipe Basic Wheat Starch Dough (page 27) or Basic Glutinous Rice Flour Salt Dough (page 28)

Vegetable oil for panfrying

Red vinegar and julienned ginger for dipping

Chile oil (page 225)

To make the filling, heat a small sauté pan or wok over medium-high heat. When the pan is hot, add the peanut oil. Add the scallion, garlic and ginger to the pan, stir-frying for 1 minute. Add the black beans and cook for 1 minute more. Add the sake and vegetable stock and cook until most of the liquid has evaporated and only a few tablespoons remain when you tilt the pan. Stir in the butter until it melts and is well incorporated. Remove the pan from the heat.

Mix the crumbled tofu and chopped broccoli together in a bowl. Mix the brown sugar and cornstarch together until well blended and sprinkle over the tofu and broccoli. Pour the hot black beans over the mixture and stir until the filling comes together and is homogenous. Cover and refrigerate for 1 to 2 hours until the filling is cold and has firmed up a little bit.

To form your wrappers, roll the dough into a 1-inch (2.5-cm)-thick rope and cut into 32 pieces. Cover the dough pieces with plastic wrap and a hot, damp towel.

Form your dumplings, using a heaping teaspoon (4 g) of filling, making them one at a time as you roll out each wrapper (page 114).

To panfry, heat a wok or large sauté pan over medium-high heat. Add a few tablespoons of oil to coat the bottom of the pan. Line the dumplings in the hot pan, ensuring that they are not touching each other. Fry the dumplings until they begin to brown on the bottom, about 1 to 2 minutes. Add ½ cup (125 ml) of water and immediately cover the pan with a tight-fitting lid. Cook until all of the water has been absorbed and the dumpling skins have cooked through, about 4 to 5 minutes. When the water has evaporated let the bottoms crisp up again then flip the dumplings to brown on the opposite side, another 1 to 2 minutes. Drain on paper towels and serve hot with red vinegar, julienned ginger and chile oil.

# BBQ CHICKEN DUMPLINGS ✓

I like the convenience of using cooked meat for dumpling filling. This is a great way to have some fun with leftover chicken. The Asian-style barbecue sauce keeps the filling moist and juicy. Similarly, you can use sauce as a marinade for raw chicken or pork and roast or barbecue the meat. A slightly yeasted dough works well for this dumpling, adding a lighter texture to the wrapper.

➢ MAKES 32 DUMPLINGS
➢ Preferred Cooking Method: Deep-fried

## FILLING

12 oz (340 g) cooked chicken meat, dark meat preferably

¼ cup (15 g) minced scallion, white and green parts

1 tsp (5 g) minced garlic

1 tsp (5 g) minced ginger

2 tbsp (30 ml) maple syrup or dark brown sugar

1 tbsp (15 ml) oyster sauce

1 tbsp (15 ml) soy sauce

1 tbsp (15 ml) apple juice or cider

1 tbsp (10 g) cornstarch

1 tbsp (15 ml) Chinese red vinegar or rice vinegar

1 tsp (5 ml) sambal paste or Sriracha

½ tsp dry mustard powder

¼ tsp ground white pepper

1 recipe Bao Dough (page 30)
Oil for deep-frying

To make the filling, chop the cooked chicken meat into small ½-inch (1.3-cm) pieces and shred. In a separate bowl, mix the remaining ingredients until smooth. Fold the sauce into the cooked chicken meat until well combined. Refrigerate for at least an hour.

Divide your dough into 4 pieces. Roll each piece into a 1-inch (2.5-cm)-thick rope and cut into ½-inch (1.3-cm) pieces. Keep the dough covered with a damp towel.

Roll each dough ball into a 3-inch (7.5-cm) round wrapper using a rolling pin, about ⅙-inch (0.4 cm) thick. Fill each wrapper with 1 tablespoon (12 g) of filling. Lightly wet the edges of the wrapper and form the dumpling using the round or puck-shaped fold. Keep the dumplings covered on a lightly floured tray or plate.

Preheat the deep-frying oil to 350°F/176°C. Carefully fry the dumplings in small batches until the skin is golden brown and the dumplings are floating in the oil, about 3 to 4 minutes, gently tossing the dumplings in the oil so all sides cook evenly. Drain on paper towels. Allow the oil to come back to 350°F/176°C before frying the next batch. Serve immediately with the dipping sauce of your choice.

# LAMB AND SCALLION DUMPLINGS

The rich flavor of lamb pairs well with aromatic scallions. I love serving these dumplings with tangy, seasoned Greek yogurt and black vinegar.

➤ MAKES 32 DUMPLINGS
➤ Preferred Cooking Method: Panfried

## FILLING

2 tbsp (30 ml) sesame oil

2 cups (100 g) scallion greens, cut into 4" (10 cm) batons

10 oz (285 g) ground lamb shoulder

1 oz (30 g) ground pork fatback

1 tbsp (15 g) minced garlic

1 tbsp (15 ml) oyster sauce

¼ cup (6 g) minced cilantro

1 tsp (5 g) salt

½ tsp ground white pepper

1 recipe Basic Glutinous Rice Flour Salt Dough (page 28) colored with 2 tbsp (30 ml) spinach juice (page 25)

## SZECHUAN SESAME YOGURT

1 cup (235 ml) Greek yogurt

2 tsp (10 g) Szechuan peppercorns, toasted and ground

2 tbsp (30 g) roasted sesame seeds, lightly crushed or ground

1 tbsp (15 ml) freshly squeezed lime juice

½ tbsp honey

½ tsp salt

Oil for panfrying
Black Vinegar Dipping Sauce (page 219)

To make the filling, heat a sauté pan or wok over high heat. When the pan is hot, add the sesame oil and the scallion greens. Stir-fry for 1 minute, until the scallion greens wilt. Transfer to a bowl and refrigerate until cool. Once the scallion greens are cool, roughly chop them with a knife. Set aside.

Combine the lamb and fatback in a mixing bowl with the garlic and oyster sauce. Mix by hand, until the fatback is well distributed in the mix, being careful not to overwork the ground meat (it will become tough). Once the meat is well blended, fold in the scallion greens, cilantro, salt and pepper. Refrigerate the mixture for at least 30 minutes.

To form your wrappers, roll your dough into a 1-inch (2.5-cm)-thick rope and cut into 32 pieces. Cover the dough pieces with plastic wrap and a hot, damp towel. Form your dumplings, using 1 tablespoon (12 g) of filling and making them one at a time as you roll out each wrapper (see page 114).

Make your yogurt sauce. Combine all the ingredients in a bowl and whisk until well blended. Cover and refrigerate until needed.

To pan-fry, heat a wok or large sauté pan over medium-high heat. Add a few tablespoons of oil to coat the bottom of the pan. Line the dumplings in the hot pan, ensuring that they are not touching each other. Fry the dumplings until they begin to brown on the bottom, about 1 to 2 minutes. Add ½ cup (125 ml) of water and immediately cover the pan with a tight-fitting lid. Cook until all of the water has been absorbed and the dumpling skins have cooked through, about 4 to 5 minutes. When the water has evaporated let the bottoms crisp up again then flip the dumplings to brown on the opposite side, another 1 to 2 minutes. Drain on paper towels and serve with the yogurt and dipping sauce.

# ROOT VEGETABLE DUMPLINGS WITH BROWN BUTTER CRÈME FRAÎCHE

The natural sweetness of root vegetables pairs well with the nuttiness of sesame and the salinity of fish sauce. I like making these dumplings with fresh wheat dough, for that classic dumpling texture, and panfrying them. Brown butter and tangy crème fraîche complement the warmly spiced filling.

➣ MAKES 32 DUMPLINGS
➣ Preferred Cooking Method: Panfried

## FILLING

4 oz (115 g) carrots, peeled and cut into small pieces

4 oz (115 g) parsnips, peeled and cut into small pieces

4 oz (115 g) turnips or rutabaga, peeled and cut into small pieces

4 oz (115 g) red beet or celeriac, peeled and cut into small pieces

2 tbsp (30 ml) sesame oil

2 tbsp (30 g) finely grated ginger

1 tbsp (10 g) minced garlic

1 tbsp (15 g) lightly toasted white or black sesame seeds

1 tsp (5 g) five-spice powder

1 tsp (5 g) ground cumin

½ tsp ground coriander

¼ tsp ground allspice

¼ tsp cayenne pepper

1½ tsp (7 g) salt

1 tbsp (15 ml) Shaoxing rice wine

1 tbsp (15 ml) honey

1½ tbsp (20 ml) fish sauce

1 cup (50 g) minced scallion, green parts only

1 tbsp (10 g) cornstarch

To make the filling, pulse each of the vegetables separately in a food processor until broken down into small pieces (⅛ inch [0.3 cm]). Combine the minced root vegetables in a bowl.

Heat a nonstick sauté pan over high heat. Add the sesame oil and grated ginger, garlic and sesame seeds and cook for 15 seconds until fragrant. Add the minced root vegetables and stir-fry for 2 minutes. Add all the spices, mix well and stir-fry for another 2 minutes. Add the rice wine, honey and fish sauce, stirring to coat, and cook for another minute. Fold in the scallion and remove the pan from the heat immediately. Transfer the filling to a plate to cool to room temperature. When it has cooled, stir in the cornstarch and then cover and refrigerate the filling for an hour.

To make the brown butter crème fraîche, cut the butter into small pieces and place in a small sauté pan. Cook the butter over high heat, gently shaking the pan, until the butter begins to boil and foam. Reduce the heat to medium-high and continue to cook until it begins to turn a light amber color. At this point the fat solids will begin to brown very quickly. Remove the pan from the heat and continue to gently swirl the pan until the butter turns a deep amber brown and has a nutty (hazelnut-like) aroma. Pour the butter and browned solids into a heatproof bowl and allow the butter to cool to room temperature, until it solidifies slightly. Whisk the brown butter together with the crème fraîche, rice vinegar, soy sauce and sugar until smooth. Cover and refrigerate until needed.

Working on a lightly floured surface, roll the dough into two 1-inch (2.5-cm)-thick ropes and divide the ropes into 4 pieces each. Divide each piece into 4 more pieces, for a total of 32 pieces of dough. Keep the dough covered in plastic wrap or with a damp towel.

Using a small rolling pin, roll each piece of dough into a 3-inch (7.5-cm) circle about ⅟₁₆ inch (0.2 cm) thick. You may roll out all the wrappers at once if you keep them lightly floured and covered.

Fill each wrapper with 1 tablespoon (12 g) of filling. Lightly wet the edges of the wrapper and form the dumpling using the round or puck-shaped fold. Keep the dumplings covered on a lightly floured tray or plate.

Heat a wok or large nonstick frying pan over high heat. Add ½ tablespoon (7.5 ml) of oil to the hot pan, tilting the pan to coat the bottom. Place the dumplings in a single layer in the hot pan and cook until the bottoms are golden brown, 1 to 2 minutes. Add ½ cup (125 ml) of water and immediately cover the pan with a tight-fitting lid. Cook until all of the water has been absorbed and the dumpling skins have cooked through, about 5 to 6 minutes.

## BROWN BUTTER CRÈME FRAÎCHE

6 tbsp (85 g) unsalted butter
½ cup (120 ml) crème fraîche
1 tsp (5 ml) rice vinegar
1 tsp (5 ml) soy sauce
¼ tsp sugar

1 recipe Fresh Wheat Flour Dough
(page 22)
Oil and butter for panfrying

When all the water has evaporated, remove the lid from the pan and add 1 tablespoon (15 g) of butter to the pan, allowing it to melt and gently basting the dumplings in the melted butter with a spoon, until the dumpling bottoms get crisp again. Transfer the finished dumplings to a plate. Repeat with the remaining dumplings. Serve with brown butter crème fraîche on the side.

# CHAPTER 7

# PARCEL FOLD

➤ I remember the first time I had a parcel shaped dumpling. It was made with wheat starch dough and filled with spinach, shrimp and water chestnuts. I recall thinking how much the dumpling looked like a miniature gift, and to my delight, it was a two-bite savory gift indeed.

# HOW TO FOLD

This dumpling is great because it's easy to make. You can use fresh dough or wrappers, square or round. If using a square shape, simply place the dumpling filling in the middle of the wrapper, wet the edges of the wrapper using a pastry brush or your finger and bring the two opposite corners together over the filling, using water to pinch the two corners together. Bring the remaining two corners to the center and seal all the edges together with a gentle pinch. You may use this technique with round wrappers also to achieve either a square (four seams) or a triangle (three seams).

Using a round wrapper, lightly wet the edges of the dough with water.

Spoon the filling in the middle.

Bring the edges of the wrapper together toward the center.

Press the edges together to seal (there will be three sealed edges).

Pinch the dough in the center where the edges meet and press to seal.

There are two methods for the square wrapper: place the filling in first.

Wet the edges of the wrapper. Bring the opposite corner together over the center of the dumpling.

Bring the other two corners together to meet in the center.

Press and seal the edges and center.

For the second method, lightly wet the dumpling edges and bring the center of each edge together.

Press and pinch to seal.

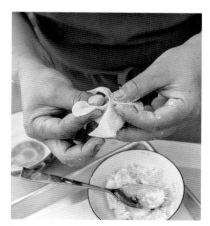

The dumpling should almost look like a pinwheel.

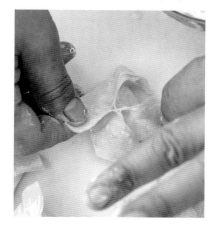

# STEAMED SPINACH DUMPLINGS

This dim sum classic is a vegetarian favorite. Spinach and tofu make a tender filling for the chewy, translucent, steamed wheat starch wrapper. The filling is perfect for any type of wrapper though, and is an all-star whether steamed, boiled, panfried or deep-fried. Serve with the dipping sauce of your choice.

➢ MAKES 24 DUMPLINGS
➢ Preferred Cooking Method: Steamed

## FILLING

10 oz (225 g) spinach leaves, washed and dried

6 oz (85 g) extrafirm tofu, crumbled

½ cup (25 g) minced garlic chives

¼ cup (45 g) finely diced carrot

4 dried shiitake mushrooms, rehydrated (see page 239), stems removed, finely diced

2 tbsp (30 ml) dark soy sauce

2 tsp (10 ml) Shaoxing rice wine

2 tsp (10 ml) rice vinegar

1 tsp (5 ml) sambal or Sriracha

1 tsp (5 g) sugar

3 tbsp (30 g) cornstarch

1 tbsp (15 g) lightly toasted sesame seeds

1 recipe Basic Wheat Starch Dough (page 27) or Glutinous Rice Flour Salt Dough (page 28)

To make the filling, bring a small pot of water to a boil. Add the spinach leaves, stirring to submerge. Cook the leaves for 30 seconds, and then transfer to a bowl of ice water to stop the cooking. Drain the spinach leaves and firmly squeeze any excess liquid from the cooked spinach. Chop the spinach into small pieces using your knife or pulse in the food processor.

Combine the chopped spinach with the remaining ingredients for the filling. Refrigerate for at least an hour.

Working on a lightly floured surface, roll the dough into a 1-inch (2.5-cm)-thick rope and divide the dough into 4 pieces. Divide each piece into 6 more pieces, for a total of 24 pieces of dough. Keep the dough covered in plastic wrap or with a damp towel.

Using a small rolling pin, roll each piece of dough into a 4-inch (10-cm) circle about 1/16 inch (0.2 cm) thick. You may roll out all the wrappers at once if you keep them lightly floured and covered.

Place 1 tablespoon (12 g) of filling in the center of each wrapper. Using a pastry brush or your finger, lightly wet the edges of the wrapper and bring them together to make a point in the center and carefully seal the three edges that have formed. Press the edges together firmly to seal, making sure there are no holes or breaks in the wrapper. Place the formed dumplings on a lightly floured tray and keep covered and refrigerated until you are ready to cook them.

Place the formed dumplings into a steamer lined with lightly greased parchment or waxed paper punched with holes, ensuring the dumplings are not touching each other in the steamer basket. Keep a layer of plastic wrap weighted with a lightly damp towel on top of the finished dumplings so they do not dry out. Remove the plastic wrap and towel before cooking. Cover and steam the dumplings for 6 to 8 minutes, until they are fully cooked and the wrappers are translucent. Serve with the dipping sauce of your choice.

# SWEET POTATO AND CHILE DUMPLINGS

Dried spices can be a vast playground for flavor discovery. I prefer to keep whole spices instead of ground spices because the flavor and aroma last much longer. I love the Indo-Asian combination of spices in this dumpling. These are great panfried or deep-fried—the little bit of crispiness on the wrapper accentuates the soft sweetness of the sweet potato.

➤ MAKES 36 DUMPLINGS
➤ Preferred Cooking Method: Panfried

## FILLING

1 tsp (5 g) Szechuan peppercorns
1 tsp (5 g) whole coriander seed
2 tsp (10 g) brown or black mustard seed
2 tsp (10 g) whole cumin seed
4 whole dried red chiles
1 lb (450 g) sweet potatoes or garnet yams, peeled and cut into ¼" (0.6 cm) dice
2 tsp (10 g) salt
1 tbsp (15 ml) sesame oil
2 tbsp (30 g) butter
½ cup (120 g) minced shallot
2 tbsp (20 g) minced garlic
1 tbsp (15 ml) fish sauce
1 tbsp (15 ml) lime juice
2 tbsp (5 g) minced cilantro, plus more for garnish

## YOGURT SAUCE

1 cup (235 ml) Greek yogurt
2 tbsp (30 g) toasted sesame seeds, lightly crushed
1 tbsp (15 ml) honey
Pinch of salt

36 round or square dumpling wrappers
1½ cup (355 ml) water
1½ tbsp (9 g) flour
Oil for panfrying
Fish Sauce Caramel (page 226)

To make the filling, in a small dry sauté pan lightly toast the peppercorns, coriander seed, mustard seed, cumin seed and dried red chiles over medium heat until fragrant, about 3 minutes, stirring often. Pulse the spices in a spice grinder or crush using a mortar and pestle. Set aside.

Place the diced sweet potatoes in a wide sauté pan in a single layer and add enough water to just cover the tops of the sweet potatoes. Add the salt to the water and bring to a boil over high heat. As soon as the water boils, drain the potatoes and discard the cooking water. Spread the potatoes on a sheet tray to cool.

In a large sauté pan, heat the sesame oil and butter over medium-high heat. Once the butter melts, add the minced shallot, cooking until soft and translucent, 3 minutes. Add the garlic, stir for another minute, then add the sweet potatoes and crushed spices. Cook the potatoes, stirring occasionally, for 5 minutes over medium heat until they are tender. Add the fish sauce, lime juice and cilantro and stir once more. Transfer the potato mixture to a bowl to cool. Refrigerate until cold.

To make the sauce, in a small bowl, combine the yogurt, sesame seeds, honey and salt. Stir well and refrigerate until needed.

Fill each wrapper with 1 tablespoon (12 g) of filling. Lightly wet the edges of the wrapper and form the dumpling using the technique of your choice (see pages 114 and 130). Keep the dumplings covered on a lightly floured tray or plate.

In a liquid measuring cup, mix the water with the flour until the flour has dissolved into the water and the mixture is cloudy. Heat a large wok or nonstick pan over medium-high heat. Add 1 tablespoon (15 ml) of vegetable oil to the pan and place a third of the dumplings in the pan, lined up next to each other, and cook until the bottoms of the dumplings turn golden brown, about 1 to 2 minutes. Add ½ cup (125 ml) of the flour and water mixture to the pan. It will react with the hot pan and steam and splatter a bit; be ready with a lid to fit the pan. As soon as you add the flour and water mixture, cover the pan with a tight-fitting lid.

Cook the dumplings, covered, until almost all of the water has evaporated and a thin golden crust begins to form in the bottom of the pan, 5 to 6 minutes. Remove the lid and cook until all the water has evaporated. Carefully remove the dumplings from the pan. Repeat with the remaining dumplings. Garnish with the cilantro and serve with the fish sauce caramel and sesame yogurt.

# GINGER CRAB RANGOON DUMPLINGS WITH SWEET AND SOUR SAUCE ✓

Crab rangoon is a Chinese-American favorite, commonly found on most take-out menus. You can use real crabmeat (I like Jonah crabmeat for its sweetness) or canned or imitation crabmeat, in which case I prefer the Japanese kani crab stick you would use for sushi.

⮞ MAKES 24 DUMPLINGS
⮞ Preferred Cooking Method: Deep-fried

## FILLING

8 oz (225 g) crabmeat, picked through and excess moisture removed, or kani crab stick, chopped into small pieces and gently shredded

½ cup (25 g) minced scallion, white and green parts

4 oz (110 ml) cream cheese, softened

2 tbsp (30 ml) mayonnaise

2 tbsp (30 g) finely minced ginger

1 tsp (5 g) salt

½ tsp sugar

¼ tsp ground white pepper

24 square wonton wrappers

## SWEET AND SOUR SAUCE

⅓ cup (80 ml) rice vinegar

¼ cup (50 g) brown sugar

2 tbsp (30 g) ketchup

1 tbsp (15 ml) soy sauce

2 tbsp (20 g) cornstarch dissolved in ¼ cup (60 ml) water

Oil for deep-frying

To make the filling, combine all the ingredients in a mixing bowl and stir until well blended. Refrigerate the filling for at least an hour.

Place 1 tablespoon (12 g) of filling in the middle of the square wrapper and wet the edges of the wrapper using a pastry brush or your finger. Bring the two opposite corners together over the filling, using water to pinch the two corners together. Bring the remaining two corners to the center and seal all the edges together with a gentle pinch. You may use this technique with round wrappers to achieve either a square (four seams) or a triangle (three seams).

To make the sauce, combine all of the ingredients in a small saucepan. Bring to a boil while whisking and then reduce to a simmer. The cornstarch will thicken the sauce rapidly; whisk until smooth and then remove from the heat.

Preheat a few inches of oil to 340°F/170°C in a heavy-bottomed pot. Add the dumplings a few pieces at a time to the oil. Gently turn the dumplings in the oil, cooking until all sides are golden brown, about 3 minutes. Drain the dumplings on paper towels. Make sure the heat of the oil stays at 340°F while frying the dumplings, and return the oil to this temperature before adding new dumplings. Serve warm with the sweet and sour sauce.

# LES SMOKED SALMON DUMPLINGS

This dumpling pays homage to one of my favorite neighborhoods in New York City and its Jewish deli establishments of yore. A little bit of wasabi gives the filling a complementary horseradish kick. I like serving these with a little bit of watercress and tomato, but they are perfect on their own.

➤ MAKES 16 DUMPLINGS
➤ Preferred Cooking Method: Deep-fried

## FILLING

3 oz (85 ml) cream cheese, softened

1 tbsp (15 ml) mayonnaise

1 tsp (5 ml) prepared wasabi paste

1 tbsp (15 g) toasted sesame seeds

¼ cup (15 g) minced scallion

3 oz (85 g) smoked salmon, sliced and then cut into ¼" (0.6 cm) dice

1 recipe Fresh Wheat Flour Dough (page 22)

Oil for deep-frying

Watercress for garnish (optional)

Chopped tomato for garnish (optional)

To make the filling, blend the cream cheese, mayonnaise, wasabi paste and sesame seeds with a spoon until smooth and homogenous. Stir in the minced scallion and diced smoked salmon. Mix until well blended. Refrigerate the filling for an hour.

Working on a lightly floured surface, roll the dough into a 1-inch (2.5-cm)-thick rope and divide the dough into 4 pieces. Divide each piece into 4 more pieces, for a total of 16 pieces of dough. Keep the dough covered in plastic wrap or with a damp towel.

Using a small rolling pin, roll each piece of dough into a 3-inch (7.5-cm) circle about 1/16 inch (0.2 cm) thick. You may roll out all the wrappers at once if you keep them lightly floured and covered.

Place 1 tablespoon (12 g) of filling in the center of each wrapper. Using a pastry brush or your finger, lightly wet the edges of the wrapper and bring them together to make a point in the center and carefully seal the three edges that have formed. Press the edges together firmly to seal, making sure there are no holes or breaks in the wrapper. Place the formed dumplings on a lightly floured tray and keep covered and refrigerated until you are ready to cook them.

Preheat a few inches of oil to 340°F/170°C in a heavy-bottomed pot. Add the dumplings a few pieces at a time. Gently turn the dumplings in the oil, cooking until all sides are golden brown, about 3 minutes. Drain the dumplings on paper towels. Make sure the heat of the oil stays at 340°F/170°C while frying the dumplings, and return the oil to this temperature before adding new dumplings.

Serve the fried dumplings warm with watercress and chopped tomato or as is.

# SNOW PEA AND GOAT CHEESE DUMPLINGS

The sweetness of green peas and the tang of goat cheese make for a fresh new take on the classic snow pea and tofu filling. Any way you decide to cook these will be a winner, but I love these panfried with a bit of butter.

➢ MAKES 24 DUMPLINGS
➢ Preferred Cooking Method: Panfried

## FILLING

1 tbsp (15 ml) vegetable oil or lard

4 cups (600 g) snow pea tendrils and leaves

½ cup (75 g) fresh or frozen green peas

2 oz (60 g) extrafirm tofu, crumbled

2 oz (60 ml) fresh goat cheese

1 tsp (5 g) finely grated ginger

1 tsp (5 ml) soy sauce

1 tsp (5 ml) fish sauce

1 tbsp (2 g) finely minced mint

1 tbsp (10 g) cornstarch

½ tsp salt

1 tsp (5 g) sugar

1 recipe Fresh Wheat Flour Dough (page 22) or 24 round or square wrappers

Vegetable oil and butter for frying

To make the filling, heat a large sauté pan over high heat. When the pan is hot, add the oil and snow pea tendrils. Stir-fry for 30 seconds until the tendrils wilt. Transfer the pea sprouts to a plate to cool.

Bring a small pot of heavily salted water to a boil and blanch the green peas briefly, until they float, about 2 minutes. Transfer the peas to ice water for 30 seconds, then drain on paper towels.

When the pea tendrils are cool, chop them into small pieces and mix in a bowl with the drained peas and remaining filling ingredients until well blended. Cover and refrigerate for at least an hour.

If using homemade dough, let the dough rest in the refrigerator for 1 hour. Working on a lightly floured surface, roll the dough into a 1-inch (2.5-cm)-thick rope and divide the dough into 4 pieces. Divide each piece into 6 more pieces, for a total of 24 pieces of dough. Keep the dough covered in plastic wrap or with a damp towel.

Using a small rolling pin, roll each piece of dough into a 4-inch (10.5-cm) circle about ¹⁄₁₆ inch (0.2 cm) thick. You may roll out all the wrappers at once if you keep them lightly floured and covered.

Place 1 tablespoon (12 g) of filling in the center of each wrapper. Using a pastry brush or your finger, lightly wet the edges of the wrapper and bring them together to make a point in the center and carefully seal the three edges that have formed. Press the edges together firmly to seal, making sure there are no holes or breaks in the wrapper. Place the formed dumplings on a lightly floured tray and keep covered and refrigerated until you are ready to cook them.

Heat a wok or large nonstick frying pan over high heat. Add ½ tablespoon (7.5 ml) of oil to the hot pan, tilting the pan to coat the bottom. Place the dumplings in a single layer in the hot pan and cook until the bottoms are golden brown, 1 to 2 minutes. Add ½ cup (125 ml) of water and immediately cover the pan with a tight-fitting lid. Cook until all of the water has been absorbed and the dumpling skins have cooked through, about 5 to 6 minutes. When all the water has evaporated, remove the lid from the pan and add 1 tablespoon (15 g) of butter, allowing it to melt and gently basting the dumplings in the melted butter with a spoon, until the dumpling bottoms get crisp again. Transfer the finished dumplings to a plate. Repeat with the remaining dumplings.

# BLACK SESAME PEANUT BUTTER DUMPLINGS

Sesame has a natural nutty flavor, so I love the moist cake this filling forms when the dumpling is lightly fried. These are perfect served with warm chocolate sauce or even a fruit jam.

➢ MAKES 36 DUMPLINGS
➢ Preferred Cooking Method: Deep-fried

½ cup (80 g) lightly toasted black sesame seeds

¼ cup (50 g) sugar

¼ cup (60 g) unsalted butter, at room temperature

¼ cup (45 g) creamy peanut butter

1 large egg, lightly beaten

2 tbsp (30 ml) milk

1 cup (100 g) all-purpose flour

1 tsp (5 g) baking powder

½ tsp fine sea salt

36 square dumpling wrappers

Oil for deep-frying

In a food processor, pulse the sesame seeds until they begin to break down into a rough grain, about 1 minute. Add the sugar and pulse a few seconds more. Add the butter and peanut butter and pulse until well blended, making sure you scrape down the sides of the bowl.

Add the egg and milk to the mix and pulse until incorporated. In a separate bowl, whisk together the flour, baking powder and sea salt. Add the flour a little at a time, pulsing until incorporated (do not let the food processor run continuously), until all of the flour has been added. Refrigerate the filling for at least an hour.

Place 1 tablespoon (12 g) of filling in the center of each wrapper. Using a pastry brush or your finger, lightly wet the edges of the wrapper and bring them together to make a point in the center and carefully seal the four edges that have formed. Press the edges together firmly to seal, making sure there are no holes or breaks in the wrapper. Place the formed dumplings on a lightly floured tray and keep covered and refrigerated until you are ready to cook them.

Preheat a few inches of oil to 340°F/170°C in a heavy-bottomed pot. Add the dumplings a few pieces at a time. Gently turn the dumplings in the oil, cooking until all sides are golden brown, about 3 minutes. Drain the dumplings on paper towels. Make sure the heat of the oil stays at 340°F/170°C while frying the dumplings, and return the oil to this temperature before adding new dumplings. Allow the dumplings to cool slightly before serving, because the filling will be very hot.

# RUMAKI DUMPLINGS

Rumaki is one of my favorite Polynesian appetizers and one of the first things my mom taught me how to make. Traditional forms of rumaki sometimes utilize chicken livers, skewered with a piece of sweet pineapple and a slice of crunchy water chestnut, then wrapped in bacon and glazed in soy sauce and pineapple juice. The same key ingredients make this dumpling a stand-alone, no need for dipping sauce.

➢ MAKES 40 DUMPLINGS
➢ Preferred Cooking Method: Deep-fried

4 oz (115 g) bacon, cut into ¼" (0.6 cm) dice

6 oz (170 g) ground chicken, dark meat preferred

4 oz (120 g) crushed pineapple, drained and juice reserved

4 oz (115 g) water chestnuts, diced

1 oz (30 g) chicken liver, diced (optional)

1½ tbsp (20 ml) dark soy sauce

1 tbsp (15 ml) pineapple juice (from crushed pineapple)

½ tbsp (6 g) sugar

1 tbsp (10 g) cornstarch

40 square wonton wrappers

Oil for deep-frying

In a large sauté pan, render the bacon until it is completely cooked and crispy. Transfer the bacon to a food processor and reserve 2 tablespoons (30 ml) of the rendered bacon fat.

Once the bacon has cooled, pulse the bacon into small bits and transfer to a mixing bowl. Add the ground chicken, crushed pineapple, water chestnuts, diced chicken liver, dark soy sauce, pineapple juice, sugar, cornstarch and the reserved bacon fat. Mix well. Refrigerate the filling for at least an hour.

Place 1 tablespoon (12 g) of dumpling filling in the middle of the square wrapper and wet the edges of the wrapper using a pastry brush or your finger. Bring the two opposite corners together over the filling, using water to pinch the two corners together. Bring the remaining two corners to the center and seal all the edges together with a gentle pinch. You may use this technique with round wrappers to achieve either a square (four seams) or a triangle (three seams).

Preheat a few inches of oil to 340°F/170°C in a heavy-bottomed pot. Add the dumplings a few pieces at a time. Gently turn the dumplings in the oil, cooking until all sides are golden brown, about 3 minutes. Drain the dumplings on paper towels. Make sure the heat of the oil stays at 340°F/170°C while frying the dumplings, and return the oil to this temperature before adding new dumplings. Serve warm.

# TOASTED ALMOND COOKIE DUMPLINGS

I love the light sweetness of traditional almond pastry cream, otherwise known as frangipane. Make sure you allow these to cool slightly before serving, because the filling will be very hot!

➤ MAKES 40 DUMPLINGS
➤ Preferred Cooking Method: Deep-fried

8 tbsp (115 g) unsalted butter, cut into small cubes

¾ cup (100 g) confectioners' sugar

¾ cup (75 g) almond meal or almond flour*

1 large egg

1½ tbsp (15 g) cornstarch

1 tsp (5 ml) almond extract

¼ tsp vanilla extract

¼ tsp salt

½ cup (85 g) lightly toasted sliced almonds

40 round or square dumpling wrappers

Oil for deep frying

Confectioners' sugar for dusting

Using an electric mixer, cream the butter on low speed until soft and whipped. Add the confectioners' sugar and beat on high for 30 seconds. Add the almond meal and beat for 30 seconds more. Add the egg, cornstarch, almond and vanilla extracts, and salt. Mix on low speed until well incorporated, about 1 minute. Fold in the toasted sliced almonds using a spatula. Cover and refrigerate the filling for at least an hour.

Place 1 tablespoon (12 g) of filling in the middle of a square wrapper and wet the edges of the wrapper using a pastry brush or your finger. Bring the two opposite corners together over the filling, using water to pinch the two corners together. Bring the remaining two corners to the center and seal all the edges together with a gentle pinch. You may use this technique with round wrappers also to achieve either a square (four seams) or a triangle (three seams).

Preheat a few inches of oil to 340°F/170°C in a heavy-bottomed pot. Add the dumplings a few pieces at a time. Gently turn the dumplings in the oil, cooking until all sides are golden brown, about 3 minutes. Drain the dumplings on paper towels. Make sure the heat of the oil stays at 340°F/170°C while frying the dumplings, and return the oil to this temperature before adding new dumplings. Serve warm, dusted with confectioners' sugar.

* You can usually find almond meal or almond flour in your grocer's health food or all-natural aisle where they sell various wheat-free products and other baking flours. If you can't find almond flour you can make it by simply pulsing blanched almonds (untoasted) in a food processor until the almonds break down into a small-grain flour, about 1 minute. (Do not overprocess or it will turn into almond butter.)

# CHAPTER 8

# WONTONS

➤ The most widely known sister to the dumpling is the wonton. Found in its namesake soup, in stir-fries, with noodles or on their own with a dipping sauce, wontons can be gobbled down in dozens of ways. I love wontons for their versatility and recognized appeal. My fondest memory of wontons was going with my parents and brother to Plum Blossom, the local Chinese restaurant in Troy, New York, where I grew up. As a child, I used to dig them out of my soup with my chopsticks and pour duck sauce all over them before taking tiny little bites until the wonton was gone. It's still a now-not-so-secret habit I have as an adult, except I'm usually devouring the wonton in one bite, kind of like the Cookie Monster. That's me. The Wonton Monster. Some things we never outgrow.

This is the perfect fold for the beginner, and it allows quite a bit of filling for a bigger dumpling. Whether you are using a fresh dough or premade wrapper, these dumplings look just like little packages and are easy to assemble.

# HOW TO FOLD

Wontons are traditionally made with thin square wrappers, and can be folded a number of different ways. Truth be told, it doesn't really matter how you do it, just as long as there is a tight seal around the filling. It looks great any way you fold it, cook it and serve it.

The easiest fold—and one that is great for boiling, panfrying and deep-frying—is the triangle fold. Simply place your filling (about 1 teaspoon [4 g]) in the middle of a square wrapper, moisten the edges of the wrapper with water using a pastry brush or your finger and fold the wrapper diagonally in half, pressing the edges to seal and eliminating any air bubbles with the filling.

You can take that wonton one step further by crossing the two pointed ends over each other, like crossed arms, and pinching with a little bit of water to seal.

Wet the edges of your wrapper. Fold your wrapper in half.

Press the edges to seal.

Fold the top corner back.

Bring the long corners away from the folded top.

Cross the corners and press to seal.

The wonton will resemble a tortellini.

Another fold you can do is gathering and crimping the dumpling. Form the dumpling by folding and sealing the wrapper in half diagonally. Holding one end of the folded dumpling loosely in the cradle where your thumb meets your forefinger, begin gathering and pleating the remaining dough edges, gently crimping and then squeezing the pleated dough to seal the neck of the wonton. It should look like a beggar's purse; this is a very easy fold and looks particularly beautiful deep-fried.

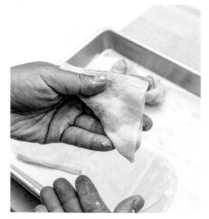
Fold the wrapper in half.

Use one hand to hold the dumpling.

Begin to gather and crimp the wrapper between your thumb and forefinger.

Use your thumb and forefinger to press and seal the dumpling.

The finished dumpling should resemble a beggar's purse.

The classic wonton shape is similar to that of a tortellini. For this shape, fold the moistened wrapper in half into a rectangle or half-moon, pressing the seal into the filling. Bring the two folded corners together and pinch to seal.

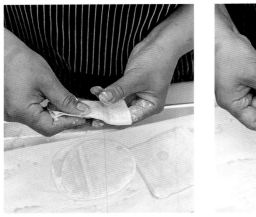

Wet the edges of your wrapper. Fold in half and press and seal the wrapper.

Fold the top edge of the wrapper back toward you.

Take the corners and fold them forward away from you.

Have the corners meet and pinch to seal.

The finished dumpling should look like a tortellini.

A simple fold: wet the edges of your wrapper.

Press the edges to seal.

Fold the corners together and pinch to seal.

The finished dumpling should look like arms embracing.

# PORK AND CABBAGE WONTONS

Another king of classics, the pork and cabbage wonton is versatile, juicy and delicious. I love the supple, slick mouthfeel of the wonton wrapper when these are boiled and simply doused in chile oil and black vinegar.

➣ MAKES 40 WONTONS
➣ Preferred Cooking Method: Boiled

1 tbsp (15 ml) sesame oil
6 cups (2,044 g) finely shredded and chopped (1" [2.5 cm] pieces) Chinese cabbage
8 oz (225 g) ground pork
1 tbsp (10 g) minced garlic
1 tbsp (15 g) minced ginger
¼ cup (15 g) minced scallion, white parts only
2 tbsp (30 ml) soy sauce
1 tsp (5 g) salt
½ tsp ground white pepper
¼ tsp sugar
1 tbsp (10 g) cornstarch
40 wonton wrappers
Black vinegar
Chile oil (page 225)

Heat a large sauté pan over high heat. Add the sesame oil and shredded cabbage. Using tongs, gently cook down the cabbage, turning and stirring often, until the cabbage wilts completely, about 6 minutes. Reduce the heat to medium and cook for another 5 minutes, then transfer to a fine-mesh sieve positioned over a bowl. Allow the cabbage to drain at room temperature for at least 30 minutes. Squeeze the excess moisture from the cabbage, patting dry with a paper towel, and combine in a large bowl with the ground pork, garlic, ginger, scallion, soy sauce, salt, pepper, sugar and cornstarch. Mix until well combined and refrigerate for at least 1 hour.

Form each wonton, using 1 tablespoon (12 g) of filling per wonton and folding in the style of your choice (page 148). Keep the wontons covered on a lightly floured tray. Wrap and refrigerate or freeze.

Bring a large pot of water to a boil. Add the dumplings to the pot in 3 or 4 batches, adding only 10 to 12 wontons to the pot at one time. When the water boils again, add ½ cup (120 ml) of cold water. When the water boils again, add another ½ cup (120 ml) of cold water. When the water boils again (the wontons should be floating), strain out the wontons. Return the water to a boil and repeat with the remaining wontons. Serve hot garnished with the black vinegar and chile oil.

# PANANG CURRY WONTONS

You can certainly make your own Panang curry paste, a flavorful mild Thai curry, but it is commonly available at Asian grocery stores in a can or jar. You can add more chile pepper if you want an extra kick, but a little goes a long way, especially if you are using small chiles such as Thai birds. Any type of protein will work well for the filling—chicken, pork, beef, tofu or seafood.

➤ MAKES 40 WONTONS
➤ Preferred Cooking Method: Deep-fried

## FILLING

12 oz (340 g) ground chicken, dark meat preferred

1 tbsp (15 g) minced shallot

2 tbsp (20 g) finely chopped peanuts

2 tsp (5 g) minced garlic

¼ tsp seeded and minced fresh chile pepper, such as Thai bird

1 tbsp (15 ml) Panang curry paste

1 tbsp (15 ml) coconut cream, such as Coco Lopez

¼ cup (6 g) minced cilantro

¼ cup (6 g) minced Thai basil

1 tbsp (10 g) cornstarch

## PANANG CURRY SAUCE

2 tbsp (30 ml) Panang curry paste

2 tbsp (30 ml) fish sauce

3 tbsp (45 g) palm sugar or brown sugar

2 (14-oz [385 ml]) cans coconut milk

1 tbsp (15 ml) coconut cream, such as Coco Lopez

Juice of 1 lime

Salt and white pepper to taste

40 wonton skins

Oil for deep-frying

Chopped peanuts for garnish

Fried Shallots (page 231) for garnish

Chopped cilantro for garnish

Chopped Thai basil for garnish

To make the filling, combine all the ingredients in a bowl and mix until well blended. Refrigerate for at least an hour.

To make the curry sauce, combine the curry paste, fish sauce, palm sugar, coconut milk and coconut cream in a small saucepan. Bring the mixture to a simmer over medium heat. Whisk until well blended and the sugar has dissolved, about 5 minutes. Simmer for another 15 minutes, until it has reduced by one-third, then remove from the heat and whisk in the lime juice and salt and pepper to taste.

Form each wonton, using 1 tablespoon (12 g) of filling per wonton and folding in the style of your choice (page 148). Keep the wontons covered on a lightly floured tray. Wrap and refrigerate or freeze.

Preheat a few inches of oil to 340°F/170°C in a heavy-bottomed pot. Add the wontons a few pieces at a time to the oil. Gently turn the wontons in the oil, cooking until all sides are golden brown, about 3 to 4 minutes. Drain the wontons on paper towels. Make sure the heat of the oil stays at 340°F/170°C while frying the wontons, and return the oil to this temperature before adding new ones.

Serve the fried wontons in a pool of Panang curry sauce, sprinkled with chopped peanuts, fried shallots, and chopped cilantro and Thai basil for garnish.

# DAN DAN PORK WONTONS

Easily one of my favorite recipes, dan dan noodles are a famous Szechuan dish, renowned for its tahini-based sauce and spicy flavor profile. Here I love these as boiled wontons, smothered in dan dan sauce and doused in mouth-tingling chile oil.

➤ MAKES 40 WONTONS
➤ Preferred Cooking Method: Boiled

## FILLING

12 oz (340 g) ground pork

½ cup (25 g) minced scallion, white and green parts

½ cup (100 g) minced preserved Szechuan vegetables

1 tbsp (15 g) finely grated ginger

1 tbsp (10 g) minced garlic

1 tbsp (15 ml) soy sauce

1 tbsp (15 ml) Shaoxing rice wine

1 tbsp (10 g) cornstarch

1 tsp (5 g) granulated sugar

1 tsp (5 g) ground Szechuan peppercorns

½ tsp salt

## DAN DAN SAUCE

1 tbsp (15 ml) sesame oil

2 tsp (10 g) minced ginger

2 tsp (5 g) minced garlic

¼ cup (50 g) minced preserved Szechuan vegetables

½ tsp crushed red pepper flakes

1 tsp (5 g) ground Szechuan peppercorns

1 tbsp (15 g) brown sugar

2 tbsp (30 ml) light soy sauce

¼ cup (60 ml) Chinkiang black vinegar

¼ cup (60 ml) Shaoxing rice wine

½ cup (120 ml) sesame tahini paste, stirred*

1 cup (240 ml) chicken stock (page 215)

Salt to taste

40 wonton skins

Szechuan chile oil (page 225)

Minced scallion for garnish (optional)

Cilantro leaves for garnish (optional)

Sesame seeds and/or chopped peanuts for garnish (optional)

To make the filling, combine all the ingredients in a bowl and mix until well blended. Refrigerate the filling for at least an hour.

To make the dan dan sauce, in a small saucepan, heat the sesame oil and sweat the ginger and garlic over medium heat until fragrant, about 2 minutes. Add the minced preserved vegetables, red pepper flakes and Szechuan peppercorns. Sauté the mixture for another 2 minutes. Add the brown sugar, soy sauce, black vinegar, wine, tahini paste and chicken stock, whisking until well blended. Simmer for 5 minutes and then remove from the heat. Season with salt to taste.

Form each wonton, using 1 tablespoon (12 g) of filling per wonton and folding in the style of your choice (page 148). Keep the wontons covered on a lightly floured tray. Wrap and refrigerate or freeze.

Bring a large pot of water to a boil. Add the wontons to the pot in 3 or 4 batches, adding only 10 to 12 wontons to the pot at one time. When the water comes to a boil again, add ½ cup (120 ml) of cold water. When the water boils again, add another ½ cup (120 ml) of cold water. When the water boils again (the wontons should be floating), strain out the wontons. Return the water to a boil and repeat with the remaining wontons. Serve the wontons hot, covered in dan dan sauce and garnished with chile oil, scallion, cilantro and sesame seeds.

* It's always best to stir your tahini paste before using. The sesame solids will separate from the natural oil; this is normal. I find a sturdy wooden chopstick or metal fork works best for stirring and reblending the thick and sludge-like solids with the natural oil. Get to the bottom of the container and stir. The ideal consistency will resemble a runny peanut butter.

# HAMBURGER WONTONS WITH LYCHEE KETCHUP

Back in 2003, when I was working at The French Culinary Institute in New York City as their Executive Chef of Events and Continuing Education, I had a very simple epiphany. Throughout the week it would often be just me and an assistant cooking for multiple events—hors d'oeuvres, wine pairing classes, etc. At the time, my buddy Shannon, who now owns two Mexican restaurants in Seattle, was helping me out. I had recently shown him how to fold dumplings and wontons, and we had some leftover ingredients in the fridge and were feeling enterprising. We decided to make these hamburger wontons with lychee ketchup. Let me tell you something—they were so satisfying and familiar and fun and delicious all at the same time. Our coworkers devoured them, happily surprised by the fast food mash-up. And that's when my epiphany happened: "You really can put anything in a dumpling wrapper and people are going to love it."

➢ MAKES 40 WONTONS
➢ Preferred Cooking Method: Deep-fried

## FILLING
12 oz (340 g) ground beef sirloin

⅓ cup (40 g) American or cheddar cheese, shredded or cut into ¼" (0.6 cm) dice

¼ cup (50 g) minced yellow onion

¼ cup (40 g) minced dill pickles

1 tbsp (15 ml) yellow mustard

1 tbsp (15 ml) bottled steak sauce

1 tbsp (10 g) cornstarch

½ tsp salt

¼ tsp freshly ground black pepper

## LYCHEE KETCHUP
¼ cup (50 g) diced yellow onion

1 clove garlic, minced

1 tsp (5 g) seeded and minced jalapeño pepper

1 tbsp (15 ml) tomato paste

1 tbsp (15 ml) soy sauce

3 tbsp (45 ml) rice vinegar

2 tbsp (30 ml) dark brown sugar

1 cup (235 ml) crushed tomatoes, with liquid

¼ cup (60 ml) pitted, drained and chopped fresh or canned lychee fruit

Salt

40 wonton wrappers
Oil for deep-frying

To make the filling, combine all the ingredients in a bowl and mix until well blended. Refrigerate for at least an hour.

To make the lychee ketchup, combine all the ingredients in a small saucepan. Bring the mixture to a simmer over medium heat. Whisk until well blended and the sugar has dissolved, about 5 minutes. Simmer for another 10 minutes, then remove from the heat. Pour into a blender or food processor and process until smooth (be careful when blending hot items—start on low speed and always make sure the lid is secure). Add water as needed for texture and season to taste with salt. Allow to cool to room temperature before covering and refrigerating. The ketchup will thicken slightly when cold.

Form each wonton, using 1 tablespoon (12 g) of filling per wonton and folding in the style of your choice (page 148). Keep the wontons covered on a lightly floured tray. Wrap and refrigerate or freeze.

Preheat a few inches of oil to 340°F/170°C in a heavy-bottomed pot. Add the wontons a few pieces at a time to the oil. Gently turn the wontons in the oil, cooking until all sides are golden brown, about 3 to 4 minutes. Drain the wontons on paper towels. Make sure the heat of the oil stays at 340°F/170°C while frying the wontons, and return the oil to this temperature before adding new ones.

Watch your favorite sporting event or movie on your television. Serve the hamburger wontons warm with the lychee ketchup.

# CHICKEN PAD THAI WONTONS

One of the most well-known and popular dishes in Thai cuisine takes its turn as a tasty wonton (I like to think of it as portable pad Thai). You may substitute ground peeled shrimp or superfirm tofu (crumbled) for the chicken. These are great boiled or deep-fried. The familiar flavors and fresh textures are sure to be a crowd-pleaser!

➢ MAKES 75 DUMPLINGS
➢ Preferred Cooking Method: Deep-fried

## FILLING

1 oz (30 g) rice stick noodles, rehydrated with hot water until al dente and drained

1 lb (450 g) ground breast meat chicken

1 cup (25 g) raw bean sprouts, chopped into ¼" (0.6 cm) pieces

1 cup (50 g) minced scallion, white and green parts

3 tbsp (5 g) minced cilantro

3 tbsp (30 g) chopped roasted peanuts

2 tbsp (20 g) minced garlic

1 tsp (5 g) finely grated ginger

1 large egg, scrambled, cooled and diced

1 Thai bird chile, seeded and minced, or ¼ tsp ground dried chile

2 tbsp (30 g) palm sugar

2 tbsp (30 ml) tamarind concentrate

2 tbsp (30 ml) fish sauce

75 square yellow wonton skins

## SPICY PEANUT DIPPING SAUCE

¼ cup (60 ml) hoisin sauce

¼ cup (60 ml) creamy peanut butter

¼ cup (60 ml) sesame oil

3 tbsp (45 ml) rice vinegar

2 tbsp (30 ml) sambal or Sriracha

1 tbsp (15 ml) soy sauce

1 tbsp (15 g) sugar

Oil for deep-frying

Chopped cilantro for garnish

To make the filling, chop the rehydrated rice noodles into ½" (1.3 cm) pieces. Combine the chopped noodles in a bowl with the ground chicken, bean sprouts, scallion, minced cilantro, peanuts, garlic, ginger, scrambled egg and Thai chile. Mix until well combined.

In a separate small bowl, mix the palm sugar, tamarind and fish sauce until the sugar dissolves and the mixture is smooth. Add this sauce to the filling mixture and combine until well incorporated.

Form the wontons using the beggar's purse fold (page 149). Place 1 tablespoon (12 g) of filling in the center of each wonton skin. Fold the skin diagonally, eliminating any air in the middle around the filling. Gather and crimp the wonton skin from corner to corner, pressing to seal the wonton. Place on a lightly floured parchment-lined baking sheet. Repeat until all the filling and skins are used. Cover and refrigerate until ready to cook.

To make the sauce, combine all the ingredients using a whisk, food processor or blender. Process until smooth and homogenous. Refrigerate until needed.

Preheat a few inches of oil to 350°F/176°C. Carefully drop the wontons one by one into the hot oil, frying in small batches and being sure not to overcrowd the oil. Cook the wontons for 2 minutes, until the filling is cooked and the exterior is golden brown. Drain on paper towels. Repeat with the remaining wontons until all are cooked, making sure the oil temperature returns to 350°F/176°C before frying the next batch. Serve immediately with the spicy peanut dipping sauce, topped with chopped cilantro.

# VEGETABLE WONTONS WITH APRICOT MUSTARD

This is an easy crowd-pleaser, especially for the vegetarian set who are sometimes overlooked at meals and parties. Use a food processor on the pulse mode to chop your vegetables to a small, even size. Note that the measurements for the vegetables are the measured yield of the chopped product.

➢ MAKES 50 WONTONS
➢ Preferred Cooking Method: Deep-fried

### FILLING

2 tbsp (30 ml) sesame oil

3 cups (1,020 g) finely chopped green cabbage

½ cup (90 g) finely chopped carrot

½ cup (35 g) stemless finely chopped shiitake mushrooms

½ cup (75 g) stemless finely chopped snow peas

3 tbsp (45 ml) Shaoxing rice wine

3 tbsp (45 ml) soy sauce

1 tsp (5 g) salt

½ tsp sugar

¼ tsp ground white pepper

½ cup (25 g) minced scallion, white and green parts

3 tbsp (5 g) minced cilantro

1 tbsp (10 g) toasted sesame seeds (optional)

2 tbsp (20 g) cornstarch

50 wonton wrappers
Oil for deep-frying
Apricot Mustard (page 226)

To make the filling, heat a large sauté pan or wok over high heat. Add the sesame oil and the cabbage and carrots. Stir-fry the vegetables for 2 minutes, then add the shiitake mushrooms. Cook for another 4 minutes, stirring and gently shaking the pan to keep the vegetables moving. Add the snow peas, wine, soy sauce, salt, sugar and pepper. Sauté until the liquid has completely evaporated, about 3 minutes more. Quickly stir in the scallion, cilantro and sesame seeds and remove the pan from the heat. Transfer the filling to a rimmed baking sheet and spread into a thin layer to cool. Allow the filling to cool slightly before placing the tray in the refrigerator. Chill for at least 30 minutes.

Transfer the filling to a bowl, including the released liquid, and stir in the cornstarch. Refrigerate for another 10 minutes.

Form each wonton, using 1 tablespoon (12 g) of filling per wonton and folding in the style of your choice (page 148). Keep the wontons covered on a lightly floured tray. Wrap and refrigerate or freeze.

Preheat a few inches of oil to 350°F/176°C in a heavy-bottomed pot. Add the wontons a few pieces at a time. Gently turn the wontons in the oil, cooking until all sides are golden brown, about 3 to 4 minutes. Drain the wontons on paper towels. Make sure the heat of the oil stays at 350°F/176°C while frying the wontons, and return the oil to this temperature before adding new ones. Serve the wontons hot with the Apricot Mustard.

# SARDINE GINGER WONTON SOUP

Of all the recipes in this book, this is one of my favorites. Sardines have always gotten a bad rap, and the canned variety is usually the first to come to mind. I happen to love canned sardines but the fresh kind can be a revelation, so you need to make sure you are getting them from a reputable seafood source. The origins of this soup stem from my first trip to Japan when my friend Shinji, a food tour guide in Tokyo, took me to a restaurant that specialized solely in sardine cuisine. I had a classic Japanese soup, iwashi tsumire—sardine meatball miso soup—that changed the way I thought about fresh sardines. It was rich and satisfying, not fishy at all. This recipe pays homage to that wonderful moment of culinary enlightenment. #TEAMSARDINE

≫ MAKES 40 WONTONS
≫ Preferred Cooking Method: Boiled

## FILLING

2 lb (900 g) fresh sardines, cleaned*
1½ tbsp (20 g) finely grated ginger
½ cup (25 g) minced garlic chives
1 tbsp (15 ml) dark soy sauce
1 tbsp (15 ml) shiro (white) miso paste
3 tbsp (30 g) cornstarch

## SOUP BASE

Sardine carcasses from the filling
1 piece kombu seaweed, 3" (7.5 cm) square
10 cups (2.3 L) water
1 tbsp (15 g) finely grated ginger
1 cup (130 g) thinly sliced onion
3 tbsp (5 g) dashi stock granules, or 2 cups (20 g) loosely packed bonito flakes
½ cup (120 ml) dry sake
½ cup (120 ml) mirin
2 tbsp (30 ml) soy sauce

40 wonton skins
1 cup (140 g) finely julienned carrot
½ cup (25 g) garlic chives, cut into 2" (5 cm) batons
4 cups (300 g) Asian greens, such as chrysanthemum greens or bok choy, chopped into 1" (2.5 cm) pieces
½ cup (120 ml) shiro (white) miso paste
Salt

To make the filling, remove the sardine fillets from the bodies using a sharp paring knife. Carefully separate the skin from the fillets and discard the skin. Reserve the fish bones and heads for the soup base.

Carefully remove any pin bones from the fillet using tweezers. Chop the sardines into a fine dice using a large knife. Add the remaining filling ingredients to the sardines on your cutting board and mix in using a chopping and scraping motion with your knife, folding the mixture over until it is well blended. Transfer the filling to a bowl and refrigerate for an hour.

To make the soup base, preheat the oven to 475°F/245°C. Place the sardine carcasses on a parchment- or foil-lined baking sheet and roast until they begin to color, about 8 minutes.

Transfer the roasted bones to an 8-quart stockpot. Add the kombu, water, ginger and onion and bring to a boil over high heat, then reduce to medium-low heat and simmer for 20 minutes. Add the dashi granules or bonito flakes, stirring to saturate, simmer for 1 minute, and then remove the pot from the heat. If using bonito flakes, allow the stock to steep until all of the flakes have sunk to the bottom of the pot.

Strain the stock through a fine-mesh strainer or colander lined with a lint-free towel into a clean pot. Discard the solids. Place the stock back on the stove and add the sake, mirin and soy sauce. Simmer over medium heat for another 10 minutes. Keep warm or refrigerate until needed.

Form each wonton, using 1 tablespoon (12 g) of filling per wonton and folding in the style of your choice (page 148). Keep the wontons covered on a lightly floured tray. Wrap and refrigerate or freeze.

Bring a large pot of water to a boil. Add the wontons to the pot in 3 or 4 batches, adding only 10 to 12 wontons to the pot at one time. When the water comes to a boil again, simmer the wontons for 3 to 4 minutes (the wontons should be floating), then strain out the wontons and hold them in a single layer in a covered baking dish with 1 inch (2.5 cm) of warm water in the bottom. Return the water to a boil and repeat with the remaining wontons.

(continued)

Bring the sardine stock to a boil over high heat, and add the julienned carrot, garlic chives and greens. Reduce the heat and simmer until the vegetables are just tender, about 2 minutes. Place the miso paste in a small bowl and ladle 1 cup (240 ml) of the hot stock into the bowl, whisking until well blended to thin out the miso paste. Whisk the miso paste into the soup. Season to taste with salt. Drain the wontons from the warm water and add to the soup. Serve immediately.

When shopping for fresh sardines, make sure you visit a reputable fishmonger. The sardines should be shiny but not slimy. The eyes should be clear and intact, not cloudy and damaged. The flesh should be firm to the touch. Softer flesh denotes older sardines. The odor should be of the sea, but not fishy.

\* To clean the sardines, rinse each sardine under cold water, gently removing the scales with your thumbs or the back of a knife with a gentle scraping motion. Usually the sardines are gutted. If by chance your purchase them whole, simply run a sharp paring knife up the belly of the sardine and remove the innards with your fingers, fish tweezers or a knife. Rinse the inside under cold water, using a toothbrush to gently scrub away any blood, or remaining innards. Pat the sardines dry inside and out. Using a knife, slit the remainder of the belly to the tail. Snip the head off the sardine at the neck. Firmly grip the spine of the fish and pull it down and away from the body of the fish through the slit-open belly; the bones should pull away easily from the flesh. Use your paring knife to gently scrape the flesh away from the bones if they stick.

# SWEET CHEESE AND DATE WONTONS

These little numbers are perfect for the holiday season, with a hint of warm spice in the dough and a touch of candied citrus in the filling. I am particularly fond of snacking on these with a boozy glass of rich eggnog. You can substitute premade wonton skins for the fresh dough.

➤ MAKES 40 WONTONS
➤ Preferred Cooking Method: Deep-fried

## FILLING

12 oz (350 ml) ricotta cheese, full-fat preferred

4 oz (120 g) pitted dates, minced into 1/8" (0.3 cm) dice

1 large egg, beaten

1 tsp (5 g) minced candied orange peel, or 1/4 tsp fresh orange zest

1/4 cup (30 g) confectioners' sugar

2 tbsp (20 g) finely chopped marcona almonds or toasted salted almonds

1/2 tsp vanilla extract

1/4 tsp salt

Pinch of ground cinnamon

Pinch of freshly ground nutmeg

## SWEET CINNAMON DOUGH

2 cups (200 g) all-purpose flour

1/2 tsp cinnamon

1/4 tsp ground allspice

1/8 tsp freshly ground nutmeg

1/4 cup (30 g) confectioners' sugar

1 large egg plus 1 egg yolk, lightly beaten

2 tbsp (30 ml) ice water

Oil for deep-frying
Cinnamon sugar for dusting

To make the filling, combine all the ingredients in a bowl and mix until well blended. Refrigerate for at least 30 minutes.

To make the dough, whisk the flour, cinnamon, allspice, nutmeg and confectioners' sugar in a bowl until well blended. Make a well in the center of the flour and add the egg and the ice water. Slowly mix the flour and liquid until the dough begins to come together. You may need to add more water to the dough if it is dry, or if the dough is sticky, a touch more flour. Once the dough comes together, turn it out onto a lightly floured surface and knead the dough lightly for 3 to 4 minutes, until it can be kneaded into a smooth ball. Wrap the dough in plastic wrap and refrigerate for at least 1 hour.

Working on a lightly floured surface, roll the dough into a 2-inch (5-cm)-thick rope and divide the dough into 8 even pieces. Roll each piece into a 1-inch (2.5-cm)-thick rope and cut into 5 pieces, for a total of 40 pieces. Keep the dough covered in plastic wrap or with a damp towel.

Using a small rolling pin, roll each piece of dough into a 3-inch (7.5-cm) circle about 1/16 inch (0.2 cm) thick. You may roll out all the wrappers at once if you keep them lightly floured and covered.

Form each wonton, using 1 tablespoon (12 g) of filling per wonton and folding in the style of your choice (page 148). Keep the wontons covered on a lightly floured tray. Wrap and refrigerate or freeze.

Preheat a few inches of oil to 340°F/170°C in a heavy-bottomed pot. Add the dumplings a few pieces at a time. Gently turn the dumplings in the oil, cooking until all sides are golden brown, about 3 to 4 minutes. Drain the dumplings on paper towels. Make sure the heat of the oil stays at 340°F/170°C while frying the dumplings, and return the oil to this temperature before adding new dumplings. Lightly sprinkle the fried wontons with cinnamon sugar and serve warm.

# CHOCOLATE BACON WONTONS √
# WITH CARAMEL SABAYON

I've been on the bacon chocolate train for decades at this point, even if it was canned chocolate frosting and Bacos as my guilty pleasure in high school (potato chips and chocolate frosting was another one). The salty-smoky flavor of bacon pairs well with sweet, rich chocolate.

➤ MAKES 32 WONTONS
➤ Preferred Cooking Method: Deep-fried

## WONTONS

4 oz (115 g) bittersweet chocolate
½ lb (225 g) bacon, cut into ¼"
(0.6 cm) dice
6 tbsp (70 g) sugar
2 large eggs
6 tbsp (40 g) all-purpose flour
½ tsp baking powder
1 tbsp (10 g) unsweetened cocoa powder
32 round or square wonton skins
Oil for deep-frying

## CARAMEL SABAYON

2 large eggs
1 egg yolk
½ cup (95 g) sugar
¼ cup (60 ml) water
1 cup (235 ml) heavy cream
¼ tsp salt

To make the wontons, bring a small pot of water to a boil over high heat. Reduce the heat to medium. Place a metal or Pyrex bowl on top of the pot (the bowl should be large enough to rest snugly in the rim of the pot). In the top of this double boiler place the chocolate and allow to melt slowly. Stir occasionally until melted, about 5 minutes.

Render the diced bacon in a nonstick sauté pan until the bacon is crisp. Drain the bacon on paper towels and strain the bacon fat through a fine-mesh sieve. Reserve 6 tablespoons (90 ml) of the bacon fat.

Remove the chocolate from the heat once melted and stir in the reserved bacon fat and the sugar until smooth. Add the eggs, flour, baking powder and cocoa. With an electric mixer, beat at medium-high speed until pale and very thick, about 5 minutes. Fold the crispy bacon bits into the chocolate batter. Cover and chill the filling for at least 2 hours.

Form each wonton, using 1 tablespoon (12 g) of filling per wonton, and folding in the style of your choice (page 148). Keep the wontons covered on a lightly floured tray. Wrap and refrigerate or freeze.

Preheat a few inches of oil to 340°F/170°C in a heavy-bottomed pot. Add the wontons a few pieces at a time. Gently turn the wontons in the oil, cooking until all sides are golden brown, about 4 to 5 minutes. Drain on paper towels. Make sure the heat of the oil stays at 340°F/170°C while frying the wontons, and return the oil to this temperature before adding new ones.

Allow the wontons to cool slightly before serving with the caramel sabayon.

To make the caramel sabayon, in an electric mixer beat the eggs and egg yolk until they are fluffy and pale. Cook the sugar and water in a saucepot over high heat, stirring constantly, until the sugar reads 290°F/143°C on a candy thermometer and begins to turn a deep golden brown. Immediately remove the mixture from the heat. With the mixer on, pour the hot sugar into the beaten eggs, taking care to pour slowly down the side of the bowl, avoiding the whip. Continue to whip the mixture until it has cooled. In a separate bowl, whip the heavy cream to stiff peaks and fold in the caramel mixture. Season with salt. Serve immediately.

# CHAPTER 9

# SOUP DUMPLINGS: XIAOLONGBAO

➤ Shanghai-style xiaolongbao (little steamed buns) have long been revered for their delicate skin encasing a flavorful, steamy hot broth and filling, which is why they are served with a soupspoon. These single-bite works of art are a dumpling lover's dream and one of my absolute favorites.

The secret to the "soup" in the dumpling is to first make a flavorful stock or broth with gelatin or naturally occurring gelatin (such as in pig bones and skin or chicken feet and wings). Once chilled, the stock becomes an aspic or jelly that can be mixed with the filling. When the dumplings are steamed, the aspic liquefies from the heat, creating the juicy filling that makes these dumplings tricky timing-wise to eat: too soon and you'll scald your mouth; let them sit too long and you lose that wonderful burst-in-your-mouth sensation that makes xiaolongbao so special.

To eat, I like to poke a little hole in the top of my soup dumpling with my chopstick to allow steam to escape. Other times I'll let it sit for a minute, until it's not visibly pumping steam, and then enjoy the whole dumpling all at once. It's the kind of experience that makes me close my eyes, breathe deep, and silently thank the genius who created this Chinese national treasure. They are laborious to make, the necessary steps taking a few days, but worth every minute. Once you get the hang of making these exquisite dumplings

# HOW TO FOLD

Fresh dough is best for xiaolongbao. Roll your dough into a 1 inch (2.5-cm)-thick rope and cut into small pieces, ¾ inch (1.9 cm) thick. Roll each ball of dough into a 3-inch (7.5-cm) round wrapper using a rolling pin or cleaver to flatten. Add 1 tablespoon (12 g) of filling to the center of the wrapper and wet the edges with a pastry brush or your finger. Begin to gather the edge of the wrapper and make tiny overlapping pleats, keeping the center of the dumpling as the focal point, until you have gathered all of the dough and the dumpling is formed. Gently pinch the pleats to seal the dumpling. Store on a lightly floured tray, covered with plastic wrap. Refrigerate or freeze as needed.

Mix your gelatinized stock with your filling.

Place in the middle of your dumpling wrapper.

Gather your wrapper, making small pleats toward the center of the dumpling.

Pinch the top of the xiaolongbao to seal.

# PORK AND CRAB SOUP DUMPLINGS

My very first xiaolongbao was at the original Joe's Shanghai, which resides on Pell Street in New York City's Chinatown. I had read all about their famously plump and juicy steamed delights in many various local food publications, so I was compelled to try them for myself. Forewarned by many who had devoured before me, I knew to be careful with the first bite, as these dumplings were notorious for the hot broth inside that could easily burn and injure. Whatever your plan of attack is, these will surely become a favorite, as they are mine. No kidding, the sky could be falling, but if I have a dim sum steamer full of xiaolongbao, I'll be fine. These dumplings take a whole day or two to make, so get the soup stock going first. By sundown, you'll have fresh soup dumplings in the comfort of your own home—what I consider to be one of the true secret keys to happiness.

≥ MAKES 40 DUMPLINGS
≥ Preferred Cooking Method: Steamed

## SOUP GELATIN

2 lb (900 g) chicken wings and/or feet*

8 oz (225 g) pork belly, with skin

4 oz (115 g) Chinese ham or bacon

8 cups (2 quarts) water

3 whole scallions, minced

1" (2.5 cm) piece ginger, thinly sliced

3 cloves garlic, lightly crushed

2 tbsp (30 ml) Shaoxing rice wine, chilled

1 tbsp (15 ml) soy sauce

## FILLING

8 oz (225 g) ground pork

4 oz (115 g) crabmeat, cleaned and picked through, or shrimp, peeled, deveined and minced

½ cup (25 g) minced scallion, white and green parts

2 tbsp (30 ml) soy sauce

1 tbsp (15 ml) Shaoxing rice wine

½ tbsp (7.5 ml) sesame oil

2 tsp (10 g) sugar

1 tsp (5 g) salt

1 tsp (5 g) finely grated ginger

¼ tsp ground white pepper

To make the soup gelatin, rinse the chicken and pork under cold water, then pat dry with paper towels. Using a large knife or cleaver, chop the chicken wings and feet in half to expose the bone. Dice the pork belly and ham into large chunks. Combine with the water, scallion, ginger and garlic in a large stockpot. Bring the water to a boil and then reduce to a rolling simmer. Skim the foam and impurities that rise to the surface of the stock for a clearer broth. Cook the broth for 2½ hours. Strain the stock through a fine-mesh sieve or colander lined with a lint-free towel into a clean pot. Discard the solids (or pull the braised meat from the wing bones and chop and use for dumpling filling, stir-fry, salad, stew or sandwiches).

Place the strained broth back on the burner. Add the wine and soy sauce. Bring the broth to a rolling simmer and reduce until you only have 2 cups (475 ml) of liquid remaining. Pour the soup into a shallow baking dish. Allow the soup stock to cool enough to stop steaming, then cover and place in your refrigerator. Chill the stock for several hours, until it is completely cold and set, like Jell-O. Using a fork, scrape up the gelatin and gently mash it to break it up into small pieces.

To make the filling, combine the ingredients in a bowl. Mix well. Stir in the soup gelatin until it is well distributed. Cover and refrigerate the filling.

## SOUP DUMPLING DOUGH

2 cups (200 g) packed all-purpose flour

1 cup (235 ml) boiling water

1 tbsp (15 ml) sesame oil

Black or Red Vinegar Dipping Sauce
(pages 219 or 220)

Chile oil (page 225)

To make the dough, place the flour in a bowl and make a well in the center. Pour the boiling water and sesame oil into the center of the well and stir with a fork or pair of chopsticks until the dough begins to come together. You may need to add more water if it is dry, or if the dough is sticky, a touch more flour. Once the dough comes together, turn it out onto a lightly floured surface and knead lightly for 3 to 4 minutes, until it can be kneaded into a smooth ball. Wrap the dough in plastic wrap and refrigerate for at least 1 hour.

Working on a lightly floured surface, roll the dough into a 2-inch (5-cm)-thick rope and divide the dough into 10 even pieces. Roll each piece into a 1-inch (2.5-cm)-thick rope and cut into 4 pieces, for a total of 40 pieces. Keep the dough covered in plastic wrap or with a damp towel.

Using a small rolling pin, roll each piece of dough into a 4-inch (10-cm) circle about $\frac{1}{16}$ inch (0.2 cm) thick. You may roll out all the wrappers at once if you keep them lightly floured and covered.

Add a heaping tablespoon (12 g) of filling to the center of the wrapper and wet the edges with a pastry brush or your finger. Begin to gather the edge of the wrapper and make tiny overlapping pleats, keeping the center of the dumpling as the focal point, until you have gathered all of the dough and the dumpling is formed. Gently pinch the pleats to seal the dumpling. Store on a lightly floured tray, covered with plastic wrap. Refrigerate or freeze as needed.

To steam the xiaolongbao, arrange the dumplings at least 1½ inches (4 cm) apart in a dim sum steamer lined with blanched napa cabbage leaves or greased parchment paper that has holes punched in it. Place the dim sum basket over several inches of water in a wok (the water should reach just below the bottom tier of the first basket). Bring the water to a boil and steam the dumplings for 6 to 8 minutes, adding more water to the bottom pan as necessary. Serve hot with black or red vinegar dipping sauce and chile oil.

\* Chicken feet happen to be great for making stock because of the natural gelatin and collagen they contain, and the price is usually pretty low if you can find fresh or frozen chicken feet. Wings are my other option as I find the meat can be pulled from the bones later on and used for a variety of recipes, and the meat adds great flavor to the stock.

# TOM YUM SOUP DUMPLINGS

Tom yum soup is one of the most well-known and revered dishes in Thai cuisine. Pack all that flavor into a dumpling and—ta-da! Soup dumpling magic.

➤ MAKES 40 DUMPLINGS
➤ Preferred Cooking Method: Steamed

## SOUP GELATIN

3 lb (1.4 kg) chicken wings and feet
4 oz (120 g) shrimp shells
10 cups (2.4 L) water
2 stalks lemongrass, crushed and minced
4 kaffir lime leaves, crushed and minced
1" (2.5 cm) piece galangal, thinly sliced
1" (2.5 cm) piece ginger, thinly sliced
5 cloves garlic, crushed
1 Thai bird chile, or ½ tsp crushed red pepper flakes or dried ground chile
1 cup (160 g) chopped ripe tomato
1 cup (235 ml) coconut milk
½ tsp nam prik pao (Thai chile paste)
1 tbsp (15 ml) fish sauce
1 tbsp (15 ml) freshly squeezed lime juice

## FILLING

6 oz (170 g) ground pork
6 oz (170 g) shrimp, peeled, deveined and minced
2 tsp (5 g) minced garlic
2 tsp (5 g) minced lemongrass
1 kaffir lime leaf, finely minced
1 tbsp (15 g) minced shallot
2 tbsp (15 g) minced red bell pepper
2 tbsp (15 g) minced green bell pepper
1 tbsp (5 g) minced cilantro
1 tbsp (5 g) minced Thai basil
1 tbsp (15 ml) fish sauce

1 recipe Soup Dumpling Dough (page 171)

To make the soup gelatin, rinse the chicken under cold water, then pat dry with paper towels. Using a large knife or cleaver, chop the chicken wings and feet in half to expose the bone. Combine the chicken bones with the shrimp shells, water, lemongrass, kaffir lime leaf, galangal, ginger, garlic, chile, chopped tomato and coconut milk in a large stockpot. Bring the soup to a boil and then reduce to a rolling simmer. Skim the foam and impurities that rise to the surface off the stock. Cook for 2 hours. Strain the stock through a fine-mesh sieve or colander lined with a lint-free towel into a clean pot. Discard the solids.

Place the strained stock back on the burner. Bring to a rolling simmer and reduce until you only have 2 cups (475 ml) of liquid remaining. Whisk in the chile paste, fish sauce and lime juice. Pour the soup gelatin into a shallow baking dish. Allow to cool enough to stop steaming, then cover and place in your refrigerator. Chill the stock for several hours, until it is completely cold and set, like Jell-O. Using a fork, scrape up the gelatin and gently mash it to break it up into small pieces.

To make the filling, combine the ingredients in a bowl. Mix well. Stir in the soup gelatin until it is well distributed. Cover and refrigerate the filling.

Working on a lightly floured surface, roll the dough into a 2-inch (5-cm)-thick rope and divide the dough into 10 even pieces. Roll each piece into a 1-inch (2.5-cm)-thick rope and cut into 4 pieces, for a total of 40 pieces. Keep the dough covered in plastic wrap or with a damp towel.

Using a small rolling pin, roll each piece of dough into a 4-inch (10-cm) circle about ¹⁄₁₆ inch (0.2 cm) thick. You may roll out all the wrappers at once if you keep them lightly floured and covered.

Add 1 tablespoon (12 g) of filling to the center of the wrapper and wet the edges with a pastry brush or your finger. Begin to gather the edges of the wrapper and make tiny overlapping pleats, keeping the center of the dumpling as the focal point, until you have gathered all of the dough and the dumpling is formed. Gently pinch the pleats to seal the dumpling. Store on a lightly floured tray, covered with plastic wrap. Refrigerate or freeze as needed.

To cook the soup dumplings, arrange the dumplings at least 1½ inches (4 cm) apart in a dim sum steamer lined with blanched napa cabbage leaves or greased parchment paper that has holes punched in it. Place the dim sum basket over several inches of water in a wok (the water should reach just below the bottom tier of the first basket). Bring the water to a boil and steam the dumplings for 6 to 8 minutes, adding more water to the bottom pan as necessary. Serve hot.

# CHICKEN TRUFFLE SOUP DUMPLINGS

This beauty is a luxurious combination of Chinese technique and Japanese and French flavors. I keep this recipe for special occasions or when I really want to bring the wow factor to the dinner table. The unctuous and aromatic truffle, part of the fungi family, is a prized and pricey ingredient. Thankfully, truffle products such as oil, salt, and preserved truffles can give you that impact and flavor without spending a few thousand dollars on fresh truffles.

➤ MAKES 40 DUMPLINGS
➤ Preferred Cooking Method: Steamed

## SOUP GELATIN

3 lb (1.4 kg) chicken wings and/or feet

10 cups (2.4 L) water

1 cup (240 ml) dry sake

½ large onion, thinly sliced

1 medium carrot, sliced into coins

1" (2.5 cm) piece ginger, sliced into coins

3 cloves garlic, crushed

2 tbsp (30 ml) soy sauce

2 tsp (10 g) dashi soup stock granules

2 tbsp (30 g) minced preserved black truffle

1 tbsp (15 ml) mirin

## FILLING

10 oz (285 g) ground chicken

4 or 5 fresh shiitake mushrooms, stems removed, pulsed in a food processor (¼ cup [20 g])

¼ cup (45 g) finely grated Parmesan cheese

¼ cup (15 g) minced scallion, white and green part

2 tsp (10 g) finely grated ginger

1 tbsp (15 ml) black truffle oil

1 tbsp (15 ml) soy sauce

½ tsp sugar

1 recipe Soup Dumpling Dough (page 171)

To make the soup gelatin, rinse the chicken under cold water, then pat dry with paper towels. Using a large knife or cleaver, chop the chicken wings and feet in half to expose the bone. Combine with the water, sake, onion, carrot, ginger and garlic in a large stockpot. Bring the water to a boil and then reduce to a rolling simmer. Skim the foam and impurities that rise to the surface of the stock for a clearer broth. Cook the broth for 2½ hours. Strain the stock through a fine-mesh sieve or colander lined with a lint-free towel into a clean pot. Discard the solids.

Place the strained broth back on the burner. Bring the broth to a rolling simmer and reduce until you only have 2 cups (475 ml) of liquid remaining. Whisk the soy sauce, dashi granules, minced truffle and mirin into the broth. Pour the broth into a shallow baking dish. Allow the soup stock to cool enough to stop steaming, then cover and place in the refrigerator. Chill the stock for several hours until it is completely cold and set, like Jell-O. Using a fork, scrape up the gelatin and gently mash it to break it up into small pieces.

To make the filling, combine the ingredients in a bowl. Mix well. Stir in the soup gelatin until it is well distributed. Cover and refrigerate the filling.

Working on a lightly floured surface, roll the dough into a 2-inch (5-cm)-thick rope and divide the dough into 10 even pieces. Roll each piece into a 1-inch (2.5-cm)-thick rope and cut into 4 pieces, for a total of 40 pieces. Keep the dough covered in plastic wrap or with a damp towel.

Using a small rolling pin, roll each piece of dough into a 4-inch (10-cm) circle about 1/16 inch (0.2 cm) thick. You may roll out all the wrappers at once if you keep them lightly floured and covered.

Add 1 heaping tablespoon (12 g) of filling to the center of the wrapper and wet the edges with a pastry brush or your finger. Begin to gather the edge of the wrapper and make tiny overlapping pleats, keeping the center of the dumpling as the focal point, until you have gathered all of the dough and the dumpling is formed. Gently pinch the pleats to seal the dumpling. Store on a lightly floured tray, covered with plastic wrap. Refrigerate or freeze as needed.

To cook the soup dumplings, arrange the dumplings at least 1½ inches (4 cm) apart in a dim sum steamer lined with blanched napa cabbage leaves or greased parchment paper that has holes punched in it. Place the dim sum basket over several inches of water in a wok (the water should reach just below the bottom tier of the first basket). Bring the water to a boil and steam the dumplings for 6 to 8 minutes, adding more water to the bottom pan as necessary. Serve hot.

# CHAPTER 10

# BAO

➤ Growing up ABC (American-born Chinese) in upstate New York gave me limited access to authentic Chinese food. My mother is a fantastic self-taught cook, but she never had the recipe box full of my grandmother's best secret dishes. Occasionally she would cook Chinese for our family; she'd usually drive out to Albany to get ingredients from one of the few Asian markets in the area. The best part about her going to the market was when she'd come home with a box full of char siu bao, Chinese roasted barbecue pork buns. Fluffy, white steamed bread buns full of savory-sweet meaty pork were a favorite snack of mine growing up. To my delight, when I moved to New York City, I realized I could find bao at any number of Chinese bakeries.

In technical terms, bao are similar to dumplings—dough wrapped around a filling—but the dough for bao contains leavening agents to give the signature bread-like quality to the wrapper. Bao are also represented in a variety of sizes, preparations and fillings, and are usually steamed or baked. The giant dumplings (dabao) are at least 4 to 5 inches (10 to 12.5 cm) in diameter, and one or two of them can easily make a meal, having been my grab-and-go food for years. Xiaobao, small buns, are more commonly served in restaurants, and usually fit three to ten pieces in a dim sum basket. I like to think of them as mini bao, and I've seen friends cram two at a time into their mouths. Regardless of size, bao have been a wildly popular food in China for almost two millennia, and America is finally beginning to catch on to an experience that makes me close my eyes, breathe deep, and silently thank the genius who created this Chinese national treasure. They are laborious to make, the necessary steps taking a few days, but worth every minute. Once you get the hang of making these exquisite dumplings at home, you'll never need to go out to find them.

# HOW TO FOLD

Divide the proofed dough into 16 small balls. Keep the dough balls covered with plastic wrap and a lightly damp towel to prevent them from drying out. Flatten each ball into a 4- to 5-inch (10 to 13-cm) round, using a small rolling pin if necessary, leaving the dough about ¼-inch (0.6 cm) thick. The edges of the dough should be thinner than the center.

Place 2 tablespoons (24 g) of filling in the center of the dough, bring the edges of the dough together in the center to encase the filling, gently pinch the seam and twist the center to seal the bao. Place a lightly greased 2-inch (5 cm) square of parchment paper on the bottom of the bao, with the seam side facing upward.

# CHAR SIU BAO (BARBECUE ROAST PORK BUNS)

Back in 2003, I was part of the opening team for Jean-Georges Vongerichten's Chinese restaurant 66 in Tribeca. The kitchen staff was comprised of half American cooks—the classically trained fine dining restaurant variety. The other half consisted of Chinese cooks; non-English-speaking culinary masters—geniuses in their own right through sheer skill and talent, whether it was carving a carrot into a phoenix or a butterfly using only a cleaver, creating a perfect sauce in a giant wok, or hand folding thousands of intricately detailed dumplings. These cooks possessed generations of history and culture in every move they made, every perfect dish they created. It was fascinating for me to watch and learn, as I was still a young line cook working the hot apps station. The benefit of working at this high-pressure, grueling station was that I was next to the dim sum station. Every third day the dim sum cooks would make massive amounts of mini char siu bao during the morning prep hours. I'd stand next to them, quietly joking with them while half begging for the first char siu bao to come out of the steamer. On a good day, they'd let me sample one from each tray, which could add up to at least six or seven baos. I called myself "quality control," aka The Char Siu Bao Monster. Your biggest challenge is not eating all the pork filling before you make your bao. Once you steam these beauties, you can individually freeze them. Just thaw and re-steam for that authentic Chinatown taste.

> MAKES 32 SMALL BAO
> Preferred Cooking Method: Steamed

## CHAR SIU PORK

2 lb (900 g) pork butt, cut into 1½" (4-cm)-thick strips with the grain

1 tsp (5 g) five-spice powder

1 tsp (5 g) ground white pepper

¼ cup (50 g) maltose syrup or brown sugar

¾ cup (180 ml) Shaoxing rice wine or dry sherry

½ cup (120 ml) soy sauce

To make the char siu pork, rinse the pork butt strips under cold water and pat dry thoroughly with a paper towel. Place the pork butt into a large baking dish or into a gallon-size zip-top plastic bag.

In a large bowl, combine the remaining ingredients, whisking until well blended. Reserve ¼ cup (60 ml) of marinade for glazing the pork. Pour the remaining marinade over the meat, and using your hands (make sure they are clean or you are wearing disposable gloves), massage the marinade into the meat by gently squeezing and tossing the pork strips until they are thoroughly coated. If you are using a plastic bag, squeeze most of the air out of the bag and seal it closed. You can now massage the meat in the bag without the mess. Allow the meat to marinate for at least 12 hours and no more than 24 hours.

¼ cup (60 ml) hoisin sauce

¼ cup (60 ml) honey

¼ cup (60 ml) fermented red bean curd, mostly liquid (optional)

2 tbsp (30 g) finely grated ginger

1 tbsp (10 g) crushed and finely minced garlic

1 tbsp (15 ml) sesame oil

## CHAR SIU FILLING

1½ cups (120 g) diced char siu pork

¼ cup (15 g) minced scallion, white parts only

2 tbsp (30 ml) soy sauce

2 tbsp (30 ml) oyster sauce

1 tbsp (15 ml) hoisin sauce

1 tbsp (15 g) sugar or honey

1 tsp (5 ml) sesame oil

1 tsp (3 g) cornstarch

¼ tsp ground white pepper

1 recipe Bao Dough (page 176)

Preheat the oven to broil (high). Set the oven rack 6 inches (15 cm) below the broiler. Place a baking pan filled with 1 inch (2.5 cm) of water on the bottom of the oven or on the lowest rack. Remove the pork strips from the marinade, allowing excess marinade to drip off. Arrange the pork in a single layer on an ovenproof baking rack set on top of a sheet pan. Brush both sides of the pork with the reserved marinade. Place the pan in the oven under the broiler. Roast the pork for 12 to 15 minutes, brushing the pork with the reserved marinade and turning the pork every 2 minutes, until the pork is cooked through and the outside is caramelized. Remove the pork from the oven and allow the meat to cool to room temperature before slicing.

To make the filling, combine the diced pork and scallion together in a bowl. In a separate bowl, whisk together the soy sauce, oyster sauce, hoisin, sugar, sesame oil, cornstarch and white pepper. Add to the pork and scallion and mix until well blended.

Divide the proofed dough into 16 small balls. Keep the dough balls covered with plastic wrap and a lightly damp towel to prevent them from drying out. Flatten each ball into a 4- to 5-inch (10 to 13-cm) round, using a small rolling pin if necessary, leaving the dough about ¼-inch (0.6 cm) thick. The edges of the dough should be thinner than the center.

Place 1 tablespoon (12 g) of filling in the center of the dough, bring the edges of the dough together in the center to encase the filling, gently pinch the seam and twist the center to seal the bao. Place a lightly greased 2-inch (5 cm) square of parchment paper on the bottom of the bao, with the seam side facing upward. Repeat with the remaining dough balls and filling.

Arrange the finished bao on a baking sheet and keep covered with a layer of plastic wrap. Allow the covered bao to proof again for 10 to 15 minutes in a warm area before placing them in a steamer, spaced at least 1 inch (2.5 cm) apart. Place the lid on the steamer and steam the buns over high heat for 10 to 12 minutes, until the dough is cooked and fluffy. Remove the bao from the steamer immediately and place on a cooling rack. Repeat with the remaining bao.

# CHICKEN, LEEK AND BACON BAO

Some of my greatest gastronomic joys date back to my time in culinary school at the French Culinary Institute, when I was a young, green thing, just learning about food and discovering the craft of cooking. One of the simplest pleasures was the combination of salty, smoky bacon lardons (strips of salt pork) and buttery, fragrant leeks. You really can put any sort of filling in bao dough, but I am particularly fond of this French-inspired filling with a little Japanese twist. You can, of course, steam these bao, but I love panfrying them for an extra crispy exterior.

➤ MAKES 32 SMALL BAO
➤ Preferred Cooking Method: Panfried

---

8 oz (225 g) boneless, skinless chicken thighs

1 tbsp (15 g) finely grated ginger

1 tsp (3 g) minced garlic

1 tbsp (15 ml) sake

1 tbsp (15 ml) mirin

1 tbsp (15 ml) soy sauce

3 tbsp (45 ml) chicken stock, store-bought or homemade (page 215)

1 tbsp (15 g) sugar

4 slices bacon, cut into small ¼" (0.6 cm) dice

1 tbsp (15 ml) unsalted butter

2 cups (400 g) halved, washed, thinly sliced leeks, white part only

2 tsp (5 g) cornstarch
Salt and black pepper to taste

1 recipe Bao Dough (page 30)

Oil for panfrying

Toasted sesame seeds for garnish

Minced scallions for garnish

Place the chicken thighs in a shallow bowl. Whisk together the ginger, garlic, sake, mirin, soy sauce, chicken stock and sugar, stirring until the sugar dissolves. Pour the marinade over the chicken thighs and stir to coat. Refrigerate the chicken for at least 4 hours to allow the flavors to develop.

While the chicken is marinating, cook the bacon and the leeks. Add the bacon to a large sauté pan and cook over medium-high heat until the bacon is cooked through and crisp and has rendered all its fat. Remove the cooked bacon from the pan, transfer to a cutting board and chop into tiny pieces. Reserve 1 tablespoon (15 ml) of the bacon fat in the pan (keep the leftover bacon fat for future use!). Reduce the heat to medium. Add the butter to the bacon fat in the pan and then stir in the sliced leeks. Gently sweat the leeks, stirring often, until they are soft, translucent and tender, about 10 minutes. Stir the cooked crumbled bacon into the leeks. Transfer the mixture to a clean bowl and cover and refrigerate until needed.

Add the chicken and the marinade to a small 6-to 8-inch (15-to 20-cm) sauté pan. Place the pan over medium-high heat and bring the chicken and liquid to a simmer, then reduce the heat to low. Gently poach the chicken until it is just cooked through (165°F/73°C), turning once, 5 to 8 minutes, depending on how thick the chicken thighs are. Remove the thighs from the pan and allow the chicken to cool on a cutting board. Reserve the cooking liquid. Once the chicken is cool, dice it into small, ¼-inch (0.6-cm) pieces. Add the chicken to the chilled leeks and bacon, as well as 3 tablespoons (45 ml) of the cooking liquid and the cornstarch. Mix well and season to taste with salt and black pepper. Refrigerate the filling for at least an hour.

Divide the proofed dough into 32 pieces. Roll each piece of dough into a small 3- to 4-inch (7.5- to 10-cm) circle, keeping the edges thinner than the center of the dough. Place 1 tablespoon (12 g) of filling in the middle and then fold the bao, gathering the edges of the dough toward the center using small pleats. Seal the edges of the dough by twisting and pinching where the dough comes together, forming your enclosed bao.

Place the bao on a lightly oiled sheet tray and cover with plastic wrap. Allow the dough to proof again for 10 minutes in a warm place.

Heat a wok or large nonstick frying pan over high heat. Add ½ tablespoon (7.5 ml) of oil to the hot pan, tilting the pan to coat the bottom. Place the bao in a single layer in the hot pan, spaced 1 inch (2.5 cm) apart, and cook until the bottoms are golden brown, 1 to 2 minutes. Add enough hot water to cover ½ inch (1.3 cm) of the bao and immediately cover the pan with a tight-fitting lid. Cook until all of the water has been absorbed, about 5 to 6 minutes. Remove the lid and allow the remaining water to boil off until the bottoms of the bao begin to crisp again. Remove from the pan and repeat with the remaining bao. Serve immediately, garnished with the toasted sesame seeds and minced scallion, or allow to cool and then refrigerate or freeze.

# PEKING DUCK BAO

Roast duck buns are fairly common in the contemporary Asian food scene. The origins of traditional Peking duck dates back over six centuries to Beijing. The artful preparation of this national dish is laborious and time-consuming because of the process of boiling and glazing the whole duck to drain all of the excess fat, yielding an extra-thin, crispy skin when the duck enters the oven for roasting. This bao uses tender duck legs confit as its filling, accented with traditional flavors. If you don't feel like making your own duck confit, you can buy it already cooked at most gourmet food stores. The cucumber (and/or Asian pear) adds a tender crunch to the filling. Serve these buns alone or with Quick Pickled Cucumbers and a splash of hoisin.

≽ MAKES 16 SMALL BAO
≽ Preferred Cooking Method: Steamed

2 lb (900 g) whole duck legs

1½ tbsp (20 g) kosher salt

1 tsp (5 g) five-spice powder

10 cloves garlic, lightly crushed

1" (2.5 cm) piece ginger, sliced into thin coins

1 tsp (5 g) Szechuan peppercorns, toasted and lightly crushed

1 piece whole star anise

1" (2.5 cm) piece cinnamon

4 cups (945 ml) duck fat or vegetable oil

2 tbsp (30 ml) hoisin sauce

2 tbsp (30 ml) plum sauce

2 tbsp (30 g) finely minced ginger

¼ cup (15 g) thinly sliced scallion, white parts only

¼ cup (45 g) peeled and diced cucumber or Asian pear

2 tsp (5 g) cornstarch

1 recipe Bao Dough (page 176)

Quick Pickled Cucumbers (page 230)

Hoisin or plum sauce for serving

Remove the skin from the duck legs and set aside to make cracklings. Rinse the duck legs under cold water and pat dry. Place the duck legs in a shallow, ovenproof baking dish or pan. Mix the salt and five-spice powder together and season all sides of the duck legs, gently rubbing the mixture into the meat. Cover and refrigerate the duck for at least 8 hours, allowing the salt to season the duck meat.

While the legs are curing, cut the skin into small ¼-inch (0.6-cm) dice. Place the skin in a small saucepan and cover with at least 2 inches (5 cm) of water. Bring the water to a boil and reduce to a rolling simmer. Cook the skin until all of the water evaporates, stirring often to prevent the skin from sticking to the bottom of the pot. As the water evaporates and the skin cooks it will render its fat. Once all of the water is gone, the cracklings will continue to cook in the rendered duck fat. At this point you will need to stir the cracklings often, using a wooden spoon to scrape the bottom of the pan. Once the cracklings are golden brown and crispy, drain them on paper towels, spreading them out to cool (they will continue to crisp once cooled). Season the cracklings with salt while they are still hot. Refrigerate in an airtight container once finished. To bring the cracklings back to life, warm them briefly in a single layer on a tray in your toaster oven or oven set at 350°F/176°C until hot and sizzling again.

Preheat the oven to 250°F/121°C. Remove the duck from the pan and rinse the legs and pan separately, drying with a paper towel afterward. Place the legs back into the baking dish and sprinkle the garlic cloves, ginger coins and peppercorns over the duck legs. Add the star anise and cinnamon stick to the dish. Gently warm the duck fat in a small pot to melt it (do not boil). Pour the fat over the duck legs and gently press the duck legs down to submerge them. Cover the pan with aluminum foil and place in the oven. Cook the duck until it is tender and falling off the bone, about 2 to 3 hours.

Remove the duck confit from the oven and allow the legs to cool to room temperature. (At this point the legs can be stored in the fat for several weeks in your refrigerator.)

To make the filling, remove the legs from the duck fat and gently warm the fat if necessary. Wipe away any excess fat and oil from the legs. Take the meat off the bones and transfer to a cutting board. Gently chop the confit into small ½-inch (1.3-cm) dice or shreds. Add the meat to a bowl and combine with the hoisin sauce, plum sauce, minced ginger, scallion, cucumber, cooked duck cracklings and cornstarch. Mix until well blended. Refrigerate the mixture for at least an hour.

Divide the proofed dough into 32 small balls. Keep the dough balls covered with plastic wrap and a lightly damp towel to prevent them from drying out. Flatten each ball into a 3-inch (7.5-cm) round, using a small rolling pin if necessary. The edges of the dough should be thinner than the center.

Place 2 tablespoons (25 g) of filling in the center of the dough, bring the edges of the dough together in the center to encase the filling and gently pinch the seam and twist the center to seal the bao. Place a lightly greased 2-inch (5-cm) square of parchment paper on the bottom of the bao, with the seam side facing upward. Repeat with the remaining dough balls and filling.

Arrange the finished bao on a baking sheet and keep covered with a layer of plastic wrap. Allow the covered bao to proof again for 10 to 15 minutes in a warm area before placing them in the steamer, spaced at least 1 inch (2.5 cm) apart. Place the lid on the steamer and steam the buns over high heat for 10 to 12 minutes, until the dough is cooked through and fluffy. Remove the bao from the steamer immediately and place on a cooling rack. Repeat with the remaining bao. Serve with the pickled cucumbers and hoisin or plum sauce.

# CHAPTER 11

# EXOTIC STYLES

➤ This chapter is a glimpse into the true possibilities of where you can take your dumplings. By now you should be familiar with the traditional styles of doughs, fillings and folds. These recipes will illustrate that you can make a dumpling out of just about anything (or turn anything into a dumpling). New textures, shapes and presentations will wow your audience, even if it's just you eating all the dumplings.

# FRIED MOCHI PORK DUMPLINGS

These dumplings, otherwise known as ham sui gok, are one of the most popular dumplings on the dim sum circuit. The glutinous rice dough fries up chewy and slightly crispy to encase a filling of tasty pork, mushrooms and carrots. It is important when you deep-fry these to keep your oil at an ideal temperature so the dough cooks thoroughly but does not absorb any oil and become heavy or grease laden (usually due to the oil temperature being too low). These filling morsels are easily recognizable by their football-like shape and golden, puffy exterior, certain to become an indulgent favorite in your dumpling cache.

➢ MAKES 24 DUMPLINGS
➢ Preferred Cooking Method: Deep-fried

## FILLING

8 oz (225 g) ground pork or finely diced pork tenderloin

3 tbsp (45 ml) oyster sauce

1 tbsp (15 ml) sesame oil

2 cloves garlic, finely minced

½ cup (85 g) finely diced or grated carrot

2 dried shiitake mushrooms, rehydrated and finely minced

½ cup (25 g) finely minced scallion, white and green parts

1 tbsp (15 ml) soy sauce

1 tsp (5 g) sugar

¼ tsp salt

¼ tsp ground white pepper

1 recipe Basic Glutinous Rice Flour Salt Dough (page 28)

Oil for deep-frying

To make the filling, combine the pork, oyster sauce, sesame oil and garlic in a small bowl. Allow to marinate for 30 minutes in the refrigerator. Heat a large nonstick sauté pan over medium-high heat. Cook the pork until just pink and halfway cooked, stirring frequently with a wooden spoon and shaking the pan vigorously, about 2 minutes. Add the minced carrot, shiitakes and scallion. Stir-fry for 1 minute more. Add the soy sauce, sugar, salt and pepper. Stir-fry for 2 minutes more, then remove the pan from the heat. Transfer the filling to a large plate or baking sheet to cool. Cover and refrigerate for at least 2 hours or until chilled and firm.

Divide the dough into 24 pieces. Keep the dough covered with plastic wrap or a damp towel. Roll each piece into a small ball between the palms of your hands (keep your hands lightly floured in wheat starch). Flatten each ball into a round disk, about 3½ inches (9 cm) in diameter and ¹⁄₁₀ inch (0.2 cm) thick, and then use your thumbs and forefingers to gently press the disk into a small cup. Spoon a tablespoon (12 g) of the filling into the middle and fold the dough in half, pinching the edges to seal. Repeat with the remaining dough and filling.

Preheat the oil to 375°F/190°C. Fry the dumplings a few pieces at a time, tossing in the oil gently so that the dumplings brown evenly. Fry for 4 to 5 minutes, maintaining the oil temperature at 360°F/182°C (the oil temperature will drop once you add the dumplings), until the dumpling begins to turn a light golden brown. Drain on paper towels. Return the oil to 375°F/190°C before frying your next batch. Repeat with the remaining dumplings. Allow to cool slightly before serving.

Form the dough into a small cup.          Spoon filling inside and bring edges together to pinch and seal.

(continued)

# FRIED MOCHI PORK DUMPLINGS (CONTINUED)

Bring edges together to pinch and seal.

Make sure all edges are sealed.

Gently shape the dumpling into a football shape.

Deep-fry until the dumpling begins to puff, float, and turn deep golden brown.

# RAMEN DUMPLINGS

Let's face it—the world is in the midst of noodle mania. Specifically, ramen worship. This traditional, humble Japanese soup and noodle dish has fed millions and spawned hundreds of inspired styles, from regional versions such as Hokkaido- and Tokyo-style ramen, to creative offshoots such as the ramen burger, first made by my friend Keizo Shimamoto. These dumplings are best fried, giving the ramen noodle wrapping a seriously delightful crunch. You can serve these alone with a dipping sauce or float them in a savory, rich broth. Either way, it's the best of both worlds as you get your noodles and dumplings all at once.

➢ MAKES 16 DUMPLINGS
➢ Preferred Cooking Method: Deep-fried

## DUMPLINGS

¾ lb (340 g) ground pork or chicken

½ cup (25 g) minced scallion, white and green parts

¼ cup (70 g) minced bamboo shoots

1 tbsp (10 g) minced garlic

1 tbsp (15 ml) mirin

1 tsp (5 ml) soy sauce

1 tsp (5 ml) miso paste (preferably shiro)

1 tbsp (10 g) cornstarch

Oil for deep-frying

1 lb (450 g) fresh ramen or chow mein noodles, precooked*

## SOUP

3 cups (700 ml) rich pork or chicken stock (page 216 or 215)

2" (5 cm) square kombu seaweed

1 clove garlic, crushed and finely minced

2 tbsp (30 ml) miso paste

1 cup (180 g) fresh bean sprouts

Minced scallion greens for garnish

Beni shoga pickled ginger for garnish

To make the dumplings, combine the ground pork, scallion, bamboo shoots, garlic, mirin, soy sauce, miso and cornstarch in a mixing bowl and stir until well combined. Divide the filling into 16 balls. Form each ball into a football shape and place on a baking sheet or plate, spaced apart. Cover with plastic wrap and refrigerate for at least 1 hour.

Preheat several inches of oil in a wide-bottomed pot or pan to 350°F/176°C. Pull 2 or 3 strands of cooked cold ramen noodles and line the ends up together so the noodles are hanging between your thumb and forefinger. Pinch the noodles together and place the noodle strand at one end of the chilled meatball. Carefully wrap the dumpling filling with the noodles, pulling the noodles slightly taut around the meatball as you rotate and wrap, until the entire meatball is wrapped in noodles, like an outer shell. Tuck the ends of the noodles into the rest of the noodles and gently pinch to bind.

Carefully fry the dumplings in small batches until the noodles are golden brown and the dumplings are floating in the oil, about 2 to 3 minutes, gently tossing the dumplings in the oil so all sides cook evenly. Drain on paper towels. Allow the oil to come back to 350°F/176°C before frying the next batch. At this point you can serve the dumplings by themselves or make a quick soup base to float them in.

To make the soup, in a medium-size pot, heat the pork stock and kombu seaweed over high heat until it begins to boil. Remove the kombu from the stock. Reduce the heat to a simmer and stir in the crushed garlic. Ladle ¼ cup (60 ml) of hot stock into a small bowl with the miso paste and mix until the miso dissolves into a smooth puree. Add the miso puree to the rest of the hot soup and stir until well blended.

To serve, arrange the dumplings in a deep platter or divided among bowls. Garnish the dumplings with a heavy pinch of fresh bean sprouts, minced scallion and pickled ginger. Ladle a desired amount of miso soup over the dumplings and garnish. Serve immediately.

* You can usually find prepackaged par-cooked ramen or chow mein noodles at Asian groceries in the refrigerated section or freezer section. If they are dried ramen noodles, cook the noodles in boiling water according to the package until al dente (the noodles will not be raw in the center but will still be slightly chewy), and then drain and shock in ice water to stop the cooking. Drain the noodles from the ice water—never allow noodles to sit in liquid, hot or cold, until you are ready to eat—the noodles will continue to absorb liquid and soften. Dry the noodles well (remember oil and water do not mix) and use the freshly blanched noodles to wrap your dumplings.

(continued)

# RAMEN DUMPLINGS (CONTINUED)

Form the meat filling into a small football.

Lay your noodles on the cutting board and carefully roll the noodles around the meat filling.

The dumpling filling should be encased in ramen noodles.

Fry to crispy perfection!

# SCOTCH EGG DUMPLINGS

The best part about Asian-style dumplings is what's inside. Sometimes it's a surprise … is it pork? Is it shrimp? This recipe marries two favorite foods: Scotch eggs and dumplings. You can use any type of ground meat you choose—beef, lamb, chicken, pork or a blend; they all will be delicious and lend a unique flavor profile depending on what you decide to go with. Quail eggs can be found at Asian markets as well as gourmet or specialty markets and occasionally your neighborhood butcher. Fresh dough is a must for this recipe. You can, of course, panfry or steam these, but I love the crispy texture of the deep-fried shell. The surprise inside is a perfectly cooked little quail egg beneath a layer of savory meat. Just wait for the ooohs and ahhhs.

➤ MAKES 12 LARGE DUMPLINGS
➤ Preferred Cooking Method: Deep-fried

## FILLING

12 quail eggs

6 oz (170 g) ground pork, lamb, beef, chicken or a blend

1 clove garlic, minced

¼ cup (15 g) minced scallion, white and green parts

1 tbsp (15 ml) soy sauce

1 tbsp (15 ml) Shaoxing rice wine

½ tsp sugar

¼ tsp salt

¼ tsp ground black pepper

Flour for dusting

1 recipe Fresh Wheat Flour Dough (page 22)

Oil for deep-frying

Miso Mustard Sauce or Black Vinegar Dipping Sauce (page 220 or 219)

To make the filling, have an ice water bath ready to go in a small bowl. Find the smallest pot you have and place the quail eggs gently in the bottom in a single layer. Cover the eggs with water by at least 1 inch (2.5 cm). Bring the eggs to a boil over high heat. Once the water boils, remove the pot from the heat immediately, count to 90, then remove the eggs from the water and transfer to the ice bath to stop the cooking. Gently crack the eggs on the side of the bowl to allow the ice water to seep in under the eggshells and cool the eggs in the ice bath for at least 5 minutes. Gently and carefully peel away the eggshells, leaving the egg intact. Refrigerate the hard-boiled quail eggs until needed.

In a food processor, combine the ground meat, minced garlic, chopped scallion, soy sauce, wine, sugar, salt and black pepper. Pulse several times until a paste is formed. Refrigerate the paste until needed.

Working on a lightly floured surface, roll the dough into a 1-inch (2.5-cm)-thick rope and divide into 12 pieces. Keep the dough covered in plastic wrap or with a damp towel.

Using a small rolling pin, roll each piece of dough into a large 4-inch (10-cm) circle, about ⅟₁₆ inch (0.2 cm) thick. You may roll out all the wrappers at once if you keep them lightly floured and covered.

Roll the cooked quail eggs in flour and shake off the excess. Divide the pork paste into 12 small balls, keeping your palms lightly wet with water to prevent the pork paste from sticking to your hands. Rinse and wet your hands again with cold water. Flatten each ball of pork paste between your palms to create a 3-inch (7.5-cm) disk about ¼ inch (0.6 cm) thick. Place the quail egg in the center of the paste and gently gather the paste around the egg to form a meatball. The egg should be completely encased in meat. Repeat with the remaining eggs and meat.

Preheat the oil to 350°F/176°C. Place a meatball in the center of a wrapper. Form your dumpling using the classic potsticker pleat (see page 34). You can trim away any excess dough with a knife. The dumpling will be slightly larger than your usual dumpling because of the egg inside. Deep-fry the dumplings, a few pieces at a time, making sure the oil temperature remains at 350°F/176°C, until the dumplings are golden brown and crispy and the filling is cooked through on the inside, about 4 minutes. Drain on paper towels. Serve immediately with the dipping sauce.

(continued)

# SCOTCH EGG DUMPLINGS (CONTINUED)

Press the pork paste into your hand.

Place the lightly floured quail egg in the middle.

Gently wrap the pork around the egg.

Make sure the egg is completely encased in pork paste.

# SHRIMP TOAST DUMPLINGS

I love shrimp toast. In its greasy, crunchy goodness it's always on the list when calling for takeout. This recipe turns this favorite into a delicious dumpling. The key to perfect (nongreasy) dumplings is an accurate oil temperature. Watch the oil temperature closely, as the bread wrapper will brown quickly. This nontraditional all-star is sure to become the talk of your table.

➢ MAKES 24 DUMPLINGS
➢ Preferred Cooking Method: Deep-fried

## FILLING

4 oz (115 g) shrimp, peeled and deveined, plus 3 oz (85 g) peeled, deveined and chopped into ¼" (0.6 cm) pieces

4 tbsp (60 g) unsalted butter, softened

½ tbsp soy sauce

½ tbsp dry sherry or Shaoxing rice wine

1 tsp (5 ml) sesame oil

½ tsp salt

¼ tsp white pepper

¼ tsp sugar

¼ cup (15 g) minced scallion, white parts only

¼ cup (30 g) minced water chestnuts

24 slices white bread

2 eggs, beaten

Oil for deep-frying

Sesame Seeds for garnish

Apricot Mustard or Soy Ginger Dipping Sauce (page 226 or 219)

To make the filling, in a food processor combine the 4 ounces (115 g) of shrimp and the butter. Pulse until a fine paste is made, scraping down the sides of the bowl. Add the soy sauce, sherry, sesame oil, salt, pepper and sugar and pulse again until the mousse is emulsified and well blended. Transfer the shrimp mousse to a bowl. Fold in the 3 ounces (85 g) of chopped shrimp, scallions and water chestnuts.

Using a rolling pin, flatten each slice of white bread so it is about ⅛ inch (0.3 cm) thick. Cut out the flattened bread with a 3½-inch (9-cm) round cookie cutter. Make each dumpling one at a time. Using a pastry brush, brush one side of the bread circle with egg wash. Spoon ½ tablespoon (7.5 g) of filling into the center of the wrapper and fold it in half to form a half-moon shape, gently molding the moistened bread around the filling and sealing the dumpling around the edges by pressing. Brush the outside of the dumpling with a very light layer of egg wash and place on a parchment-lined baking sheet. Sprinkle a pinch of sesame seeds on each dumpling and gently press to adhere. Repeat with the remaining bread and filling.

Preheat the deep-frying oil to 330°F/176°C. Preheat the oven to 250°F/120°C to keep the dumplings warm. Fry the dumplings in small batches, tossing often in the oil, until they float and are golden brown, about 4 minutes. Drain on paper towels and keep warm in the oven until ready to serve. Serve with mustard or dipping sauce.

Use your rolling pin to flatten each slice of bread.

Cut your wrapper using a ring cutter.

(continued)

# SHRIMP TOAST DUMPLINGS (CONTINUED)

Brush the bread with beaten egg.

Place the shrimp filling in the center.

Carefully fold in half.

Press the edges to seal.

Brush the exterior with beaten egg.

Decorate the dumpling with sesame seeds.

# STEAMED CHICKEN AND RICE DUMPLINGS

These dumplings take a little bit of time to make and cook, but the presentation is always worth the effort. Found in both Chinese and Japanese cuisine, these meatballs coated in steamed rice come in several versions and are often called "pearl balls" for their unique appearance. I like to use chicken here for both its aroma and flavor. A dim sum steamer basket works best for cooking, but if you don't have one you can always improvise with a regular steaming setup, though you may have to cook your dumplings in several batches. Sweet (glutinous) rice works best for this preparation, though you can substitute a good-quality sushi rice if you don't have sweet rice.

➤ MAKES 24 DUMPLINGS
➤ Preferred Cooking Method: Steamed

---

1 cup (210 g) sweet (glutinous) rice, soaked overnight in cold water (cover by 2" [5 cm])

1 lb (450 g) ground chicken meat, preferably dark meat

3 tbsp (10 g) minced Chinese chives or cilantro

3 tbsp (20 g) finely diced water chestnuts

2 tsp (10 g) finely grated ginger

2 tsp (10 ml) soy sauce

1 tbsp (15 ml) sake or Shaoxing rice wine

1 tbsp (10 g) cornstarch

1 large egg, beaten

1 tsp (5 g) salt

Pinch of togarashi pepper or Chinese five-spice powder (optional)

Blanched lettuce or cabbage leaves for steaming

Soy Ginger Dipping Sauce (page 219)

Drain the soaked rice and dry the grains well, spreading them out on a sheet pan and patting dry with a paper towel.

Combine the ground chicken, chives, water chestnut, ginger, soy sauce, sake, cornstarch, egg, salt and pepper in a mixing bowl. Mix until well blended. Divide the mix into 24 meatballs, lightly wetting the palms of your hands with water to help shape them. Refrigerate for 20 minutes to firm up.

Roll the meatballs in the soaked rice, ensuring the entire meatball is covered in rice grains.

Prepare a steamer basket lined with blanched cabbage leaves or lightly greased parchment paper. Place the dumplings in the steamer basket, being careful to space them about 1 inch (2.5 cm) apart so they are not touching. Cover with a lid and place the steamer over boiling water, then reduce the heat to medium-high. Steam the dumplings for 15 to 20 minutes until the rice grains are cooked through. Serve with the dipping sauce.

# WHOLE PRAWN DUMPLINGS

This dumpling takes advantage of the natural beauty of fresh prawns (freshwater shrimp) and other colorful ingredients. If you can't find freshwater prawns, shrimp will do just fine (for an impressive treat, use size 16/20 count, but 2½ 5 count is also a good substitution for the prawns).

➤ MAKES 12 DUMPLINGS
➤ Preferred Cooking Method: Steamed

## FILLING

12 large freshwater prawns or shrimp (16/20 count)

6 oz (170 g) boneless skinless chicken breast, finely minced

½ link Chinese lap cheong sausage or salty ham, outer casing removed, meat finely minced

2 tsp (10 ml) Shaoxing rice wine

1 tsp (5 ml) soy sauce

1 tsp (5 g) sugar

¼ tsp salt

12 large cilantro leaves

1 recipe Basic Wheat Starch Dough (page 27)

Soy Ginger Dipping Sauce or Red Vinegar Dipping Sauce (page 219 or 220)

To make the filling, remove the heads and the shell around the body of the prawns, leaving the last section of shell and tail intact. Split the prawns along their underside, not cutting fully through. Remove and discard the intestinal vein and flatten or butterfly the prawn cut-side down on your cutting board.

In a small bowl, combine the minced chicken, lap cheong sausage, rice wine, soy sauce, sugar and salt. Mix until well blended. Divide the ground paste into 12 portions.

Place a portion of the chicken filling on the top of each prawn, folding the edges of the prawn upward as if to flip the prawn inside out. Spread the filling gently to the prawn edges and use the palm of your hand to help shape and mold the dumpling. Place a cilantro leaf on top of the filling. Repeat with the remaining prawns.

Divide the dough into 12 balls. Roll each ball into a 4-inch (10-cm) disk about 1/16 inch (0.2 cm) thick, making sure the wrapper is big enough to enclose the prawn dumpling. Wrap each prawn, keeping the prawn tails exposed; seal the wrapper on the underside by pinching together.

Place the finished prawn dumplings on a lightly greased plate, spaced apart. Place in a large steamer and cook for 8 to 10 minutes, until the prawns are fully cooked (pink) and the chicken meat is white. Serve immediately with the dipping sauce.

# CRISPY SHREDDED SHRIMP DUMPLING

This recipe is as simple as it gets but the end result is definitely a crowd-pleaser. These texturally fun dumplings can be steamed or deep-fried. I like to deep-fry them because the finely shredded strands of wrapper turn crispy and golden, encasing a savory seafood filling.

➤ MAKES 32 TO 36 DUMPLINGS
➤ Preferred Cooking Method: Deep-fried

14 oz (400 g) shrimp, peeled, deveined and roughly chopped

1 tsp (5 g) salt

1 tsp (5 g) sugar

2 tsp (10 ml) soy sauce

2 tbsp (30 ml) sake or Shaoxing rice wine

3 tbsp (30 g) cornstarch or all-purpose flour, plus more for dusting

¾ cup (40 g) minced scallion, white and green parts

Oil for deep-frying

32 to 36 wonton or spring roll wrappers

Water or beaten egg

Sweet and Sour Sauce or Thai Basil Sauce (page 223 or 220)

Combine the shrimp, salt, sugar, soy sauce, sake and cornstarch in a food processor. Pulse until you have a rough paste, scraping down the sides of the food processor bowl, about 1 minute. Transfer the shrimp paste to a mixing bowl and fold in the minced scallion.

Lightly dust your hands in flour. Take a tablespoon (12 g) of filling and gently roll it into a ball with the palms of your hands. Place the shrimp balls on a plate, spaced apart, and cover with plastic wrap. Refrigerate for at least 30 minutes.

Preheat several inches of deep-frying oil to 330°F/165°C. Remove the shrimp balls from the refrigerator. Using a knife, cut the wonton wrappers or spring roll wrappers into fine shreds or strips about 1 inch (2.5 cm) long by 1/16 inch (0.2 cm) wide. Peel apart the shreds as you cut them so they sit in a loose pile.

Brush the shrimp balls lightly with water or beaten egg. Roll the shrimp balls in the shredded wrappers, gently pressing so all sides and surfaces of the shrimp ball are covered. Deep-fry the dumplings at 330°F/165°C, tossing frequently, until the shredded wrappers are golden brown and the filling is cooked through, about 3 or 4 minutes. Drain on paper towels. Serve while warm with dipping sauce.

# CARROT GINGER DUMPLINGS

I love the natural sweetness of these dumplings and their vibrant color from the use of carrot juice in the dough. Tofu gives an airy texture to these vegetable wonders, but you can easily substitute meat or seafood for a different version. These are delicious panfried and served with Apricot Mustard or Kimchi Vinaigrette.

➤ MAKES 32 DUMPLINGS
➤ Preferred Cooking Method: Panfried

1 tbsp (15 ml) sesame oil

1 tbsp (15 ml) butter

¼ cup (60 g) finely minced shallot

1 cup (180 g) peeled and finely chopped carrot

1 cup (160 g) fresh bean sprouts, chopped into small pieces

½ cup (75 g) corn kernels

½ tsp salt

2 tbsp (30 ml) honey

2 tbsp (30 ml) dark soy sauce

3 tbsp (45 ml) pureed ginger

½ cup (110 g) pressed and crumbled firm tofu

½ tsp lime zest

1 tbsp (15 ml) lime juice

2 tbsp (4 g) minced shiso or sesame leaf

1 recipe Basic Wheat Starch Dough (page 27) colored with carrot juice (see page 25)

Oil for panfrying

Carrot fronds, or chives, for garnish

Apricot Mustard (page 226) or Kimchi Vinaigrette (page 227)

Heat a sauté pan over medium-high heat and add the sesame oil and butter to the pan. Add the shallots and cook while stirring for 3 minutes, until the shallots are translucent. Add the carrots and cook for another 3 minutes, then stir in the bean sprouts and corn kernels. Season with the salt and cook for another 2 minutes. Stir in the honey, soy sauce and ginger, cook for another minute, then transfer the mixture to a bowl to cool.

Once the mixture has cooled, stir in the tofu, lime zest, lime juice and shiso. Check the filling for seasoning and refrigerate as needed.

Divide your dough into 2 pieces. Roll each piece into a 1-inch (2.5-cm)-thick rope and cut into 1-inch (2.5-cm) pieces. Keep the dough covered with a damp towel.

Roll each dough ball into a 6-inch (15.25-cm) round using a rolling pin (about 1/16-inch [0.2-cm] thick). Cut the dough in half and then into quarters so you have 4 equal wedges. Carefully take one wedge of dough and roll it gently into a cone around your finger, using the pointed end as the apex. Press the wrapper together at the seam to seal. Fill each dumpling with 1 tablespoon (12 g) of filling. Enclose the filling by sealing the top edges of the dumpling, forming a carrot shape. Keep the dumplings covered on a lightly greased sheet pan.

Place the dumplings in a parchment of cabbage leaf-lined steamer basket, spaced apart. Steam the dumplings for 5 to 6 minutes until the skins are cooked through. Garnish the tops of the carrot dumplings with carrot fronds or chives. Repeat with the remaining dumplings. Serve with the mustard or vinaigrette.

(continued)

# CARROT GINGER DUMPLINGS (CONTINUED)

Roll your carrot dough into a large round and cut into quarters.

Using your thumb and forefinger roll a quarter of the dough into a small cone.

Press the edges together to seal.

Carefully stuff the cone with filling.

Press and seal the top together.

The dumpling should resemble a small carrot.

# HIJIKI TOFU DUMPLINGS

After high school, I had a part-time job at a popular restaurant in New York, named Dojo, which was famous for its soy burgers and hijiki-tofu burger. At the time, I didn't have an appreciation for Japanese cuisine and preferred hamburgers over seaweed-tofu patties. Now that I eat more vegetables than meat, both hijiki and tofu are regular staples in my diet. This recipe pays homage to my first job and its still very popular hijiki-tofu burger. The wrapper itself is unique by using yuba (tofu) skin. Finding fresh yuba is not easy, but this recipe calls for dried sheets, which can be found in most Asian grocers. You can find frozen "fresh" sheets, which are also great to use and don't require rehydration.

➢ MAKES 36 DUMPLINGS
➢ Preferred Cooking Method: Panfried

---

¼ cup (60 ml) dry sake

¼ cup (60 ml) mirin

2 tbsp (30 ml) soy sauce

1 tsp (5 ml) rice vinegar

1 tsp (5 g) sugar

¼ cup (10 g) dried hijiki seaweed

1 tbsp (15 ml) sesame oil

½ cup (90 g) grated carrot

1 tbsp (10 g) minced garlic

1 tbsp (15 g) finely minced ginger

2 tbsp (30 ml) miso paste (preferably shiro) mixed with 1 tbsp (15 ml) water

½ cup (25 g) chopped scallion, white and green parts

3 tbsp (30 g) toasted white sesame seeds

14 oz (900 g) firm tofu, water gently pressed out*

12 to 15 sheets dried yuba

1 egg, beaten, or a mixture of ½ cup (120 ml) water and 1 tbsp (10 g) flour

Oil for panfrying

Miso Mustard Sauce (page 220)

Whisk together the sake, mirin, soy sauce, rice vinegar and sugar until the sugar dissolves. Add the dried hijiki to the liquid and allow the seaweed to fully rehydrate and absorb the liquid, about 30 minutes.

Heat a small sauté pan over medium-high heat and add the sesame oil to the pan once it is hot. Add the grated carrot, garlic, ginger, rehydrated hijiki and liquid, and diluted miso paste to the pan and sauté for 1 minute, until fragrant and soft. Remove from the heat and stir in the scallion and sesame seeds, mixing well. Transfer the vegetables to a plate or baking sheet to cool in the fridge.

Crumble the pressed tofu into a large bowl with your hands. Add the cooled vegetables, pressing and mashing the filling together with your hands until it is thoroughly mixed. Refrigerate the filling for at least 30 minutes (the seaweed will continue to hydrate).

Take a linen napkin or lint-free towel and place on your cutting board. Take a sheet of dried yuba and soak it in a shallow wide pan of water so the entire sheet is immersed. The sheet will begin to soften after 20 seconds and should become pliable. Gently pull the yuba skin from the water. Cut the sheet in half lengthwise, forming three 3-inch-(7.5-cm) wide strips.

Working one at a time, with the yuba facing vertically, pat the yuba skin dry with a paper towel, then brush with the beaten egg or flour and water mixture. Spoon a heaping tablespoon (12 g) of filling onto the bottom of the strip. Fold the two sides in so they are parallel to each other, covering the filling. Carefully roll the dumpling forward, brushing the exposed surface with egg or flour and water. The finished dumpling should resemble a loose egg roll.

Heat a large nonstick pan or wok over medium-high heat. Add a thin layer of oil to the pan, swirling to coat. Fry the dumplings in small batches, about 3 minutes on each side until they are crispy and golden brown. Drain on paper towels and serve with the mustard or dipping sauce of your choice.

* To press tofu, remove the tofu from the package and drain off all the water. Place the tofu block on a baking sheet or large flat plate in a clean sink. Cover with a piece of plastic wrap and place another large plate or baking sheet directly on top of the tofu so that it is weighing down the tofu. Elevate one edge of the baking sheet or plate by a few inches and place a towel or an object underneath to secure. Place another lightweight object (about 1 pound [450 g]) on top of the top plate so the tofu is weighted but not being crushed. The tofu will slowly release water and trickle off the bottom plate into the sink. Allow the tofu to press for at least 30 minutes to an hour. Use the tofu immediately.

(continued)

# HIJIKI TOFU DUMPLINGS (CONTINUED)

Brush your dried yuba skin with water.

Place filling in the middle and fold the sides in, parallel to each other covering the filling.

Roll the dumpling forward to form a loose egg roll.

# SESAME JIN DUI

This traditional sweet Chinese delicacy has a special place in my heart. I think I may have been four years old. It was the middle of the day. My mom and dad were working. My older brother Ian was in school and I was home with Amah, my non-English-speaking Chinese grandmother. I decided that I wanted to make peanut butter cookies. My little mind and hands got to cheffing, even though I could barely reach over the kitchen counter. Oats, eggs, peanut butter, sugar and milk. I had seen Mommy do it so many times. I was close. (Not really.) I was standing on a stepstool so I could reach over the counter. Wet, gloppy batter on the toaster oven tray. Then TOAST. Dark setting. As I stared intently into the toaster oven, my face reflecting the red glow of the toaster's heating element, eyes wide with the wild hope that crispy peanut butter cookies would come out when the toaster went DING!, Amah walked into the kitchen to see what all the noise was about. I remember smiling up at her and pointing to the toaster oven at the wet mess slowly toasting into a slightly less wet mess. She chuckled and then proceeded in what seemed like minutes to make the classic Chinese dumpling dessert jin dui–fried sesame balls. We did it together. I helped her roll the dough and stuff the jin dui. It was like magic. It was also my first and only time making dim sum with my grandmother. This one's for you, Amah, and for all the other grandmothers who have shared their love and legacy through food.

➢ MAKES 24 DUMPLINGS
➢ Preferred Cooking Method: Deep-fried

---

## FILLING

½ lb (225 g) dried red adzuki beans, soaked for at least 2 hours in cold water*

4 cups (1 L) water

6 tbsp (90 ml) vegetable oil

1 cup (200 g) packed brown sugar

1 recipe Sweet Glutinous Rice Flour Dough (page 28)

8 oz (225 g) untoasted white and/or black sesame seeds, or a blend of both

Oil for deep-frying

To make the filling, drain the soaked beans and discard the soaking liquid. Bring the beans to a boil with the 4 cups (1 L) of water in a small pot and reduce to a low simmer. Cook the beans until they are tender and most of the liquid has evaporated. Mash the beans with a fork.

Heat a large nonstick pan or wok over medium heat and add the oil to the hot pan. Stir in the sugar and the bean paste, stir-frying until well blended and dry and the sugar has dissolved, about 2 to 3 minutes. Spread the paste out on a parchment-lined plate or baking sheet to cool. Transfer to an airtight container and refrigerate until chilled.

Roll the chilled red bean paste into 24 ½-inch (1.3-cm) balls.

Divide the dough into 24 equal portions. Keep the dough covered to prevent it from drying out. Roll each dough piece into a small ball and flatten with the palms of your hand into a 2-inch (5-cm) circle.

Make an indentation in the center of the disk. Place the red bean filling in the center and wrap the dough completely around it, pinching and rolling the dough between your palms to form a ball, making sure there are no cracks or breaks in the outer dough shell.

Dip each ball into a bowl of cold water, shake off the excess, then roll in the sesame seeds, making sure all sides are completely coated. Roll each ball between the palms of your hands to gently press the sesame seeds in and make a nice round ball.

Preheat the oil to 325°F/162°C in a large wok or deep pot. Fry the dumplings a few pieces at a time. Gently press them under the oil to submerge as they cook using a deep-fry spider—they will puff up nicely when submerged in the oil. Toss the jin dui and monitor the oil temperature to make sure they brown and puff evenly, about 3 to 4 minutes. The jin dui will float in the oil once fully puffed and cooked. Drain on paper towels. Allow to cool slightly. Serve while still warm.

* You may purchase red bean paste in place of cooking your own; one 18-ounce (510 ml) can is sufficient.

(continued)

# SESAME JIN DUI (CONTINUED)

Form the dough into a small cup.

Place the red beans inside.

Enclose the dough around the filling.

Pinch away any excess dough.

Roll the jin dui into a ball.

Dip in water.

Then roll the jin dui in sesame seeds until they are completely coated.

Gently roll the jin dui one more time to secure the sesame seeds.

# CHAPTER 12

# STOCKS, DIPPING SAUCES AND CONDIMENTS

➤ Every now and then I buy jarred sauces if I don't have time to make my own. On the other hand, I'm not a fan of the "extra goodies" one will tend to find in them: preservatives, food coloring, crazy chemical compounds I've never even heard of. The benefits of making your own sauces and condiments from scratch are:

· You can say you made it from scratch.

· You know exactly what's going into your recipe and you have the ability to adjust to suit your needs and tastes. In other words, you get consistent quality.

· You can make the sauces and stocks ahead of time, or when you have free time, and store them in your refrigerator or freezer so you'll be able to create your own recipes knowing you've used fresh, quality ingredients.

· It's just as convenient on the back end—if you have your pantry of homemade sauces already done, it saves you time when you are ready to make a fantastic new dumpling recipe.

· The sauces are not only for dumplings. The thrill of cooking is being able to discover new flavor and ingredient combinations. So make the sauce. Taste the sauce. And choose your own adventure from there.

# STORAGE

I recommend refrigeration for most fabricated products if you don't plan on using them right away, and freezing is always a good option. One of my favorite tricks is using an ice cube tray to freeze stocks, sauces and condiments. Simply allow your finished product to cool to room temperature before pouring or spooning into an ice cube tray. Wrap your ice cube tray in plastic wrap and then freeze. Once the cubes have frozen solid, you can pop them out and keep them in a freezer bag, portioned for your convenience, rather than trying to thaw a brick of sauce. The sauce cubes can be defrosted and thawed naturally, or gently heated and stirred.

When freezing liquids, watery or thin liquid will tend to separate after the thawing process. This is natural; do not discard the liquid, as it is part of the prefrozen product. Most times agitation, such as stirring, whisking, blending and/ or heating, will help the sauce come back together. Freezer shelf life for most sauces and condiments is 3 to 6 months. Dairy-based products do not freeze particularly well and tend to curdle and separate when reheated.

# STOCKS

There is nothing more soul satisfying than hot, homemade broth. I never throw any bones out, whether they are meat, poultry or seafood. I wrap them individually in plastic wrap and date them, then throw them into a large freezer bag with similar bones. Once you accumulate enough bones to make stock (and you really don't need a lot), you can also portion and freeze your stock for convenience. These are five of my Asian-style favorites, great on their own to float a few dumplings in, or able to transform into a rich sauce or soup base. Boil your dumplings in a separate pot of water before adding to the stock.

# CHICKEN STOCK

I love getting whole chickens and taking care of the butchering myself. If you are not as handy with a knife yet, you can always buy a whole chicken at the butcher shop or meat counter and then ask your butcher to cut it off the bone (halved, quartered or in eight pieces), and to give you the filleted meat and the carcass. For a rich stock high in collagen, gelatin and flavor, I like to use chicken feet and chicken wings. Roasting your bones first will give a deeper flavor and darker color to your (brown) stock. When making a "white" chicken stock, instead of roasting you blanch the bones first (procedure below). The benefit of using chicken wings is they add a rich, meaty quality to the broth, and once you strain the stock, you can pull the meat off the wings and use for soups, chicken salad or dumpling filling!

MAKES 10 CUPS (2.4 L)

3 lb (1.4 kg) chicken wings, feet, necks and/or carcass pieces

2 cups (260 g) sliced yellow onion

6 scallions, ends trimmed, green and white parts roughly chopped

3" (7.5 cm) piece ginger, crushed and roughly chopped

1 clove garlic, crushed

16 cups (3.8 L) water

1 cup (235 ml) Shaoxing rice wine or dry sake

1 tsp (5 g) salt

If making a brown stock, preheat your oven to 400°F/204°C. Do not rinse the bones but pat them dry with a paper towels. Place the bones in a single layer in a lightly oiled roasting pan. Roast the bones in the oven until caramelized and golden brown, about 40 to 45 minutes, turning once after 20 minutes. Transfer the bones to a deep stockpot and add the onion, scallion, ginger, garlic and water.

If making a white stock, rinse the bones under cold water and pat dry. Place in a deep stockpot with enough water to cover the bones. Bring the water to a boil over high heat. Remove from the heat and drain and discard the water, keeping the bones in the stockpot. Add the onion, scallion, ginger, garlic and water.

Bring the stock to a boil and reduce to a simmer over medium-low heat, skimming off the impurities that rise to the surface as necessary. Cook the stock for about 3 hours and then strain through a fine-mesh sieve. Skim off the fat that rises to the surface of the stock (you can save this fat for cooking later on, and make sure you save any meat that can be pulled from your chicken bones). Add the wine and salt to the pot and bring to a boil again; reduce to a simmer. Taste the stock for seasoning and reduce over medium heat further if the flavor is weak. Once the stock has cooled to room temperature, transfer to an airtight container. Store in the refrigerator for up to 4 days, or portion and freeze immediately.

# PORK STOCK

I love the rich flavor of a well-made pork stock. You can actually use a combination of pork and chicken, or pork and veal bones. Either way, it's important to know that good stock cannot be rushed and can simmer for several hours to even days to develop the proper flavor and consistency. You can add a piece of star anise to give the broth another delicious layer of flavor.

MAKES 8 CUPS (1.9 L)

2 lb (900 g) pork bones—feet and/or ribs

1 lb (450 g) pork belly, skin on

2 cups (260 g) sliced yellow onion

8 scallions, ends trimmed, greens and white parts roughly chopped

4" (10 cm) piece ginger, crushed and roughly chopped

3 cloves garlic, crushed

1 tsp (5 g) white peppercorns

16 cups (3.8 L) water

½ cup (120 ml) Shaoxing rice wine or dry sake

1½ tsp (8 g) salt

Rinse the bones and pork belly under cold water and pat dry. Place in a deep stockpot with enough water to cover the bones and meat. Bring the water to a boil over high heat. Remove from the heat and drain and discard the water, keeping the bones in the stockpot. Add the pork belly, onion, scallions, ginger, garlic, peppercorns and water to the stockpot.

Bring the stock to a boil and reduce to a simmer over medium-low heat, skimming off the impurities that rise to the surface as necessary. Simmer the stock for about 4 hours and then strain through a fine-mesh sieve. Skim off the considerable amount of fat that rises to the surface of the stock (you can save this fat for cooking later on, and make sure you save any meat that can be pulled from your pork bones, as well as the belly meat, which should be falling apart tender and ready for the preparation of your choice). Add the wine and salt to the strained stock. Taste the stock for seasoning and reduce over medium heat further if the flavor is weak. Once the stock has cooled to room temperature, transfer to an airtight container. Store in the refrigerator for up to 4 days, or portion and freeze immediately.

# BEEF STOCK

I love making this stock because of its warm, rich aroma and flavor. Dumplings lend themselves perfectly as life rafts of deliciousness, floating in harmony in a sea of beefy goodness. Add fresh herbs and vegetables, maybe even some noodles, and you've got yourself a meal fit for royalty.

MAKES 10 CUPS (2.4 L)

2 lb (900 g) beef bones, such as marrow or knuckle

2 lb (900 g) beef chuck roast, diced into 2" (5 cm) cubes

1 lb (450 g) thinly sliced yellow onion

12 scallions, ends trimmed, roughly chopped

15 cloves garlic, crushed

4" (10 cm) piece ginger, sliced into thin coins

2 whole star anise

1 cinnamon stick

2 or 3 dried red chile peppers

1 tsp (5 g) white peppercorns

16 cups (3.8 L) water

1" x 4" (2.5 cm x 10 cm) strip of fresh orange peel or zest

½ cup (120 ml) Shaoxing rice wine

½ cup (120 ml) soy sauce

Salt to taste

Rinse the bones under cold water and pat dry. Blanch the bones in a small pot: cover with water and bring to a boil. Simmer the bones for 2 minutes and then drain, discarding the water. Rinse the bones again under cold water and pat dry.

Add the bones, cubed meat, onion, scallion, garlic, ginger, star anise, cinnamon, dried chiles, white peppercorn and water to a large pot. Bring the stock to a boil and reduce to a simmer, skimming off any impurities that rise to the surface. Simmer the stock over medium-low heat for 2½ to 3 hours, until the beef is tender.

Strain the stock through a fine-mesh sieve. Pull the cooked cubed meat from the solids and transfer to a cutting board. Once the meat has cooled, you can slice it thinly and add it to your soup, or use the meat (minced) for dumpling filling.

Bring the strained stock to a boil and add the orange zest, wine and soy sauce. Reduce to a simmer and cook for 10 minutes until the soup is flavorful. Taste for seasoning and reduce or add salt if necessary. Once the stock has cooled to room temperature, transfer to an airtight container. Store in the refrigerator for up to 4 days, or portion and freeze immediately.

# VEGETABLE STOCK

Save your vegetable scraps and peelings (make sure they are clean first) and keep in a freezer bag or old milk carton in the freezer. Other vegetable options for stock can add different flavor profiles, whether you employ leeks, celery or celery root, or the sweetness of parsnips.

## MAKES 10 CUPS (2.4 L)

1 lb (450 g) thinly sliced yellow onion
6 oz (170 g) carrots, peeled and sliced into 1/8" (0.3 cm) coins
8 scallions, ends trimmed, roughly chopped
4 dried shiitake mushroom or dried Chinese mushrooms
1" (2.5 cm) piece ginger, sliced into thin coins
2 cloves garlic, crushed
1 tsp (5 g) white peppercorns
12 cups (2.8 L) water
¼ cup (60 ml) Shaoxing rice wine
1½ tsp (7 g) salt

Combine the onion, carrots, scallions, dried mushrooms, ginger, garlic, white peppercorns and water in a large stockpot. Bring the water to a boil and then reduce to a simmer. Cook the stock for an hour and then remove the pot from the heat. Allow the stock to sit for 30 minutes before straining through a fine-mesh sieve into a new pot. Add the wine and salt and bring the stock to a boil again. Taste for seasoning and reduce if necessary. Once the stock has cooled to room temperature, transfer to an airtight container. Store in the refrigerator for up to 3 days, or portion and freeze immediately.

# DASHI STOCK

Dashi stock is one of those cornerstone ingredients in Japanese cooking. It is more of a finely crafted tea than a stock that simmers for hours to develop flavor. Traditional kombu dashi uses only three ingredients—kombu seaweed, dried bonito fish shavings, and spring or purified water. The reason for its widespread use in Japanese cuisine is its subtle delivery of umami—our fifth sensory taste, what we know as "savoriness." We find umami in ingredients like cooked beef, shiitake mushrooms, soy sauce, Parmesan cheese and tomato-based dishes. It's that savory flavor that keeps you craving more. Umami is present in the glutamate in the kombu seaweed. Dried bonito (part of the tuna family) is thinly shaved, providing the delicate flavor for the broth. Many people like the convenience of powdered or granulated dashi soup base, but homemade dashi simply cannot be beat for its simplicity of ingredients and nuanced aroma and taste.

## MAKES 5 CUPS (1.2 L)

1 large piece dried kombu seaweed, roughly 3" x 8" (7.5 cm x 20 cm)
5 cups (1.2 L) spring water
1½ cups (15 g) katsuobushi (bonito shavings)

Wipe the kombu with a clean cloth (do not run the kombu under water). Place the kombu in a medium-size saucepan and cover with the spring water. Allow the kombu to soak for at least 15 minutes. Place the saucepan over high heat. When small bubbles in the water begin to appear on the side of the pot (140°F/60°C) remove the kombu seaweed (you can set it aside and use for making kombu pickles, rice garnish, stir-fry, etc.). Bring the water to a simmer (160°F/71°C) and gently stir in the bonito shavings. Turn the heat off and allow the stock to steep for about 10 to 15 minutes, or until the bonito shavings sink to the bottom of the pot. Strain the broth through a fine-mesh sieve lined with a coffee filter or paper towel. The stock may be refrigerated for up to 3 days or frozen in an airtight container for up to 3 months.

# DIPPING SAUCES AND CONDIMENTS

I'm a condiment super freak. When you open my refrigerator door it's usually a sea of jams, jellies, mustards, pickles, hot sauces, oils, other gourmet flavoring agents like fish sauce and fine vinegars, and a collection of homemade sauces. That way when I'm home and want to cook a quick meal for myself, I'm already halfway there. Whether it's a piece of fish panfried and glazed in XO sauce or getting my red vinegar–ginger fix with some homemade steamed soup dumplings, I am ready to go—many of these recipes can be made well in advance and have a pretty decent shelf life in the fridge and an even longer one in the freezer. Many of these sauces are quick, easy to put together and multipurpose (meaning if you like the way it tastes, put it on whatever you want!). Try making a few on the weekend when you have some free time. You'll find weekday dinners easier to whip up when you have your flavorful, freshly made sauces, pickles and garnishes at your fingertips. By the way, have I told you how much I love condiments?

## SOY GINGER DIPPING SAUCE

This is the most classic and easiest sauce to put together. I usually use a ratio of one part soy sauce, one part vinegar or acid, and one part water. Additional flavor enhancers can include (but are not limited to) minced scallion, julienned ginger, chile paste or oil, mustard and/or minced garlic. On its own, this sauce will keep for months in the fridge.

MAKES 1 CUP

⅓ cup (80 ml) rice vinegar
⅓ cup (80 ml) soy sauce
⅓ cup (80 ml) water
1 tsp (5 g) sugar
1 oz (30 g) ginger, finely julienned

Combine the rice vinegar, soy sauce, water and sugar in a bowl. Whisk until the sugar dissolves. The sauce can be stored at this point for up to a month in the refrigerator. When ready to serve, add the julienned ginger and allow the ginger to steep for at least 30 minutes and up to 3 days, depending on your taste. You can add chile oil or sambal to the finished product for extra spice.

## BLACK VINEGAR DIPPING SAUCE

This sauce is a classic dim sum staple. The sweetness of the black vinegar works well with just about any dumpling. You can substitute balsamic vinegar with a touch of molasses whisked in if you can't find black vinegar.

MAKES ½ CUP (120 ML)

¼ cup (60 ml) Chinese black vinegar
¼ cup (60 ml) soy sauce or tamari
Julienned ginger (optional)

Combine the vinegar and soy sauce and store for up to a month in your refrigerator. Add the ginger just before serving.

# RED VINEGAR DIPPING SAUCE

This is my favorite sauce to use with soup dumplings. The bright flavor and color match well with the freshly julienned ginger.

MAKES ½ CUP (120 ML)

½ cup (120 ml) Chinese red vinegar
1 tsp (5 g) granulated or superfine sugar
Julienned ginger (optional)

Mix the vinegar and sugar until the sugar dissolves. Store for up to a month in your refrigerator. Add the ginger just before serving.

# THAI BASIL SAUCE

Feel free to add a few tablespoons of nuts to make a pesto, if you want a chunkier texture and nutty flavor.

MAKES ¾ CUP (175 ML)

2 cups (50 g) packed Thai basil leaves
1 clove garlic
2 tsp (10 g) finely grated ginger
1 tbsp (15 ml) fish sauce
1 tbsp (15 ml) rice vinegar
1 tbsp (15 g) sugar
2 tbsp (30 ml) sesame oil
¼ cup (60 ml) vegetable oil
Salt to taste

Place all the ingredients in a food processor. Pulse until you have the desired texture or blend until smooth. Store in an airtight container for up to 2 weeks in the refrigerator, or freeze.

# MISO SAUCE

You can change up this recipe just by using a different type of miso. White miso will be sweeter and milder than red or brown miso; add or reduce the sugar to suit your taste.

MAKES 1 CUP (240 ML)

3 tbsp (45 ml) white shiro miso
1 tbsp (15 g) sugar
¼ cup (60 ml) mirin
¼ cup (60 ml) rice vinegar
3 tbsp (45 ml) water
2 tbsp (30 ml) soy sauce
1 tbsp (15 ml) sesame oil

Whisk or blend together all the ingredients until smooth. Keep refrigerated for up to a month.

# MISO MUSTARD SAUCE

This recipe goes perfectly with the Ahi Dumplings (page 119).

MAKES 1¼ CUPS (295 ML)

1 recipe Miso Sauce (page 220)
3 tbsp (45 ml) Dijon mustard

Combine all the ingredients in a small bowl and mix until smooth. Keep refrigerated for up to 1 month.

# PONZU DIPPING SAUCE ✓

This is one of my favorite Japanese sauces to have on hand. If you don't have yuzu juice you can substitute a combination of fresh grapefruit juice and lemon juice or even lime juice. Add the citrus juice right before serving to keep the flavor fresh.

MAKES 1½ TO 2 CUPS (355 TO 475 ML)

¼ cup (60 ml) mirin
¼ cup (60 ml) rice vinegar
¾ cup (175 ml) soy sauce
3" (7.5 cm) square kombu seaweed
½ cup (5 g) katsuobushi (bonito shavings)
¼ cup (60 ml) yuzu juice*

Combine the mirin, rice vinegar, soy sauce, kombu and bonito shavings in a bowl and whisk until the shavings are saturated. Allow the mixture to steep for 24 to 48 hours. Strain through a fine-mesh sieve or coffee filter. You may keep the base sauce refrigerated for up to a month. Before serving, add the yuzu juice or fresh citrus juice and stir until well blended

* You may substitute ½ cup (120 ml) fresh grapefruit juice plus ¼ cup (60 ml) fresh lemon juice OR ½ cup (120 ml) fresh lemon juice plus ¼ cup (60 ml) fresh lime juice. Strain the juice through a fine-mesh sieve to remove any pulp before adding to the ponzu base.

# BLACK BEAN SAUCE

You can usually find salted (fermented) dried black beans at your Asian grocery store. Always rinse the beans briefly under cold water before using. You can of course substitute boxed stock for homemade, or even use water. This sauce is perfect for stir-frying with dumplings or as a dipping sauce.

MAKES 2 CUPS (475 ML)

2 tbsp (30 ml) vegetable oil
2 tbsp (20 g) minced garlic
2 tbsp (30 g) minced ginger
½ cup (120 ml) fermented black beans, rinsed and chopped into small pieces
3 tbsp (45 g) minced shallot
2 tbsp (30 ml) soy sauce
1 tbsp (15 g) sugar
½ cup (60 ml) Shaoxing rice wine or sake
2 cups (475 ml) chicken stock or vegetable stock (page 215 or 218)
2 tbsp (20 g) cornstarch

Heat a wok or frying pan over high heat. Add the vegetable oil, garlic and ginger. Stir-fry for 30 seconds, until fragrant, then add the black beans and shallot. Stir-fry for 1 minute more.

Add the soy sauce, sugar, ¼ cup (60 ml) of the wine, and the chicken stock. Bring the mixture to a boil and reduce the heat to a simmer. Simmer the sauce for 30 minutes over medium-low heat.

Mix the cornstarch with the remaining ¼ cup (60 ml) wine. Stir the slurry into the black bean sauce, whisking until well blended. Bring the sauce to a quick boil while stirring, then reduce to a simmer. Simmer for 1 to 2 minutes to cook out the starchy taste. Use as needed or refrigerate in an airtight container for up to 1 week.

# CORIANDER SAUCE

Straightforward and simple, this aromatic and tasty dipping sauce can double as a salad dressing, marinade or stir-fry finishing sauce. Add the vinegar and citrus juice to the sauce right before using to ensure the freshest and brightest flavor.

MAKES ¾ CUP (175 ML)

2 cups (50 g) packed cilantro leaves and stems
2 cloves garlic
1 tbsp (15 g) seeded and minced jalapeño pepper
1 tbsp (15 ml) soy sauce or fish sauce
1 tbsp (15 g) sugar or honey
½ cup (120 ml) vegetable oil
¼ cup (60 ml) rice wine vinegar
1 tbsp (15 ml) yuzu juice (see page 235) or freshly squeezed lemon juice
Salt and black pepper

Place the cilantro, garlic, jalapeño, soy sauce, sugar and vegetable oil together in a food processor. Pulse until you have the desired texture or blend until smooth. This base can be refrigerated for up to 2 weeks. Before serving, bring the sauce to room temperature and stir in the rice vinegar and yuzu juice. Season to taste with salt and pepper. Use within 48 hours.

# GOMA (SESAME) SAUCE

There are several versions of "sesame sauce," as we normally think of cold sesame noodles and the velvety, spicy sauce that clings to the noodles, usually containing peanuts or peanut butter. This Japanese version, goma, meaning "sesame," relies on toasted white sesame seeds to provide the nutty flavor. I am particularly fond of this healthy, rich sauce and I put it on everything, from dumplings to noodles to salads and meats. You can use a mortar and pestle, or the pulse setting on your food processor, for a chunkier and more rustic style of goma sauce, or puree it in your blender until smooth.

MAKES 2½ CUPS (590 ML)

1 cup (160 g) lightly toasted white sesame seeds
½ cup (120 ml) dashi stock (page 218)
6 tbsp (90 ml) soy sauce
6 tbsp (90 ml) rice vinegar
¼ cup (60 ml) mirin
¼ cup (60 g) sugar
2 tbsp (30 ml) sake
Salt to taste

Combine all the ingredients in a blender or food processor and blend to the desired consistency. Refrigerate for up to 1 month. (The ingredients will separate while refrigerated; just stir to bring back together.)

# PEANUT SESAME SAUCE

This is an adaptation of the classic cold noodle sauce first developed by Chef Shorty Tang at his restaurant in New York City in the 1970s.

MAKES ABOUT 2 CUPS (475 ML)

¼ cup (45 g) smooth peanut butter
¼ cup (60 ml) sesame tahini paste
3 tbsp (45 g) sugar
6 tbsp (90 ml) soy sauce
¼ cup (60 ml) rice wine vinegar
¼ cup (60 ml) sesame oil
¼ cup (60 ml) chile oil (page 225)

Blend all the ingredients together in a food processor or blender until smooth. Add water as needed for your desired consistency. Refrigerate in an airtight container for up to 1 month.

# SWEET AND SOUR SAUCE ✓

This classic Chinese condiment is a perfect dipping sauce for deep-fried dumplings.

MAKES ABOUT ¾ CUP (175 ML)

¼ cup (60 g) light brown sugar
1 tbsp (15 ml) ketchup
1 tbsp (15 ml) soy sauce
¼ cup (60 ml) rice vinegar
¼ cup (60 ml) pineapple juice
2 tsp (5 g) cornstarch dissolved in 1 tbsp (15 ml) water
¼ tsp salt

Combine the brown sugar, ketchup, soy sauce, rice vinegar and pineapple juice in a small saucepan, stirring to dissolve the sugar. Bring the pot to a boil and whisk in the cornstarch slurry. Simmer for 1 minute until the sauce thickens. Stir in the salt. Remove from the heat and allow to cool if serving as a dipping sauce. You may keep the sauce refrigerated in an airtight container for up to 1 week.

# SWEET CHILI SAUCE

This is a much fresher version of the bottled variety, and you can adjust the heat (spice) intensity or dial it down, depending on which fresh chile pepper you decide to use. I recommend a nice medium-spicy pepper, like red Fresno, serrano or red jalapeño. If using a small red chile, such as Thai bird, remember that a little goes a long way, so reduce the fresh chile to taste.

MAKES 1 CUP (240 ML)

1 tsp (5 g) crushed red pepper flakes
2 tsp (10 g) seeded (optional) and minced fresh red chile pepper, such as red Fresno
4 cloves garlic
1 tbsp (15 g) grated ginger
½ cup (120 ml) rice wine vinegar
¼ cup (60 ml) fish sauce
¼ cup (60 ml) water
½ cup (120 g) light brown sugar or granulated sugar
Salt to taste
1 tbsp (10 g) cornstarch dissolved in 2 tbsp (30 ml) water

Combine the red pepper flakes, minced chile pepper, garlic, ginger, rice wine vinegar, fish sauce, water and light brown sugar in a small saucepan. Bring to a boil over high heat and reduce to a simmer, cooking for 5 minutes. Whisk the slurry into the sauce and bring back to a boil, whisking often. Once the saucer thickens, about 2 minutes, remove from the heat and allow to cool to room temperature. The sauce can be refrigerated in an airtight container for up to 1 month.

# XO SAUCE

I like to keep this condiment stocked in my fridge at all times. The chunky, thick base works well for stir-fry—it can be used dry or liquid can be added for a more sauce-like consistency. Add 1 tablespoon (15 ml) of this to some panfried dumplings right before you take them out of the pan, and stir-fry for 30 seconds!

MAKES ABOUT 4 CUPS (950 ML)

¼ cup (55 g) dried shrimp

¼ cup (55 g) dried scallops

¾ cup (180 ml) vegetable oil

¼ cup (60 ml) sesame oil

½ cup (120 g) minced shallot

½ cup (75 g) minced garlic

½ cup (120 g) finely minced ginger

¼ cup (60 g) seeded and minced fresh red chile, such as Fresno

1 tsp (5 g) crushed red pepper flakes

½ cup (110 g) diced lap cheong sausage

2 tbsp (30 ml) fermented bean paste or miso paste

½ cup (120 ml) Shaoxing rice wine

¼ cup (60 ml) soaking liquid from dried seafood (above)

¼ cup (60 ml) low-sodium soy sauce

2 tbsp (30 g) brown sugar

Rinse the dried seafood under cold water. Combine the dried shrimp and dried scallops in a bowl and pour enough water to cover the dried seafood by 1 inch (2.5 cm). Allow the shrimp and scallops to soak overnight (this allows them to properly hydrate). If you are in a hurry, simply boil the water and pour over the dried seafood, allowing at least 30 minutes for rehydration. After the dried seafood has soaked, drain the shrimp and scallops, reserving ¼ cup (60 ml) of the soaking liquid. Place the shrimp and scallops in a food processor and pulse until they are finely chopped (or chop by hand using your knife).

Heat the vegetable oil and sesame oil in a large wok or frying pan over high heat. Add the shallot, garlic and ginger. Stir-fry the aromatics for 1 minute, then add the fresh minced chile and crushed red pepper flakes. Stir-fry for 1 minute more.

Add the lap cheong sausage and reduce the heat to medium-high. Sauté the sausage and aromatics together for 4 to 5 minutes, stirring often, until the sausage begins to caramelize slightly. Stir in the bean paste until the mixture is well coated and cook for 1 minute more. Add the wine, soaking liquid, soy sauce and sugar. Reduce the heat to medium-low and cook the sauce at a rapid simmer until the liquid reduces and clings to the solids. Cool the sauce to room temperature and refrigerate in an airtight container for up to 1 month.

# CHILE OIL

Homemade chile oil is probably my favorite pantry staple, and I put it on just about everything because I happen to love spice. The key is getting good-quality dried red chile, such as chile de arbol or Thai red chile. You can also flavor your chile oil with soybean paste, garlic, ginger or lemongrass. Allow the oil to steep and then strain the solids before refrigerating.

MAKES 1 CUP (240 ML)

½ cup (85 g) dried whole Thai red chile or chile de arbol, or ¼ cup (35 g) crushed red pepper flakes
¾ cup (175 ml) vegetable oil
¼ cup (60 ml) sesame oil

Grind the dried chiles in a food processor until they are in small pieces. Combine the vegetable oil and sesame oil in a small saucepan and heat to 250°F/121°C. Stir in the crushed chiles or red pepper flakes and remove the pan from the heat. Allow the chiles to steep in the warm oil for several hours until the oil cools down to room temperature. Transfer the oil to an airtight container like a clean jar or bottle and allow to steep at room temperature for at least 24 hours; you may strain out the solids or keep them in. Store in an airtight container in a cool, dark place for up to 3 months.

# SZECHUAN CHILE OIL

The addition of aromatic Szechuan peppercorns and garlic makes this oil savory and gives you that special "electric tingle" on your tongue.

MAKES 1 CUP (240 ML)

2 tbsp (30 g) Szechuan peppercorns
½ cup (85 g) dried whole red Thai chile or chile de arbol, or ¼ cup (35 g) crushed red pepper flakes
¾ cup (175 ml) vegetable oil
¼ cup (60 ml) sesame oil
2 tbsp (20 g) minced garlic
1 tbsp (15 g) minced ginger

Pulse the Szechuan peppercorns and whole dried chiles in a food processor until the chiles are chopped into small pieces. Combine the vegetable oil and sesame oil in a small saucepan and heat to 250°F/121°C. Add the garlic and ginger and simmer for 1 minute until fragrant. Stir in the crushed chiles or red pepper flakes and remove the pan from the heat. Allow the aromatics to steep in the warm oil for several hours until the oil cools down to room temperature. Allow the oil to steep at room temperature for at least 24 hours, covered. Strain out the solids through a fine-mesh sieve and transfer the oil to an airtight container. Keep in a cool, dark place for up to 2 months.

# FRIED GARLIC AND GARLIC OIL

This is one of those awesome two-for-one recipes in which nothing goes to waste. It's garlic. You can pretty much use it on anything and everything.

MAKES ½ CUP (120 ML)

½ cup (80 g) garlic cloves, minced into tiny pieces or sliced 1/16" (0.2 cm) thick
½ cup (120 ml) vegetable oil

Combine the garlic and oil in a wide shallow frying pan. Place the pan over medium-high heat. Cook the garlic and oil, stirring constantly, until the garlic begins to bubble and turns a light tan color, about 6 to 7 minutes. Remove the pan from the heat and continue to cook in the residual heat until the garlic is a deep golden brown. Be careful not to burn the garlic too much as it will become bitter and acrid. Strain the garlic through a fine-mesh sieve and reserve the oil as garlic oil (keep refrigerated for up to 1 month in an airtight container). Transfer the strained fried garlic to a paper towel and spread out to cool. The garlic will crisp up once cooled. Store in an airtight container in a cool, dark, dry place for up to 2 weeks.

# APRICOT MUSTARD

This recipe is adapted from my time at 66. All I can say about Jean-Georges Vongerichten is he is a French chef with a true love for Asian flavors and an absolute master on how to interpret and modernize cultural cuisines.

MAKES 1½ CUPS (355 ML)

1 cup (240 ml) apricot jam or preserves
1 tbsp (15 g) dry mustard powder
¼ cup (60 ml) rice vinegar
1 tbsp (15 ml) fish sauce
1 tbsp (15 g) finely minced ginger
¼ cup (60 ml) water
½ tsp salt

Combine all the ingredients in a blender and process until smooth. Refrigerate until needed. Store for up to 2 weeks.

# CHINESE MUSTARD ✓

Fellow Top Cheffer Dale Talde recently reminded me of how much I love the sinus-clearing heat of Chinese mustard. His recipe included the addition of creamy, nutty tahini paste to balance the spice of the dry mustard. This recipe is an adaptation and a nod to his Asian culinary genius.

MAKES 1 CUP (240 ML)

½ cup (120 g) Chinese or Coleman's dry mustard powder
6 tbsp (90 ml) vegetable oil
2 tbsp (30 ml) sesame oil
2 tbsp (30 ml) tahini paste
3 tbsp (45 ml) rice vinegar
1 tsp (5 g) sugar
¼ tsp salt

Blend all the ingredients together in a blender or food processor until smooth. Keep refrigerated for up to 3 months.

# FISH SAUCE CARAMEL

You can add dried spices such as a piece of star anise, a cinnamon stick or a slice of ginger to scent this sweet-sour-salty condiment.

MAKES ¾ CUP (175 ML)

½ cup (120 ml) rice vinegar
½ cup (120 g) brown sugar
¼ cup (60 g) granulated sugar
2 tbsp (30 ml) soy sauce
2 tbsp (30 ml) fish sauce

Combine the rice vinegar, brown sugar, granulated sugar and soy sauce in a small saucepan. Bring to a boil and stir until the sugar dissolves. Remove the pan from the heat and add the fish sauce. Allow the sauce to cool to room temperature before serving. Store in an airtight container in a cool, dark place for up to 3 months.

# NUOC CHAM

This classic Vietnamese dipping sauce is a perfect companion for dumplings and a wide variety of foods. You can adjust the level of spice depending on what type of chiles you use. Remember, the smaller the chile, the hotter it usually is. If you can't find Thai chiles, long red chiles or serranos work well. Make sure you wear disposable gloves when handling the chiles!

MAKES 1½ CUPS (355 ML)

2 cloves garlic
2 small Thai bird chiles, seeded
¾ cup (175 ml) hot water
6 tbsp (90 g) sugar
¼ cup (60 ml) fish sauce
¼ cup (60 ml) freshly squeezed lime juice
2 tbsp (20 g) grated carrot (optional)

Mash the garlic and chiles together with a mortar and pestle, or mince together with a knife to blend. Mix the water and sugar together until the sugar dissolves, then add the mashed garlic and chiles, fish sauce, lime juice and carrot. Use immediately or refrigerate in an airtight container for up to 3 days.

# KIMCHI VINAIGRETTE

The pungent, spicy aroma and flavor of kimchi makes a great vinaigrette or dipping sauce for salads, seafood, meats and definitely dumplings.

MAKES ½ CUP (120 ML)

¼ cup (60 ml) kimchi, drained of liquid
2 tbsp (30 ml) kimchi liquid
2 tbsp (30 ml) rice vinegar
1 clove garlic
1 whole scallion, minced
1 tbsp (15 g) sugar
½ cup (120 ml) vegetable oil
2 tbsp (30 ml) sesame oil

Combine all the ingredients together in a blender or food processor. Blend until smooth. Use immediately or within 2 days.

# CARAMELIZED ONION VINAIGRETTE

This is a fantastic dipping sauce, dressing and marinade.

MAKES ¾ CUP (175 ML)

¼ cup (60 ml) vegetable oil
¼ cup (50 g) finely minced yellow onion
1 tsp (5 g) finely grated ginger
1 tsp (5 g) sugar
3 tbsp (45 ml) soy sauce
3 tbsp (45 ml) balsamic vinegar or rice wine vinegar
2 tbsp (45 ml) sesame oil
Salt and pepper to taste

Heat 2 tablespoons (30 ml) of the vegetable oil in a small frying pan over medium heat. Add the minced onion and cook for 10 to 12 minutes, stirring often, until the onions are soft and begin to color. Add the grated ginger and sugar and cook for 30 seconds more. Add the soy sauce and balsamic vinegar, simmer for 1 minute more, then stir in the sesame oil and remove from the heat. Allow the vinaigrette to cool to room temperature, then season with salt and pepper to taste.

# GOCHUJANG AIOLI

Korean red pepper paste adds a sweet, spicy kick to mayonnaise or homemade aioli.

MAKES 1 CUP (240 ML)

1 cup (240 ml) mayonnaise or homemade aioli (page 228)
1 tbsp (15 ml) gochujang red pepper paste
1 tbsp (15 ml) rice vinegar

Blend all the ingredients together until smooth. Add water as needed for desired consistency. Refrigerate in a covered container for up to 1 week.

# HOMEMADE AIOLI

Note that raw egg yolks are not recommended for pregnant women, the elderly, infants or people with a compromised immune system. If you are concerned about using raw egg yolks, use organic eggs instead of commercially farmed eggs or use pasteurized eggs instead, which are usually available in large supermarkets.

MAKES ABOUT 1 CUP (240 ML)

1 egg yolk
2 tsp (10 ml) freshly squeezed lemon juice
1 tsp (5 ml) distilled white vinegar or rice vinegar
½ tsp Dijon mustard
½ tsp salt
¼ tsp sugar
1 cup (240 ml) canola or vegetable oil

In a small bowl, food processor or blender, combine the egg yolk, lemon juice, vinegar, mustard, salt and sugar. Blend until homogenous and smooth. While blending, add the oil gradually at first, just a few drops at a time, not adding more until the oil has been incorporated. When the emulsion starts to form (the mixture will begin to thicken as you blend) add the rest of the oil in a thin, steady stream until all of the oil has been incorporated. If the aioli is a little thick, add water a few drops at a time until you reach the desired consistency. Season to taste with salt. Refrigerate immediately in an airtight container for up to 1 week.

# YUZU AIOLI

Fragrant yuzu citrus juice adds a Japanese dimension to a classic spread. It's perfect for any application where you would use mayonnaise.

MAKES 1 CUP (240 ML)

1 cup (240 ml) mayonnaise or homemade aioli (see recipe at left)
1 tbsp (15 ml) yuzu juice (see page 235)
½ tsp sugar

Mix all the ingredients until well blended. Refrigerate in a covered container for up to 1 week.

# YUZU KOSHO

I'm a big fan of this spicy-citrus condiment. You can use red or green chiles and adjust the level of spice depending on your choice of chiles. You can use frozen yuzu zest, which you can find at a Japanese grocer. Fresh yuzu is extremely hard to find, so if you cannot get either, then substitute ¼ cup (60 g) of freshly grated lime zest and 2 tablespoons (30 g) of freshly grated grapefruit zest.

MAKES ½ CUP (120 ML)

3 tbsp (45 g) seeded and minced jalapeño pepper
2 tbsp (30 g) finely minced yuzu zest
1 tsp (5 g) salt
½ tsp sugar
2 tbsp (30 ml) yuzu juice (see page 235)

Using a mortar and pestle, muddle together the minced chile peppers and yuzu zest with the salt and sugar until you form a fragrant paste. Stir in the yuzu juice and use immediately or refrigerate in a small airtight container for up to 1 month.

# CRISPY RICE

This is a great way to utilize leftover rice. Keep the rice dehydrated and in an airtight container in a cool, dark place until you are ready to fry it.

MAKES ABOUT 4 CUPS (840 G) PUFFED RICE

2 cups (420 g) cooked, cooled white rice, preferably jasmine or good-quality medium-long grain rice

Oil for deep-frying

Salt

Spread the cooked rice in a thin, single layer on a parchment-lined baking sheet. Place the rice in a warm, dry area with air circulation to dehydrate. If you have a gas range, inside your oven is a good place (the oven is not turned on); the heat of the pilot light will dehydrate the rice in 1 to 3 days. You can also place the rice in a low oven (150°F to 175°F [65°C to 80°C] ) until the rice is completely dehydrated but not colored. A food dehydrator is even better because you can dehydrate the rice at a lower temperature (130°F to140°F [55°F to 60°C]). The rice will be brittle, hard and completely dehydrated when ready. Allow the rice to cool, and then break into small pieces. Store in an airtight container in a cool, dry place until ready to use.

To cook the crispy rice, heat a few inches of vegetable oil in a deep pot to 375°F/190°C. Have a paper towel–lined baking sheet or large heatproof tray ready stove side as the rice will cook quickly. Add the dehydrated rice in small quantities to the hot oil; be careful because the rice will cook and puff very quickly, and the hot oil will bubble and boil rapidly, so make sure the rim of the pot is at least 4 inches (10 cm) above the oil level. Stir the puffed rice in the hot oil gently using a Chinese spider strainer until the rice is cooked through and no longer rapidly bubbling in the oil, about 1 minute. Strain the puffed rice onto the paper towel–lined tray. Sprinkle lightly with salt. Ensure that the oil returns to 375°F/190°C before frying the next batch of dehydrated rice. Allow the rice to cool to room temperature before breaking apart. Store in an airtight container in a cool, dry place for up to 1 week.

# QUICK PICKLED CUCUMBERS

This is my go-to sweet and tart cucumber pickle. You can make these pickles in minutes and they are a perfect accompaniment to almost anything. Add crushed garlic, dried or fresh chiles or toasted crushed spices like coriander seed for extra flavor. You can also toss in some fresh chopped scallion or herbs like dill, mint, cilantro or basil for added dimension.

MAKES 1 CUP (240 ML)

2 seedless cucumbers or Japanese cucumbers, unpeeled
½ cup (120 g) sugar
1 cup (240 ml) rice vinegar or distilled white vinegar
Pinch of salt (optional)

Slice the cucumbers to desired thickness or shape. In a bowl, toss the sugar with the cut cucumbers until well coated, then pour the vinegar over the cucumbers. The sugar and vinegar will season the cucumbers and draw out the water. Allow the cucumbers to marinate for 1 to 2 hours, at which point they will be ready to serve, or they can be refrigerated in a covered container for up to 1 week. (Note: The color of the cucumbers will change from the acidity in the vinegar.)

# PICKLED RED ONIONS

This is also a staple garnish in my fridge, as I put pickled red onions on pretty much everything. The sliced red onions turn a lovely purple-pink color and add crunch, savory sweetness and color to any dish.

MAKES 1 CUP (240 ML)

1 red onion, halved lengthwise and sliced with the grain into ⅛"-(0.3-cm) thick slices
1 tbsp (15 g) yellow mustard seed (optional)
1 piece star anise
2 cloves garlic, crushed
2 dried whole red chiles
½ cup (120 g) sugar
1 cup (240 ml) distilled white vinegar or rice wine vinegar
1 cup (240 ml) water
½ tsp salt

Place the sliced onions in a large, heatproof container or bowl. Combine the mustard seed, star anise, crushed garlic, dried chiles, sugar, vinegar, water and salt in a small saucepan. Bring the liquid to a boil and reduce to a simmer. Simmer for 3 minutes, then remove from the heat. Allow the spices to steep in the pickling liquid until the liquid cools to room temperature. Pour the liquid and spices over the sliced onions and submerge the onions in the liquid with a paper towel. Allow the onions to marinate for 48 hours. If you are in a rush, bring the pickling liquid back to a boil after it has steeped to room temperature and pour the hot liquid over the onions. When the onions are ready they will be soft and translucent pink. You may store them, refrigerated in the pickling liquid, for up to 1 month.

# PICKLED DAIKON RADISH

This quick pickle is a traditional accompaniment to spicy Korean dishes. In addition to the fact that daikon radish is extremely healthy for you (it contains antioxidants, is anti-inflammatory, is high in vitamin C and can be used as a digestive aid, to name a few benefits), I love the crunchy texture and pungent aroma of these pickles. If your fridge smells a little funny, don't worry; it's a combination of the daikon's natural enzymes and the pickling liquid. Keep your pickles in an airtight container such as a screw-cap jar.

MAKES 2 CUPS (480 ML)

2 lb (900 g) Chinese (daikon) radish, peeled and cut uniformly into small pieces (1" [2.5 cm] cubes or ¼"[0.6 cm]-thick slices work well)
2 tbsp (30 g) kosher salt
2 tbsp (30 g) sugar
2 tbsp (30 ml) distilled white vinegar or rice vinegar
½ tsp Korean red chile flakes or crushed red pepper flakes (optional)
2 cloves garlic, crushed and mashed (optional)
2 scallions or garlic chives, cut into 1" (2.5 cm) lengths (optional)

Combine all the ingredients in a bowl and toss until well mixed. Allow the radish to marinate for at least 30 minutes before serving. Keep refrigerated in an airtight container for up to 2 weeks.

# FRIED SHALLOTS

I love crunchy oniony anything. This garnish is widely used throughout Southeast Asia and you can make these at home in a flash. The key is starting the shallots in low-temperature oil. If you drop them in hot oil, the natural sugars in the shallots will burn before they have a chance to cook and get crispy.

MAKES 1 CUP (240 ML)

Oil for deep-frying
6 to 8 large shallots, peeled and sliced into ⅛"(0.3 cm)-thick rounds
½ cup (75 g) cornstarch
½ cup (75 g) all-purpose flour
Salt

In a wide frying pan with high sides, heat 1 inch (2.5 cm) of oil over medium-low heat. Separate your sliced shallots into individual pieces. Combine the cornstarch and flour in a large bowl, and stir until well mixed. Add the shallots and toss to coat. When the oil has reached 150°F/65°C, shake off the excess coating from the shallots and add to the pan of oil. The shallots will sink and then slowly rise to the surface as the oil temperature gradually increases, about 5 to 10 minutes. When the shallots rise to the top they should be gently frying and bubbling (reduce the heat if they are browning too quickly). Slowly increase the oil temperature to 325°F/162°C, ensuring that the oil does not exceed this temperature at any time. As the shallots are cooking and bubbling (this is the action of moisture slowly dehydrating and cooking out of the shallots, which will yield the crispy texture), stir them occasionally, until the bubbling slows and the shallots are golden brown. Strain out of the oil, drain on paper towels and season lightly with salt. The shallots will crisp up once cool. Transfer to a paper towel-lined airtight container and keep in a cool, dark place for up to 3 days.

# CHAPTER 13

# THE ASIAN PANTRY

➤ Investing in a properly stocked pantry can be daunting, but like anything else in life, the more prepared you are, the easier it will be to do the job. With the booming trend in gourmet cooking at home, specialty markets are popping up everywhere across the country. Even in small towns, I am usually able to find an Asian grocery store. That being said, I also fully endorse the fact that we are living in the digital age and pretty much anything can be ordered online and delivered to your doorstep. Even online, it pays to shop around and compare prices and shipping costs, but you will find it easy to obtain everything you need in the event you can't get it locally.

A number of these ingredients may be exotic and unfamiliar to you. However, as you continue to cook with them, you will begin to understand their true potential and flavor possibilities. Quality will vary from brand to brand, which is why it is important to do your research and also TASTE everything. To be a masterful cook, you must first understand the components of a dish. We don't normally think to take a sip of the soy sauce we are using because our first reaction is, "Ugh! Salty!!!" But soy sauce is supposed to be salty, and there are literally hundreds of types of soy sauce on the market. I keep no fewer than five varieties in my own pantry, each type having a distinct level of salinity, fragrance, viscosity, mouthfeel and taste. While this may seem silly or overzealous to the average consumer, as a passionate cook, you will begin to invest in different varieties of products and you'll soon be able to tailor your pantry to your tastes (and your budget). Some of these condiments can be homemade, which I recommend for purity of ingredients, but you can use store-bought bottled and jarred condiments if you are short on time and patience.

# SAUCES

**SOY SAUCE:** Soy sauce is truly a cornerstone of Asian cuisine, and used to flavor just about everything. This ancient sauce, originating in China more than 3,000 years ago, is now produced worldwide (shoyu is the Japanese name for soy sauce). It is made from a combination of naturally fermented soybeans, grain (wheat or barley), salt and water. The mixture is usually aged, strained and then bottled. Soy sauce styles range from dark to sweet to light and thin. Some soy sauces are flavored, such as mushroom soy sauce. Others have added sugars for flavor and thickness. There is even a white soy sauce, which is lighter in color and milder and sweeter in flavor than traditional soy sauce. Reduced-sodium and gluten-free soy sauces are also popular types. There are hundreds of varieties on the market, so be sure a find a few brands that suit your tastes.

I like to store my soy sauce in the refrigerator. Although soy sauce is shelf stable, air, light, humidity and heat all affect the flavor over time, even if it sits in a cabinet.

Below is a list of soy sauces used in this book, as well as a few alternative options. Kikkoman and Yamasa are both good, all-purpose brands.

> **BREWED SOY SAUCE:** Kikkoman is a good example of an all-purpose soy sauce. Reddish brown in color, it has a rich, smooth flavor, with less saltiness than a traditional light soy sauce. This is the standard type of soy sauce for recipes in this book unless noted otherwise.

> **DARK SOY SAUCE:** Darker in color and thicker in texture, dark soy sauce is one of the two most commonly used soy sauces in Chinese cooking. It is traditionally used to add color and a deeper flavor to meats and marinades. Usually dark soy sauce contains a little bit of molasses, caramel color and starch for sweetness and thickness. The result is a richer, more full-bodied flavor.

> **KECAP MANIS:** This is a sweet, thick Indonesian soy sauce, with a syrup-like texture and a pronounced molasses-like sweetness.

> **LIGHT SOY SAUCE:** Not to be confused with low-sodium soy sauce, light soy sauce has a lighter brown color, thinner texture and pronounced salinity. This is the most commonly used soy sauce for seasoning in Chinese cooking. In Japanese cuisine, this type of shoyu is called *usukuchi*.

> **LOW-SODIUM SOY SAUCE:** Sodium levels are usually reduced by 20 to 50 percent in this seasoning alternative for health-conscious consumers. Quantities may need to be adjusted where traditional soy sauce is called for, depending on the desired taste.

> **MUSHROOM SOY SAUCE:** This is dark soy sauce with the flavor of dried mushrooms added during the fermentation and aging process. The mushroom flavor is heady and reminiscent of dried straw mushrooms and shiitake mushrooms.

> **SHIRO SOY SAUCE:** Also known as white soy sauce, this Japanese variety primarily uses wheat instead of soybeans, yielding a sauce that is very light in color (clear pale to golden brown) and mildly sweeter in flavor.

> **SUPERIOR SOY SAUCE:** Made from the first pressing of the fermentation, this soy sauce has a light, balanced flavor and aroma and is used for dipping sauces and seasoning.

> **TAMARI:** This is a type of Japanese soy sauce, made with little or no wheat. Wheat-free versions are popular with people who are gluten intolerant.

**FISH SAUCE:** A well-known seasoning staple throughout China, Southeast Asia and Japan, fish sauce is a thin, salty, amber liquid with a pungent aroma and flavor. Usually made from a single species of seafood, fish sauce is extracted from fermented fresh or dried fish with salt. Common styles can be made from fish, anchovies, shellfish, crab, shrimp, sardines and/or squid. The sharp flavor mellows when cooked or added to other ingredients. I like to keep my fish sauce refrigerated once opened, for optimal shelf life.

**HOISIN SAUCE:** This traditional Chinese condiment made from soybeans, chiles, sugar, starch and salt has a sweet, piquant flavor. It is a perfect seasoning for meats and poultry, and is commonly used to garnish dishes such as roasted pork and Peking duck.

**OYSTER SAUCE:** Another popular staple in Chinese cooking, high-quality oyster sauce is made only from cooked oysters. Most supermarket bottled varieties, however, are more "economically" produced, using sugar and salt as a base with added starch for thickening and oyster extract or essence for flavor. This sauce is a popular condiment for vegetables, stir-fries, roasted meats and seafood.

**PLUM SAUCE:** This is a sweet and sour condiment made from plums, sugar, salt, vinegar, chiles and ginger. Fruits such as apricots, peaches and pineapple may also be used in the sauce. Commonly known as duck sauce, this sauce usually accompanies fried snacks such as spring rolls and fried wontons.

**XO SAUCE:** This complex, spicy sauce gets its full flavor from a combination of dried shrimp, dried scallops, garlic, ginger and fresh chiles. It can be used to enhance a variety of dishes or served as a dipping sauce or condiment on its own. See the recipe on page 224.

**YUZU JUICE/CONCENTRATE:** Yuzu is an East Asian citrus fruit with a unique flavor similar to a blend of grapefruit and mandarin orange. Yuzu is prized for its aromatic rind and tart, distinctive flavor. You can find dried zest and juice concentrate (salt is added as a preservative) in Japanese grocery stores and occasionally in pan-Asian grocery stores and gourmet food stores.

# HOT SAUCES

**CHILE OIL:** This sauce is made by steeping dried chiles (whole or ground) in hot oil. Aromatics such as garlic, ginger and Szechuan peppercorns are commonly added for fragrance and flavor. See the recipe on page 225.

**DOUBANJIANG CHILI SAUCE:** Otherwise known as chile bean sauce, this is made from soybean paste and chiles.

**GUILIN CHILI SAUCE:** This sauce is made from salted fermented yellow soybeans, chiles and garlic. Also known as soy chili sauce or chili garlic sauce, it is slightly different in flavor from douban chili sauce.

**SAMBAL CHILI SAUCE:** There are a variety of recipes and ingredients that can comprise this Indonesian-style sauce. Sambal oelek is a paste made from pounded or chopped fresh red chiles with no additional flavorings such as garlic or spices. This is commonly found in supermarkets in the Asian grocery section.

**SRIRACHA:** A popular Thai condiment made from pureed chile peppers, vinegar, garlic, sugar and salt, Sriracha is commonly found in supermarkets in the Asian grocery section.

**SWEET CHILI SAUCE:** Commonly found in Thai and Malaysian cuisines, this chili sauce has become popular with Western palates because of its sweet-spicy taste. Made from chiles, vinegar, sugar and fruit, this versatile condiment is used as a dipping sauce or can be substituted for other chili sauces. See the recipe on page 223.

# OILS, VINEGARS AND SPIRITS

**CHINESE BLACK VINEGAR:** Otherwise known as Chinkiang vinegar, or sweet black vinegar, this condiment is made from black glutinous rice, wheat and sorghum. It has a rich, smoky, sweet and sour flavor and a malty aroma. It can be used for cooking or as a dipping sauce.

**CHINESE (DILUTED) RED VINEGAR:** Made from yeasted red rice, this bright red vinegar is sweet, salty and tart all at the same time. It lends a distinctive acidity to sauces and is perfect on its own as a dipping condiment.

**PEANUT OIL:** Several varieties of peanut oil are available on the market. The best for cooking is the highly refined variety, which has a high smoke point and is perfect for deep-frying. Roasted peanut oil has a deeper, nuttier characteristic and is used for imparting flavor as well as for cooking. Be mindful of peanut allergies when using peanut oil.

**RICE VINEGAR OR RICE WINE VINEGAR:** Made from fermented white rice, this vinegar has a milder, sweeter flavor than common Western-style vinegars. Japanese varieties tend to be pale yellow in color, while Chinese rice vinegars can range from light to dark to red in color. Another delicious variety of Japanese rice vinegar is brown rice vinegar, which has a richer, nuttier flavor.

**RICE WINE:** Made from the fermentation of rice starch, this alcoholic beverage can range in color, flavor and alcohol content. Below is a list of rice wines used in this book.

 **SHAOXING:** One of the most well-known Chinese wines originating from eastern China, Shaoxing is consumed as a beverage and also commonly used in cooking. It has a dry, savory quality, similar to dry sherry, which can be substituted if you don't have Shaoxing available.

 **SAKE:** This Japanese rice wine is made from polished rice grains through multiple fermentation and brewing processes. The alcohol content traditionally ranges from 18 to 20 percent in good-quality sakes. Traditional types of sake are categorized according to the amount of polished rice used, the maturation and aging process, and whether it is flavored or filtered. A dry sake, such as a junmai-style sake, is the best type to use for recipes in this book.

 **MIRIN:** Traditional forms of mirin, a Japanese rice wine used for cooking, are lower in alcohol content (14 percent) but higher in natural sugar due to the fermentation process. Commercially produced types of cooking mirin often contain little to no alcohol and use additional sweeteners for taste.

**SESAME OIL:** Asian-style sesame oil is made from roasted white sesame seeds, yielding a rich, amber color and aromatic, nutty flavor. Buy it in small quantities and keep in your refrigerator because it loses flavor and potency quickly. This oil is great for marinades, sauces, stir-fries and finishing applications. Sesame oil has a low smoke point, so is not ideal for deep-frying.

**VEGETABLE OIL:** Common varieties of vegetable oil are expelled from vegetable seeds such as corn, rapeseed (canola oil), safflower and sunflower. This oil is preferred in Asian cooking for its high smoke point and heat tolerance.

# PASTES

**CURRY PASTE:** Common in Indian and Thai cuisines, curry pastes are made from a blend of aromatic ingredients to give curried dishes their signature heat and flavors. Types of curry pastes will vary depending on the aromatics and spices used.

➤ **GREEN CURRY PASTE:** This type is made from lemongrass, green chiles, shallots, ginger, galangal, garlic, fish sauce, shrimp paste, coriander and basil. It is traditionally combined with coconut milk, palm sugar and lime juice to make Thai green (sweet) curry, or it can be dry-sautéed with seafood, meat and vegetables.

➤ **PANANG CURRY PASTE:** This type is made from garlic, ginger, dried chiles, lemongrass, shallots, galangal, coriander, cumin and shrimp paste. Prepared Panang curry is thickened with coconut cream to provide a rich texture and creamy flavor.

➤ **RED CURRY PASTE:** This type is made from lemongrass, red chiles, shallots, ginger, galangal, garlic, fish sauce, shrimp paste, chili powder and tomato puree. It is traditionally combined with coconut milk, palm sugar and lime juice to make Thai red curry, or it can be dry-sautéed with seafood, meat and vegetables.

➤ **YELLOW CURRY PASTE:** This type is made from lemongrass, red chiles, shallots, ginger, galangal, garlic, fish sauce, shrimp paste, turmeric, curry powder and coriander. It can be used as a base paste for curries, marinades, stews, soups and stir-fries.

**GOCHUJANG CHILI PASTE:** Also spelled kochujang, this Korean hot chile pepper condiment is made from red chiles, glutinous rice, fermented soybeans, salt and sugar or honey. It is commonly used as a condiment for barbecue or rice preparations but can also be used for sauces, emulsions and marinades. It is savory, spicy and slightly sweet at the same time, and is a signature flavor profile in Korean cuisine.

**MISO PASTE:** Made from fermented barley, rice and/or soybeans, salt and koji (the fermenting agent or fungus), miso paste is available in a wide variety, in both Chinese and Japanese styles. The ones listed below are Japanese styles called for in this book, but they can be substituted with other varieties of miso should you not be able to find a specific type.

➤ **AKA MISO:** Also known as "red miso," this miso is made from 70 percent soybeans and 30 percent rice or barley. It has a strong, salty flavor profile, with about ½ teaspoon of salt per tablespoon (15 ml) of miso (13 percent salt content).

➤ **AWASE MISO:** A blended miso, awase is usually a combination of aka and shiro misos.

➤ **GENMAI MISO:** Made from brown rice and soybeans, this miso has a rich, full-bodied flavor profile.

➤ **HATCHO MISO:** Made with 100 percent soybeans, this miso is firm, rich, dark in color and less salty than traditional barley and rice misos. Hatcho miso is rich in protein and fiber and great for use with meats, marinades, sauces, soups and stews.

➤ **SAIKYO MISO:** A form of shiro miso, this light yellow paste is the sweetest of all miso varieties. It is made with more rice and less soybean, with the shortest fermentation time. Its mild, sweet-salt balance is perfect for marinating seafood and vegetables.

➤ **SHIRO MISO:** Also known as "white miso," this yellow-beige paste is fermented for a shorter time, yielding a mellow, slightly sweet, delicate flavor. Not as salty as the darker varieties, shiro miso is great for a wide variety of uses.

**NAM PRIK PAO (THAI CHILI PASTE):** This traditional Thai chili paste has many faces and styles. It can be bought in a jar or made at home. Usually comprised of dried or fresh chiles, garlic, shallots, shrimp paste, fish sauce and sugar, additional ingredients and regional flavors distinguish the many types of nam prik pao.

**RED BEAN PASTE (SWEET):** A dark, sweet red bean paste made from cooked adzuki beans and sugar or honey, this paste is found in Chinese, Japanese and Korean desserts and confections. It can be found in cans or jars at your Asian grocer, or you can make your own at home. See the recipe on page 109.

**SESAME PASTE (TAHINI):** Made from ground, hulled sesame seeds, tahini is often used in Mediterranean, Middle Eastern and African cuisines, but it can also be found as a component in Asian-style recipes such as Dan Dan Pork Wontons (page 154). Keep your tahini refrigerated for maximum shelf life, but be sure and stir the tahini before using because the solid paste will separate from the natural oil.

**SHRIMP PASTE:** A common ingredient in Chinese and Southeast Asian cuisines, this paste is made from fermented ground shrimp and salt. Shrimp pastes often vary in pungency, texture, aroma and salinity.

**UMEBOSHI PASTE:** This paste is made from salted Japanese plums, a traditional pickle renowned for its salty-sour flavor and health benefits.

**WASABI PASTE:** Wasabi root is also known as Japanese horseradish. Fresh wasabi root is prized for its distinctive "hotness" akin to mustard. Because fresh wasabi root is expensive (and difficult to cultivate because it needs a constant water source and a cool, mountainous climate), wasabi powders and pastes often consist of horseradish, mustard and food coloring. When fresh or frozen wasabi is not available, I opt for the ready-to-use paste in tubes (S&B and House Foods are two favorite brands) rather than the powdered version, which you rehydrate yourself.

# FLOURS AND STARCHES

There are a wide variety of flours and starches you can use to make fresh dumpling dough. I highly recommend having a variety on hand so you can experiment. I like to keep my flours and starches in the freezer in an airtight zip-top freezer bag. This keeps them fresh and bug-free.

**ALL-PURPOSE FLOUR:** Good-quality brands like Gold Medal and King Arthur work well for recipes in this book. This type of flour contains a medium amount of gluten and protein (10 to 12 percent) and provides just enough structure and elasticity for a standard dumpling dough. Bleached flour will have a whiter, snowier appearance, but I prefer to use unbleached flour for its taste, gluten content (it has more protein than bleached flour), and the fact that no chemicals are used to process the flour. You can cut amounts of flour with wheat starch to make a more tender, delicate skin if you wish.

**CAKE OR PASTRY FLOUR:** More finely ground than all-purpose flour, this bleached flour has a whiter color and less gluten and protein (7 to 8.5 percent) than regular flour. It is prized for its softer texture in making delicate cakes and baked goods.

**GLUTINOUS RICE FLOUR:** Also known as "sweet rice flour," glutinous rice flour is made from ground glutinous rice. It is neither sweet nor does it contain gluten. The name refers to the sticky texture of the rice when it is cooked. It's a great flour for the gluten intolerant.

**HONG KONG FLOUR:** Similar in gluten content to pastry and cake flours, this highly bleached flour has a very soft texture and bright white color, making it popular in traditional Asian baked goods.

**MASECA FLOUR (MASA HARINA):** This instant corn flour is used for making tortillas, tamales and other corn flour–based products.

**CORNSTARCH:** Made from the endosperm of the corn kernel, cornstarch is a fine, white, powdery starch that is traditionally used as a thickening and binding agent. Heat activates the thickening powder, and cornstarch must be cooked to eliminate the "raw taste" of the starch.

**POTATO STARCH:** Derived from potatoes, this starch is used as a thickener and binder. Because it is also a root starch, like tapioca starch, it thickens at a lower temperature than does cornstarch and wheat flour, and has a silkier mouthfeel as well as a glossy texture when cooked.

**TAPIOCA STARCH:** Also known as tapioca flour, tapioca starch is a great multipurpose flour derived from the cassava root. It is used for thickening, binding and providing texture (substitute 2 tablespoons [15 g] tapioca starch for 1 tablespoon [7.5 g] cornstarch). Because it is a root starch, it thickens at a lower temperature than does cornstarch and is best added toward the end of cooking.

**WHEAT STARCH:** Wheat starch is made by removing the proteins, including gluten, from wheat flour. It is often used as a stabilizer or thickener in food applications. Because of the lack of gluten and protein, wheat starch is very fine and has a delicate structure when made into dumpling dough.

# DRY GOODS

**CHINESE FIVE-SPICE POWDER:** Available in most grocery stores in the spice aisle, this blend combines ground star anise, cinnamon, cloves, fennel seeds and Szechuan peppercorns.

**CHINESE STAR ANISE:** This star-shaped dried spice has the signature anise flavor. When cooking you may steep the seedpod in whatever you want to impart flavor to and then remove it at the desired time before consuming.

**DASHI POWDERED SOUP BASE:** Commonly found in Asian grocery stores, these dried granules are added to hot water to make instant dashi or bonito soup. Dashi adds umami to dishes.

**DRIED ADZUKI BEANS:** This easily digestible small red bean is commonly used in Asian cooking for both sweet and savory applications.

**DRIED MUSHROOMS:** There is a wide variety of dried mushroom species available in both Asian markets and specialty markets. For this book I like to use dried shiitakes for their umami flavor and rich aroma. You can experiment with different varieties of dried mushrooms, each producing a more concentrated flavor than a fresh mushroom when rehydrated. To properly rehydrate dried mushrooms, soak them in cold water overnight. Save the soaking liquid for use in soups, stews, sauces and fillings. To rehydrate quickly, bring water to a boil and pour over the dried mushrooms. Allow the mushrooms to soak for at least 2 hours.

**DRIED SEAFOOD:** Recipes for XO sauce call for dried shrimp and scallops. There are many types and varying qualities when shopping for dried seafood. A little goes a long way when used in recipes that call for it. The drying process concentrates the core flavor of the seafood, and the dried forms can be used as is or rehydrated, depending on the recipe. I like to keep my dried seafood in an airtight bag in the freezer to help maintain flavor.

**FERMENTED BLACK BEANS:** Also known as Chinese preserved black beans, these beans have been fermented and salted, which renders them soft but dry, and pungent in aroma and flavor.

**NOODLES:** Dumplings and noodles go hand in hand, so it's always good to have some dried or fresh noodles in your pantry for when you want a soup fix. Here are a few varieties I like to keep in my pantry.

➢ **CHINESE EGG NOODLES:** Also known as lo mein and chow mein (which signify their preparation, not the type of noodle), this is a super versatile noodle perfect for soups, salads, stir-fries and even deep-fried applications.

➢ **RAMEN:** Although most of us know the cheap dried variety of ramen, the noodle craze that is sweeping America has led to a wide range of fresh and precooked ramen noodles now available at your local Asian grocery store. You may also find these wheat-based noodles in dried forms and in the freezer section.

➢ **RICE STICKS:** Dried rice noodles that are easy to rehydrate and cook, and are commonly used in all Asian cuisines, especially Southeast Asian styles.

➢ **SOBA:** Traditionally made from a combination of buckwheat and wheat flours, soba has a nutty, rich flavor that is great for both hot and cold dishes.

➢ **UDON:** These thick wheat flour noodles are good for both hot and cold dishes.

**SEAWEED:** Seaweed is a key ingredient in many Asian cultures and cuisines, as well as other coastal areas around the world. Edible marine algae is consumed for its health and nutrition benefits (as well as its uniquely delicious flavors and textures). Dried forms of seaweed are readily available at Asian grocery stores and specialty markets. Here are a few we use in this book:

➢ **HIJIKI:** This brown sea vegetable is commonly used in Japanese cooking. The drying process yields a black color that is evident when rehydrated.

➢ **KOMBU:** Edible kelp, or kombu, is a cornerstone ingredient in Japanese cooking. It can be found in various forms, including dried, stewed, salted or preserved and powdered. It is a good source of glutamic acid, the amino acid that provides the savory taste known as umami.

➢ **NORI/LAVER:** This dried paper-thin seaweed made from red algae is commonly used for making sushi and onigiri.

➢ **WAKAME:** This edible seaweed commonly found in soups and salads is used most often in miso soup.

**SZECHUAN PEPPERCORNS:** As the dried red husk of the seed, this peppercorn is prized for its aromatic scent and the tingling sensation left on the palate after consumption. It is used in conjunction with dried red chiles and fresh chiles to give the signature heat and flavor to regional Chinese cuisines such as Hunan and Szechuan.

**TEA:** Various forms of loose black tea are suitable for flavoring foods and beverages. I like to use fragrant jasmine, earthy oolong and smoky Lapsang Souchong tea to give flavor to my Asian recipes. Matcha (green tea) powder is also great for both sweet and savory applications.

# AROMATICS

**CHINESE CHIVES:** Garlic chives are long and flat like blades of grass, with a deep green color, pungent aroma and garlicky flavor. The other variety has a round stem and flowering bud at the top of each piece. Commonly found in Asian grocery stores, they are used as both a vegetable and an herb.

**CILANTRO OR CORIANDER:** Also known as Chinese parsley, this flavorful herb is found throughout Asian cuisine. The plant bears seeds that are dried and used as a spice (coriander seed).

**FRESH CHILES:** There is a wide variety of fresh chiles available on the market. My rule of thumb is usually the smaller the chile is, the hotter it will tend to be. Tailor recipes that call for fresh chiles to your taste and always start with a little; you can add more later, but too much spice will ruin an entire batch of whatever you are cooking because it is hard to disguise or mask. I like to use fresh red chiles such as red Fresnos, long red and green chiles, jalapeño peppers, serrano peppers and Thai bird chiles, with each having its own distinctive aroma and level of heat or spice. Do your homework and research your fresh chile before you throw it in your recipe.

**GALANGAL:** Similar to ginger in its appearance, galangal is also a root and is commonly used in Southeast Asian cooking. It has a stronger but very different flavor from ginger. Traditionally, it is sliced and boiled or steeped for flavor.

**GARLIC:** Garlic's pungent flavor and aroma are prized in Asian-style cooking. I always use fresh garlic versus the processed jarred variety where the garlic is sitting in preservatives and water or oil. Look for fresh firm heads of garlic where the outer skin is not leathery or papery. Store garlic in a cool, dry place with a little bit of light and air circulation. Once peeled, store in an airtight container in the refrigerator.

**GINGER ROOT:** An aromatic root or rhizome found in cuisines worldwide, ginger is a key ingredient in Asian cuisine. When shopping for fresh ginger, look for roots where the skin is shiny and taut, not dry, gray and wrinkled, which denotes older ginger. Young ginger will have a thin, transparent skin, while older ginger will have a tan, thicker skin and deeper, spicier flavor. The ginger should be firm and without mold or rot. It can be sliced, crushed (for maximum aroma), minced, grated, juiced, puréed, candied or dried and ground. Store unused ginger in your vegetable crisper in a zip-top bag.

**KAFFIR LIME AND LEAVES:** Native to Southeast Asia, this citrus fruit is prized for its distinctive aroma and flavor in both the zest and the leaves of the plant, similar to citronelle. The leaves can be kept in a zip-top bag in your crisper for a few days, air-dried or wrapped and kept in your freezer.

**LEMONGRASS:** A tall perennial grass, lemongrass can be found fresh, dried, powdered and preserved. Its citrus-like aroma and flavor come from its natural oils, which can be released by crushing and pulverizing the fibers of the lemongrass. It can be kept wrapped in plastic wrap in your crisper or freezer, or dried and chopped or ground.

**SCALLIONS:** Also known as green onion. Both the white and green parts can be used for cooking and in raw preparations.

**TAMARIND:** The pulp of this edible pod fruit has a sweet and acidic taste and is used in Southeast Asian, Latin and Indian cuisines. Tamarind concentrate and/or puree can be found in specialty markets and Asian grocers.

**THAI BASIL:** Thai basil is slightly different from sweet basil in its distinctive aroma and flavor, which withstands cooking better than that of its sweet cousin. It is used throughout Southeast Asia. If you can't find Thai basil, sweet basil will work fine.

# OTHER GOOD STUFF

**BAMBOO SHOOTS:** The edible shoots of the bamboo plant can be used fresh, preserved, canned or dried.

**CHINESE BACON:** Made from pork belly and cured with a mixture of sugar, soy sauce and spices before it is smoked, Chinese bacon should be rehydrated in cold water for 6 to 24 hours before using.

**CHINESE HAM:** This salted, air-cured and air-dried ham is similar to European-style salted hams.

**EDAMAME:** The soybean in its young, green stage can be shelled from the pod or served in the pod for snacking.

**FERMENTED BEAN CURD:** A preserved, jarred condiment used in East Asian cuisine, fermented bean curd or tofu is marinated and brined to achieve a cheese-like texture and strong flavor.

**LAP CHEONG SAUSAGE:** This dried raw meat Chinese sausage is known for its fatty, rich, sweet-savory flavor. It can be made from pork, chicken, duck, beef, liver and more. Cook before consuming.

**PALM SUGAR:** Made from the sap of the sugar date palm, palm sugar has a rich, buttery, caramel-like flavor and can be used in any recipe that calls for sugar.

**PICKLES:** Having worked at a Scandinavian restaurant as my first kitchen job, I learned how to pickle just about everything. I love the range and varieties you can find in these complementary and often addictive condiments. Get into making your own pickles, if you have the time. For now, here are a few items you can buy already prepared from your local grocery store.

> **BENI SHOGA:** This pickled ginger flavored with plum and red shiso is bright red in color and usually comes with a shredded texture.

> **KIMCHI:** This traditional Korean condiment is usually made from fermented vegetables preserved in salt, spices and chiles. It is usually made with Chinese cabbage, radish, scallion and/or cucumber. The quality differs greatly in jarred varieties, so shop around!

> **PICKLED GINGER:** Also known as *gari*, this thinly sliced, sweet pickled young ginger serves as a traditional accompaniment to sushi and sashimi.

> **SZECHUAN PRESERVED VEGETABLES:** This pickle is made from the salted and preserved stem of the mustard plant. The stem is rubbed in hot chili paste before the fermentation process begins, yielding a spicy, salty, sour flavor to the finished pickle. It is usually sold in cans or jars at Asian grocery stores.

**TAKUWAN:** This yellow daikon radish pickle found in Japanese and Korean cuisine is a perfect side dish for juicy dumplings.

**SHIITAKE MUSHROOMS:** This large brown mushroom with a round cap is prized for its umami flavor and aroma. The stem is not edible.

**TOFU:** Tofu, or bean curd, is formed by combining soy milk with a coagulant, such as nigari. There are several varieties available in your local grocery store, usually categorized by texture—superfirm, firm and soft or silken. For dumpling fillings, firm or extra firm works best.

# ACKNOWLEDGMENTS

My blessed journey has taken me to kitchens and tables around the world. I'd like to give a heartfelt thank-you to everyone who contributed to my growth in getting to where I am today and the creation of this book.

I'd like to thank my family for their continued support. To my parents, thank you for fostering my creativity and equipping me for the game of life. To my Mom and both my grandmothers, my first memories of food were with you. These moments are indelible and the foundation for everything that I do.

Many thanks to Ken Goodman for your collaboration in lending your incredible talent to this book. Your beautiful photos truly captured my dumpling vision and personality, bringing it all to life on the page. Your enthusiasm for my words and recipes kept me motivated throughout our marathon three-day shoot, and I promise to have a giant platter of dumplings ready for you on your next visit to Hawaii. Special thanks to Will Chen—dumplings brought us together and now we are bonded for life. I could not have done this photo shoot without your impeccable chef skills and witty rapport.

Special thanks to all of the chefs and culinarians who have contributed recipes and words to this book: Marcus Samuelsson, Ming Tsai, Marja Samsom, Craig Koketsu, Lawrence Knapp and Dale Talde.

Thank you to my first chefs and mentors; Marcus Samuelsson, Nils Noren, Josh Eden and Andre Soltner. Your guidance, imagination and wisdom gave me the tools and fuel I needed to forge my own path through the culinary landscape.

To Saori Kawano, arigatou gozaimas for all you have done for me. Your generous spirit and giant heart serve as a constant inspiration on how make my dreams come true. Thank you to my fellow board members at The Gohan Society, our mission continues to evolve and grow in the most exciting ways.

A big thank-you to my manager, Scott Feldman, and the Two12 team—Danielle, Sarah Jane and Jessica. Thanks for always having my back and helping steer the boat.

To my TV Land compadres…. Thank-you to my Top Chef Family, Bravo and the Magical Elves; everyone at The Cooking Channel and the Food Network. Special thank you to Irene Wong and her entire team at IW Productions. I am wholeheartedly grateful for the opportunities I've been given to share my passion with a larger audience. Thanks to all of the fans, home cooks, and food enthusiasts out there, this book is for you.

Thanks to my editor, Marissa Giambelluca, and my publisher William Kiester, for your encouragement and direction. This is one of the hardest things I've ever done. Pushing me to keep writing resulted in a compendium of memories and recipes that tell the story of me, one dumpling at a time. Thank you to everyone at Page Street Publishing for this opportunity.

I have to give a big shout-out to my Supper Club homies. Our hilariously eclectic group of food lovers is one of the best group of friends I've ever had. Erin, John Mark, Jourdan, Zac, Jeff and Matt… We've laughed. We've cried. And we've eaten enough bacon to last a lifetime. I love you guys.

(continued)

Many mahalos to my new ohana— The Lee Arnolds, Brooks and Cynthia Takenaka, Hawaiian Fresh Farms, Pili Group, Street Grindz, Mana Ai, Town Restaurant, Edible HI and the culinary community. Special thanks to Doug Rigg, Bill Markevitch, Cristina and Chloe—my new home was the perfect backdrop for shooting this book. To my business partner, Kevin Hanney, and my new family at Koko Head Cafe, 12th Avenue Grill and Salt—let the adventure begin, I look forward to all that is yet to come.

To my farmer, Tristan. Your love and support has been life changing. Finding each other in one of the most beautiful places on earth has given new meaning and motivation for everything that has followed. Thank you for always telling me to "keep writing", and feeding my heart and soul. Wherever you are, that is where home is.

Lastly, thank you to my peers, students, colleagues, and friends around the world. I am incredibly lucky to have been able to meet so many people who share my passion for all things food, drink, travel and hospitality. You all continue to inspire me one remarkable experience after another, whether I am cooking side by side with you or dining at your table. It is a privilege and honor to be part of a community that continues to change the world in such positive ways. Keep cooking, you are the fundamental force in making life delicious for so many.

# ABOUT THE AUTHOR

Lee Anne Wong grew up in upstate New York with dreams of becoming a fashion designer. She moved to New York City after high school to attend the Fashion Institute of Technology, but soon traded her sewing machine for a shiny set of of knives after deciding to take her hobby of cooking more seriously. Once she donned her chef whites, she never looked back.

After graduating from The French Culinary Institute, Lee Anne jumped into the restaurant world. She immersed herself in New York's high-end fusion cuisine, taking her first job with Marcus Samuelsson at the storied Scandinavian restaurant, Aquavit. After spending several years there she went on to open Jean-Georges Vongerichten's Chinese restaurant, 66. She later became the Executive Chef of Event Operations and Continuing Ed at her alma mater, The French Culinary Institute. There she honed her event production and recipe development skills. She also coordinated the school's chef demonstration program, working alongside culinary greats such as Jacques Pepin, Andre Soltner, Ferran Adria, Tyler Florence and Martin Yan.

Lee Anne went on to broaden her culinary spectrum when she appeared on the first season of Bravo's hit series *Top Chef* in 2006, later becoming the show's Supervising Culinary Producer. She produced Seasons Two through Seven and its spin-off *Top Chef Masters*, playing an integral role in bringing the show to its Emmy Award-winning status. She also made the show more accessible, demonstrating the winning recipes on bravo.com's popular web series *The Wong Way to Cook*. Since *Top Chef* she has worked on several other projects behind the camera including her role as a consultant and culinary producer on Warner Bros. *No Reservations*, as well as PBS's *Chef Story*, Bravo's *Rocco's Dinner Party*, and most recently Delta's in-flight special *Cabin Pressure Cook Off.*

In 2011, Lee Anne returned to on-camera work, being featured as a regular contributor on The Cooking Channel's *Unique Eats*, and *Food Crawl with Lee Anne Wong*. She battled and won 2011's Halloween episode of *Iron Chef America* on Food Network, and also participated in the *Next Iron Chef: Redemption* web series. Lee Anne has made guest appearances as a judge on Food Network's hit series *Chopped* and *Rachael vs. Guy: Celebrity Chef Cook-off*. Lee Anne's gastronomic adventures have taken her into kitchens and dining rooms around the world; all over the United States, Mexico, Canada, Europe and Asia. She honed her global cuisine skills, making annual pilgrimages to Oaxaca, Mexico, in her twenties, and more recently had extensive training in cities across Japan. She has cooked in destinations such as Anguilla, Kuala Lumpur, France and Spain.

In December 2013, Lee Anne made the giant move from New York City, her home of twenty years, to Honolulu, Hawaii, to open her first restaurant, Koko Head Cafe, in March 2014. Resettled in this island paradise, Lee Anne looks forward to the next phase of her culinary career as she continues to bring her global cuisine to the masses.

Facebook: leeannewong

Instagram: leeannewong

Twitter: @leeannewong

#dumplingsalldaywong

# INDEX